Ghosts of the Gothic
AUSTEN, ELIOT, & LAWRENCE

Ghosts of the Gothic
AUSTEN, ELIOT, & LAWRENCE

Judith Wilt

PRINCETON UNIVERSITY PRESS

PRINCETON, NEW JERSEY

CONTENTS

LIST OF ILLUSTRATIONS

PREFACE

THE listener-narrator of Conrad's "Heart of Darkness" is a
bit annoyed at Marlow for shaping his narrative as a slowly
gathering palpable mist or "halo" around a mysterious
"core" rather than as a straightforward journey from definition to problem to conclusion. And so may some of my readers be with me. But it seems to me that the mode of map-
ping-defining is not equally productive on all subjects: at
this stage of our self-knowledge "the Gothic" seems better
caught, like Jupiter and Saturn, in varied bypassing circlings and ellipses. The reader will notice in these pages a
kind of circling in the form, as well as a rhetoric of "curve"
in the definitions themselves. Or, to take another metaphor
from nineteenth-century fiction, defining the Gothic ought
perhaps to be like *Bleak House*'s Phil Squod's manner of
getting to his work or his friends: he must "tack off" a hard
surface, a wall, in order to align his irresistible trajectory
outward with his desire to go inward, and when his method
works he "collides" fruitfully with his object.

The enterprise here is not only the recognition, the
partial enclosure, of the genre "Gothic" but also the recognition of that core as a material, an inheritance, in the more
comprehensive field of the "serious" or the aesthetic "mainstream" novel. In this task I do not seek to enclose Austen,
Eliot, and Lawrence within the defined Gothic (that would
be absurd) but rather to suggest that these great novelists'
imaginations function not to break out of or abandon that
core but to embrace it, along with everything else the practitioners of this ambitious genre seek to embrace—the comedy of manners, the lyric of vision, the analytic intelligence
—in a larger curve.

Surveying as I have in this large curve four fields of
literary criticism—on the Gothic, on nineteenth- and early

twentieth-century fiction, on Austen, Eliot, and Lawrence—
I have inevitably failed to do more than suggest the great
diversity and complexity of these critical fields. After my
necessary selection process, what remains is thinner perhaps
than one might wish, but I hope that it does at least, as one
early reader of the manuscript was kind enough to say,
"demonstrate a sense of the truly important" in each field
of criticism.

I am grateful to the University of California Press for
permission to use several pages on *Frankenstein* that were
originally published in my essay "*Frankenstein* as Mystery
Play" in *The Endurance of Frankenstein*, ed. George Levine
and U. C. Knoepflmacher (Berkeley and Los Angeles, 1979).
I would also like to express my gratitude to many col-
leagues whose writing and talking supplied me with energy
for my circlings and occasionally with walls against which
to tack off again at my subject: to George Levine, Joan
McTigue Zirker, and Lee Sterrenburg at Indiana University
for early conversations that validated the enterprise of
thinking about the Gothic; to Lynne Hanley, Jonathan
Arac, and Maria DiBattista at Princeton University for
stimulating discourse about English fiction. I owe thanks
too to Princeton University and to Boston College for
timely grants of money for technical and typing work, and
especially to the Educational Foundation of the American
Association of University Women for a Fellowship, 1978-
1979, which enabled me to complete this writing project
and embark on another in one smooth logical sweep.

PART I

"THIS HERETIC NARRATIVE":
APPROACHES TO A GOTHIC THEORETIC

In the last fifteen years we have been experiencing a Gothic revival—again. By the early 1970s, observers of the national culture became aware of the culture's increased fascination with things Gothic, and began studying it. The fascination lent itself partly to media analysis: like the similar interest of the 1950s, and for that matter of the formative period of the late eighteenth century, the Gothic explosion of the 1970s was sped by a new accessibility to the books—the circulating library phenomenon of the late eighteenth century, the paperback revolution of the 1950s, the move to paperback originals in this decade. Renewed interest in the Gothic yields partly to socio-political analysis, too, which often derives from guilt about a war in the immediate past and from the prospect of a pragmatic, materialistic, and narrowing immediate future. Disquietudes arising from the position of the culture on the downslope of a century and from the perceived increase in and power of "the mass" audience may also figure in both the Gothic "creation" of the late eighteenth century (even then, strictly, a "revival") and the Gothic revival of our time. And Freudian and feminist analysis offers provocative insight too into this Gothic that has acquired in many people's minds the assumed modifier "female" not only because of its main writers and readers but because of its deep revelations about gender, ego, and power.

The current revival has also generated much valuable literary analysis. Robert Hume and Robert L. Platzner conducted a provocative early quarrel in *PMLA* in 1969-1970 on the value of Gothic and Romantic writing, medium, and

APPROACHES TO A GOTHIC THEORETIC

message. Hume argued for the literary and moral primacy
of the Romantic mode, comparing it to that Coleridgean
imagination which "reconciles the discordant elements it
faces" and relegating Gothic to that activity Coleridge defined as fancy, that activity which, "however seriously it is
used, can find only paradox, never high truth . . . can find
only unresolvable moral and emotional ambiguity." Platzner responds that the Gothic works out ontological, not just
psychological, premises—that it does not "fail" to transcend
human subjective paradox but rather "succeeds" in its attempt to document as truth that which Romantic thought
rejects, the untranscendable, inexpungable paradox of
being, its embeddedness in the "mystery of evil," the "power
of blackness." In 1972, Robert Kiely assembled a Gothic
tradition behind the tremendous achievement of *Wuthering
Heights*, but he called his important book *The Romantic
Novel*. The reader-response critics Norman Holland and
Leona Sherman debated the Gothic, its Freudian and sexual
implications, in the pages of *New Literary History*, and
Ellen Moers brought significant contemporary feminist
insight to the questions of "Female Gothic" in a widely
read essay in *The New York Review of Books*, later published in her *Literary Women*. And a dozen respected Victorian scholars have just contributed essays to a book that
analyzes, and perpetuates, *The Endurance of Frankenstein*.[1]

My own offering to the literary analysis of the endurance
of the Gothic took shape in the first years of a rather schizophrenic teaching career. In the daylight I taught the great

[1] Works cited in this paragraph are: Robert Hume, "Gothic vs. Romantic: A Revaluation of the Gothic Novel," *PMLA* 84 (March 1969):
282-290; Robert Hume and Robert L. Platzner, "An Exchange," *PMLA*
86 (March 1971): 266-274; Robert Kiely, *The Romantic Novel in England* (Cambridge, Mass.: Harvard Univ. Press, 1972); Norman Holland
and Leona Sherman, "Gothic Possibilities," *New Literary History* 8
(Winter 1977): 279-294; Ellen Moers, "Female Gothic," in *Literary
Women* (Garden City, New York: Doubleday, 1976); U. C. Knoepflmacher and George Levine, eds., *The Endurance of Frankenstein*
(Berkeley: Univ. of California Press, 1979).

4

English novels of the mainstream tradition, 1750-1920, in Princeton's English department; at night I taught a four-year sequence of courses in the Gothic and the subforms it generated between 1750 and 1920—the historical novel, the detective novel, the science fiction tale—in Princeton High School's Adult School Program. This book is my attempt to put these courses, these traditions, perhaps even these institutions, together.

The book proceeds from a few basic assumptions: (1) that the theological "furniture" of early English Gothic was important in its own right, was not simply a disguise for sexual or political concerns, though these concerns entered in importantly; (2) that as a powerful public "ancestor" form, the Gothic provided tools not of imagery alone but also of plot and narrative strategy and even moral and aesthetic vision that the subtle architects of the great "serious" traditions of English fiction used as intimately as, if less colorfully than, the "entertainers," Scott, Dickens, and the Brontës, whose debt to the Gothic is so clearly marked and has been so fully studied; (3) that the Gothic works out a complicated and mystic theoretic of the topic that I see, along with Raymond Williams, as the central preoccupation of English novelists—the search for a community of individuals; (4) that Gothic romance originates from, and finally penetrates to, that emotion which Austen, Eliot, and Lawrence in their different ways locate as the birthplace of what the structuralists would call the trace of the imagination—dread.

Dread is the father and mother of the Gothic. Dread begets rage and fright and cruel horror, or awe and worship and a shining standfastness—all of these have human features, but Dread has no face. As we approach Dread, its robes flutter gaudily, its figure looms with substance, its gestures teem with a significance just short of meaning, its regard upon us is a palpable thing. Then we edge round the cowl, round the blowing hair, and are upon it. No face. But not-nothing. As E. M. Forster's Professor Godbole re-

5

marks, absence is not the same thing as nonexistence. As contemporary structuralist critics observe, the enormous significative power of the "trace," the track, of the originating impulse of anything, lies just in the fact that it is no longer there. But it has been.

At such moments, it is a great comfort to have had a psycho-historical or aesthetic education that shows us how far, how almost entirely, we have ourselves invented the coverings and uncoverings, the gestures, the imagined regard, the palpitating approach itself. Philosophers indeed posit several reasons for our fascination with exploring and concretizing our dread. Because our pain is our pleasure. Because invention, shapemaking, in any direction, is our nature and destiny. Because we seek the truth of existence in the intuited traces of the imagined ideal or supernatural as well as in the material world. Insofar as the first supposition is true alone, it accounts for the writing and the reading of *The Exorcist*, and perhaps for de Sade. Insofar as the first two are true together, they account for *The Castle of Otranto*, *The Mysteries of Udolpho*, and *The Cask of Amontillado*. Insofar as all three are true, they account for all those great works in the great artistic traditions that deal darkly with dark things—deal darkly, that is, because they resist that last temptation to utter reconciliation with dread, the giving of a terrestrial name and face to the featureless not-nothing, the unarticulated sound that is at the bottom of things: what the narrator of *Middlemarch* called "the roar on the other side of silence," what the narrator of *A Passage to India* hears as "ou-boum."

The great traditions of English fiction each have their characteristic (as critics strive to describe them) colors and purposes, but all of them reckon in some way—by caricature or appropriation or transformation, or by a living graft and grasp—with that mighty English formula for seeing giants and raising dread and crediting visions—the Gothic. Where the imagination is in English fiction—even if it is there only to be discredited or "tamed"—there is the

6

Gothic. The ghastly Tom Jones, streaming blood and brandishing sword, is taken quite properly for a Banquo vision by the sentinel guarding the rascally Northerton, and though Tom is no ghost, the man's dread of a more than human sphere of vengeance suddenly awakened is real enough for the moment for Fielding to comfortably recommend him to the study of prospective actors. At the end of Scott's *Old Mortality*, Henry Morton looks to psychology and not demonology to describe the encounter between the God-haunted covenanter Burley and an apparently invisible assailant, yet a moment of crisis occurs that seems out of scale even to deviant psychology, and Morton leaps out of the cave across the abyss with more than human power. And Charlotte Brontë's Lucy Snowe, an excellent psychologist who is even her own psychiatrist, rises from a night of unspeakable mental anguish, riven with dread, to seek "any spectacle of sincere worship, any opening for appeal to God," as a starving person seeks bread. In unreformed Villette, Lucy finds the enigmatic and personally powerful confessor who tells her that only the old vivid Gothic faith can satisfy her: "Protestantism is altogether too dry, cold, prosaic for you." The English Lucy, the Victorian Charlotte, the independent artist, will never accept that notion. Yet Lucy declines to put herself to the test of another interview with the clever priest, for that wayward hunger to deal directly with the supernatural might lead—who knows where? "The probabilities are that had I visited [him], I might just now, instead of writing this heretic narrative, be counting my beads in the cell of a certain Carmelite convent in the Boulevard of Crecy, in Villette."[2]

Brontë's happy phrase, "this heretic narrative," describes the attempt to record and probe the deep mystery of human experience in its extremities as well as its familiarities without either losing control of the probe, or facilely naming the unnameable, or using uncritically the old orthodox

[2] Charlotte Brontë, *Villette* (1853; reprint ed., New York: Dutton, 1972), p. 146.

forms and language of mystery. The phrase, the concept, I believe to some extent describes the important works in all the great fictional traditions of the nineteenth century. Between the automatism of counting beads, repeating the given formulas, and chanting the name of God, and the heresy of creating new things from the broken formulas of the old and chanting the narrative of the multiform self, the artist chooses the heresy. And a heretic, we remind ourselves, is not an atheist; rather he maintains a profound and often fruitful link with the orthodoxy that defines his terms.

I shall want to argue that the heretic/orthodoxy relationship illuminates one group of novelists particularly—Jane Austen, George Eliot, D. H. Lawrence. But first it seems proper to examine the one great tradition that the phrase does not, of course, describe: the Gothic itself, the orthodox sublime, the direct confrontation with those extremities of human experience to which dread points.

Not quite a voice, not quite a face, yet not-nothing, Dread as a positive emanation is imagined vividly in English prose fiction in a classic series of Gothic dream images. Walpole saw it as a mailed fist, disembodied, "a gigantic hand in armour . . . on the upmost bannister of a great staircase," which he remembered years later was a staircase at Trinity College. In *The Castle of Otranto* it became a giant, extinguishing or guillotining helmet and a sword so large one hundred men were required to carry it. Anne Radcliffe wouldn't tell us her dreams, wishing, as Montague Summers puts it, to be thought a lady, but these were undoubtedly of the giant hand too, so pervasive is that image in her works: "for she apprehended that the strong and invisible hand which governed her course would never relinquish its grasp until it had placed her irrecoverably beyond the reach of her lover." Robert Louis Stevenson dreamed of a potion and the image of a not-quite-unfamiliar face and, significantly enough, of "being pressed into a cabinet" where a change took place. Mary Shelley saw in her waking dream that blank face open its eyes, felt the

8

regard from the no-face, and wrote *Frankenstein*. And across the century Bram Stoker dreamed too, after a late night supper of dressed crab, of a different and more hideous meal.[3]

Thus the Sleep of Reason bred both the eighteenth-century dream of being shaken in a giant hand and the nineteenth-century dream of being transfixed by the alien eye from within. And in the twentieth century, a simpler age where Reason never sleeps but goes out to conquer day and night, the Gothic needs few mediating dream images but is a straightforward account of counterattacks by invaded foreigners intent on turning us into mindless Bolsheviks or into helpless guinea pigs for their experiments—foreigners with names like Dracula, and Yug-Soggoth, and Pazuzu from Iran, and with no name, like the Body Snatchers, whose pods are even now, in a 1978 film update of this fifties classic, coming out of California on fruit trucks.

As the Gothic has its classic plots, so it has its characteristic spaces, the special enclosures that breed the plots. Montague Summers has a lyric praise of the Gothic as significant space "with its antique courts, deserted chambers, haunted galleries, dim corridors . . . a home of memories of days gone before." Andrew Wright agrees: "the Gothic as a literary genre has a distinct and solid central feature . . . the castle," and Eino Raillo, making the image less distinct and solid and hence more compelling, reminds us that "the haunted castle" is itself a transformation of the mystically tenanted chapel, and offers us "the laboratory . . . the secret research room of a modern scientist" as the current equivalent.

Like most of the larger treatments of the Gothic, Raillo's

[3] Mary Shelley reports her dream in the 1832 preface to *Frankenstein*; Walpole and Stevenson cite theirs in letters to friends; but Stoker's grand-nephew specifies in his biography that he has been unable to establish the source of the widely reported and believed tale of Dracula's crab origins (Daniel Farsow, *The Man Who Wrote Dracula* [New York: St. Martin's Press, 1973]).

9

book suffers from that impulse to catalogue and dwell on scenery that Gothicism itself uses, or tries to use, as a suspense-holding device. But he puts his finger early on two of the major characteristics of Gothic space. First, the space is unpredictably various, full of hidden ascents and descents, sudden turnings, unexpected subspaces, alcoves, and inner rooms, above all, full of long, tortuous, imperfectly understood, half-visible *approaches* to the center of suspense. And second, all the spaces are charged with the essence of power: the empty passages crackle with the presence of the Gothic antihero, the great old one, Raillo's "tyrant-type," dead or alive, human or nonhuman, whose field of force, whose in a sense mystical body, this is. These same features characterize Mario Praz's symbol of the Gothic place, the prison. His lyric is addressed not to a castle but to Piranesi's *Carceri*, those "fantastic architectures" of stairs and bridges leading only to each other and infinity, those "mighty Daedalean buildings [with] little figures of men at the foot of them" (p. 17). This setting too has its ancestor in Gothic spaces, the madhouse, and its current topos, the mad city—settings whose scales and directions are without reference to the human and therefore support or even produce that "anxiety with no possibility of escape" which Praz affirms is the "main theme of Gothic tales."[4]

---

[4] The three seminal texts in Gothic studies are probably Michael Sadleir's "The Northanger Novels," English Association Pamphlet, no. 68 (London: Oxford Univ. Press, 1927), Eino Raillo's *The Haunted Castle* (London: Routledge, 1927), and Montague Summers' *The Gothic Quest* (London: The Fortune Press, 1939). Sadleir's book is important for its early scholarship on the works that readers of *Northanger Abbey* might have thought merely invented by Austen for caricature and for its cogent argument about Gothic fiction as a philosophically and politically "subversive" genre. Raillo's massive assembly of typological characters, settings, and icons from hundreds of works in several languages is eloquent testimony to his argument that the Gothic is less a matter of plot and character than a form for repeating with variation "definite mental images" that release emotion. Summers' quirky history remains thoroughly interesting for its ferocious comprehensiveness, its arguments against Sadleir ("not a revo-

Anxiety without escape. In the entrapping pages of books, in the fortified castles of great reputations, Harold Bloom has recently found and studied and felt the anxiety of influence and so already has written a book on the Gothic impulse in the writers of the great traditions of poetry. Bloom's poetic universe is classic Gothic in plot and space. Once inside, poets survive the great old one by way of the secret sin of poetic misprision, yet even with the glories of this guilt to spur them, the young are inevitably less great than the old: thus, "the diminishment of poetry seems . . . an inevitable realization," and "poetry in our tradition, when it dies, will be self-slain, murdered by its own past strength."[5] The murdering father, whose power fills up every passage in the haunted castle, is Bloom's covering cherub ("out of Blake, and Milton, and Ezekiel, and Genesis") who tries to fully preempt imagination and creativity. It is Walpole's Manfred with his dagger in the heart of his daughter and Radcliffe's Schedoni with his dagger at his daughter/niece's breast; it is Maturin's Melmoth and Stoker's Dracula who have simply appropriated the whole mor-

---

lutionary but a reactionary genre") and almost everybody else, and, not least, because Summers believes in ghosts. Devendra P. Varma's *The Gothic Flame* (London: Arthur Barker, Ltd., 1957) finds the heart of the Gothic in a renewed sensitivity to the quasi-religious domain of "the numinous," a point elaborated with more sophistication by several of the essayists in *The Gothic Imagination: Essays in Dark Romanticism*, ed. G. R. Thompson (Pullman, Wash.: Washington State Univ. Press, 1974). Edith Birkhead's *The Tale of Terror* (London: Constable and Co., 1921) is an important early account of the Gothic as a literary enterprise. Among the many shorter essays available on the Gothic, I have found particularly useful and provocative Andrew Wright's introduction to *The Castle of Otranto, The Mysteries of Udolpho, Northanger Abbey* (New York: Holt, Rinehart and Winston, Inc., 1963), Mario Praz's introduction to *Three Gothic Novels* (Harmondsworth, Middlesex: Penguin Books, Inc., 1968), and William F. Axton's introduction to *Melmoth the Wanderer* (Lincoln, Nebraska: Univ. of Nebraska Press, 1961).

[5] Harold Bloom, *The Anxiety of Influence* (New York: Oxford Univ. Press, 1973), p. 10.

tality of their lines and lived each generation as their own sons. It is Victor Frankenstein destroying his daughter un-actualized on the laboratory table, confronting his monster/son in the shadow of Mont Blanc with murder in his heart. And doubly Gothic is the preempting figure when it is woman: Walpole's mysterious mother receiving the seed of her son, Radcliffe's Marchesa Vivaldi, plotting the death of her son's lover, Monk Lewis's demon Matilda, who in the female incarnation, "a subordinate but crafty spirit," burns to possess Ambrosio's body and as full demon burns to possess his soul. In Gothic isolation, over all of these images broods Dante's Ugolino as Rodin saw him, gnawing his fingers and casting glances of despair and hunger at the flesh of his sons.

None of the pragmatic plot-issues surrounding these extreme illicit passions—issues of property or reputation or religious principle, or lust or jealousy or even simple life and death—seems a real correlative to the demon energies released between the parent and child figures, the great old ones and the young usurpers of life in classic Gothic. Some deep struggle for control of the springs of being itself seems to be the issue, some struggle by the parent to unmake or reabsorb the child and thus to stop time, keep power, take back freedom and life where it has inadvertently been given away. Or shared. Siblings are always at hazard, each to each, for their share—Schedoni to his brother, Jekyll to Hyde, Tom Tryon's Niles to The Other, his brother.

Classic English Gothic, we recall, took shape in the 1760s and 1770s, after a hundred years of enlightened Anglican revision of the Puritan counterreformation, after a hundred years of safer but duller parliamentary and party rule had blurred the memory of divine right tyrants and *eminences grises*, Roman, Anglican, and Puritan. The rhythm and the doctrines, not just the "props," of English religious history lie quite close to the surface of many Gothic novels. This rhythm, set up in the sixteenth century, described a movement from orthodoxy to reform powered by humanist and rationalist thought. This movement, however unretractable in the main, constantly generated a powerful counterflow back to the orthodox mysteries, when the simplifications and certainties and civilities of humanism or tolerance, latitudinarianism or deism or later liberalism were perceived as robbing life of some of its richness, nobility, or intensity. If the price of that intensity and mystery was the emotional surrender of autonomy, it was of course better paid in the national fantasy life than on the battlefield, and better still, paid by imagined well-meaning but benighted Catholic Spaniards and Italians. Not until the next century, when Scott and Hogg raised the explicit and not-long-buried ghost of British Calvinism and Bram Stoker resurrected the spirit of invading Catholic power, would the specifically English roots of the Gothic fascination with tyrant-religious establishments and dilated god-men become clear.

For the fascination first took hold disguised in scenes of Mediterranean Catholicism, amid issues of that orthodoxy's doctrines, their reformation and counterreformation. In the Gothic's rough and ready formulas, as in the treatises of enlightened churchmen and philosophers of the eighteenth century, it was the religion question again: it was even the theological question. It was even, at bottom, the Trinitarian question, that doctrine which guarded the mystery of religion in English ecclesiastical debates all through the late seventeenth and eighteenth centuries, the doctrine central to the outlook of poet-theologians from Augustine to Coleridge to Teilhard de Chardin.[6]

In a world made corruptly various by the variousness of the old gods, "the fathers" of the early Christian centuries

---

[6] In his *Coleridge and the Pantheistic Tradition* (New York: Oxford Univ. Press, 1969), Thomas McFarland has drawn attention to the way the doctrine of the Trinity served Coleridge as the dramatic choice-point between an "it is" Spinozan faith and an "I am" Augustinian faith. McFarland quotes Coleridge's assertion (from the *Philosophical Dialogues*) that the Trinity is "the great and only sure Bulwark" against atheism (p. 433).

wrestled to define in God the pure will of one being while allowing force, nature, and "person" to three entities, and "special place" to a fourth, a subordinate but crafty spirit as she would have to have been, the Virgin Mother. In its reach for the nature of God, the Trinitarian intuition has a great deal of nobility, even ecstasy about it. A triadic separateness that exists for the sharp joy of choosing communion again at every second in a seamless intense serenity —this is God in the early Christian language, or perhaps, changing the noun form to the verb form as theologian Mary Daly proposed recently, this is what it means "to God." Not so much a dying to live, but the less abstract though more mysterious rhythm-paradox of "Kenosis," the emptying out to be filled up. The Father pours himself out into the Son; the Son, knowing himself separate, makes the astonishing choice to curve that stream of being back toward the progenitor; that choice separates as person, as spirit, as Holy "Ghost" and reflects through all matter that same curve outward, with perfect confidence that its destination is inward. Thus the emptier is always filled, the spring never runs dry. There is no heat-death threatened in this universe; even the exchanges of energy take place without loss, for they are not really exchanges, body to body, but numinous participations world without end.

We remember that ideal of concepts which at once depart from and feed into one another. The Father, the Son, the Holy Ghost: the action, the passion, the sanctification; the man, man repeated, *femina genetrix*; the other, the self, the reconciler; will, choice, the faith that unites these two; violence, love, the creativity that unites these two. In eighteenth-century aesthetics this translates, perhaps, into the sublime, the beautiful, and the transcendent, by which beauty returns from its sterile symmetries and repetitions toward the expression of the jagged, the unpredictable, the sublime. We remember that ideal. But we remember too that the third term in these formulations is notoriously unstable, almost invisible; and that a great battle was fought over the first thousand Christian years to establish that orthodox, unbearable balance for a God and a Church both One and Catholic, both single and multiple. The Holy Ghost is not to be separated but "proceeds" from the Father and the Son, *filioque*; the Son is not to be separated, not even in His human nature, but in every aspect and moment is with and from and to the Father and the Holy Ghost, "begotten, not made," not the maker, all angles of the Godhead "consubstantial" as the formula had it, the formula imposed upon a divided Council at Nice by the godfather of the Church, Constantine. The point at issue is union: God is a communion, man is a community; if anyone dwell too long, fascinated, on the moment of separation let that one be, in the word of the ultimate curse, anathema, that is, separated.

In a universe shaped by the curve of God out into a consubstantial personhood, everything that moves moves together; in the words of the theologian Teilhard de Chardin, which were taken up by the modern Gothic artist Flannery O'Connor, everything that rises must converge. In such a universe, dread has the shape of an unmoving point, or a point whose movement affirms a straight line. In such a universe freedom is a long curve and slavery an obsessed straight line against all the energies of being. It is dreadful but fascinating to consider this movement against the whole outward, upward, inward sweep—to travel to the edge and leap off. Trying to account for his interest in the Gothic, a contemporary poet pounces on this insight: "But Ambrosio is the point: the point is to conduct a remarkable man utterly to damnation. It is surprising after all, how long it takes—how difficult it is—to be certain of damnation." This was John Berryman writing on *The Monk* ten years before he killed and resurrected himself in *The Dream Songs* ("Noises from underground made gibber some/ others collected & dug Henry up"), twenty-two years before he leapt off the edge into the Mississippi ("insomnia plagued, with a shovel/ digging like mad, Lazarus with a plan/ to

get his own back, a plan, a stratagem/ no newsman will unravel").[7]

Writing that long, engaged, revealing preface to M. G.
Lewis's *The Monk*, Berryman, like many a "serious" artist,
dramatizes his fascination with the rude shapes and themes
that somehow confirm and validate, as well as anchor, the
subtler, riskier formulas of his own works. In fact, artists in
the great traditions are always being asked by us about their
allegiance to or distance from popular genres. Thus we ask,
and learn, why Van Cliburn likes "The Young and the
Restless" and why Beverly Sills likes Country Charley
Pride, why Nureyev does the frug, why Edmund Wilson
doesn't care "Who Killed Roger Ackroyd" and W. H. Auden does care about "The Guilty Vicarage." And the answer
is always the same—that the energies present in these
simplest forms of the old powerful orthodox formulas provide not only a relaxation but somehow a renewal, an invitation to their own more complex imaginations. And it
seems likely for the evidence such contact affords to the artists far out from the streets and the commonality that they
are, however far out, still in the embrace of the curve, that
they are among those who go out that they may come back.
If realism is indeed "a bourgeois prejudice" as Herbert
Read engagingly asserts[8] and Ian Watt more soberly argues
in *The Rise of the Novel*, then we may well look to the
Gothic for evidence of that subconscious and slippery alliance between the "superstition-loving populace" and the
artistocrats of imagination that continues to challenge
liberal, critical accommodations.

The Gothic, so-called with a score of qualifying adjec-
tives, is one of the supreme popular genres, and the curve
out from, never separation from, the genre in the mainstream English novel is my particular interest here. For the

[7] Berryman's introduction is in the Grove Press Edition of *The Monk* (New York: 1952). The comment is on p. 13. The dream song referred to is "Opus Posthumous No. 14."

[8] See the foreword to D. P. Varma's *The Gothic Flame*, p. vii.

Gothic provides not just formulas for the child artist to absorb, the adolescent artist to parody, the mature artist to "outgrow," although this pattern supplies a useful fiction, up to a point, for the study of some careers. Nor does the Gothic simply provide a stock of hair-raising images for the artist to use clinically in the creation of terror. In low art or high art, the Gothic is upon a certain business, and part of that business, as Robert Platzner reminded Robert Hume, is affirming an ontology, a structure of being governed by mystery, not by that Romantic imagination which, however "high" or "primary," is still, for Coleridge, reason. This mystery, the Gothic suggests obliquely (even in the midst of its criticism of the institution), is that which the Church, with all its obsolete "furniture," still serviceably guards.

Joel Porte notes: "It is surprising . . . how little systematic consideration has been given to Gothic fiction as the expression of a fundamentally Protestant theological or religious disquietude."[9] It seems to me that this disquietude takes several paradoxical forms: it is at once a participation in the immense anxiety about the nature of man characteristic of the "Age of Faith" (guilt), a reenactment of the strenuous "protest" against this view characteristic of Renaissance/Reformation theology (guilt about having felt guilty), and a temporary swoon into the sublimities characteristic of the Counter-Reformational return to disquietude (guilt about having felt not guilty). Sister M. M. Tarr provides interesting examples of the fact that the details of Roman Catholic life supplied as background by early English Gothic writers are often laughably wrong.[10] But

[9] Joel Porte, "In the Hands of an Angry God: Religious Terror in Gothic Fiction," in *The Gothic Imagination*, ed. Thompson, p. 43.

[10] Sister M. M. Tarr, *Catholicism in Gothic Fiction* (Washington, D.C.: Catholic Univ. of America Press, 1946). Sister Tarr draws attention to the extensive embellishment of the topos of "taking monkish vows" in which there is "little that is specific and less that is correct," notes with some asperity that "the acceptable hours for the celebration of Mass in the Gothic novel seem to be two, the time of evening

the Counter-Reformation atmosphere is sufficiently true to warrant the supposition that it is not only the Catholic Counter-Reformation but also the Protestant one—Puritan, Presbyterian, Evangelical—that supplies the real motifs for exploration and, of course, transformation. This Puritan counterreformation's rejection of the elegant compromises, or "superstitions," of the Trinitarian, communitarian God and the resultant return to the Old Testament's solitary deity is reflected in the imagination of the age, and that choice affects the kinds of secular transformations that can be made by a later age.

Clearly, one of the prime transformations effected by classic English Gothic as it recapitulates the Reformation is the apparent demythologizing of theology into reason, of religion into enthusiasm, of church, as setting, as icon, into congregation. Further transformed in the novels of the great traditions, these become secular ideograms of considerable, though abstract, power—morality, intensity, community. Among members of the tradition that F. R. Leavis took to be greatest, the sense of a desirable curve back, the dread of that straight line out off the edge of progress, is very strong. A tradition that is, as Leavis proposes, "significant in terms of the human awareness [it] promotes," that is marked by "an intense moral interest . . . in life, . . . a profoundly serious interest in life" (p. 18), a tradition in which Lawrence counts higher than Joyce both as a thinker and as a literary technician because "he can truly say that what he writes must be written from the depth of his religious experience" (p. 125), and above all, a tradition not only whose practitioners but whose readers are commonly

---

twilight and the hour of twelve midnight" (p. 22), and concludes her examination of the treatment of Catholic matrimony thus: "It seems superfluous to say that if the officiating priests in Gothic fiction but observed the prescriptions of the Rituale with regard to the publication of banns, the expression of assent on the part of both contracting parties, and witnesses to the marriage ceremony, the major trials of the Gothic bride-to-be would be obviated" (p. 34).

"in a state of something like deracination" (p. 22) is working with Gothic material in a Gothic mood.[11]

In some ways Leavis's "Great Tradition" in prose fiction was begotten, not made, by the Gothic tradition.[12] The Gothic treats of the separated one, and the great tradition was begotten from it by heretics who wished to allow the separated one his or her mission in the outward curve—allow it and then rescue the missionary. For as Gothic fiction shows unmistakably and as Trinitarian theology implies, the most intense moral life is always lived at the edge of separation or recommunion. The terrors of the separated one are always more moving and more instructive than the terrors of the outraged community; and the *progress*, as Berryman calls it, of the self-separated one, the hero/villain, is even more significant in terms of human awareness than the progress, or rather the standfastness, of the one separated by circumstance—the "victim," the orphan, the bastard, above all, the woman.[13] Separated as he may be (usually it is a he), still, in Conrad's painful affirmation, the self-separated one is "one of us," though he confirms his separation by walking "away from the living woman [usually it is a woman] towards some shadowy ideal of conduct," as Lord Jim does, as Victor Frankenstein does.

One of us. In our fear and cowardice? In our centripetal

11 F. R. Leavis's important study, *The Great Tradition* (New York: New York Univ. Press, 1969), provokes my imagination rather the way Lord David Cecil's *Early Victorian Novelists* provoked Leavis's—as a pole of widely held and understood assumptions around which to circle, occasionally in opposition, occasionally in return.

12 What was "made" directly seems to have issued, through Godwin's Caleb Williams, Poe's Dupin, Dickens's Inspector Bucket, and Collins's Sergeant Cuff to Sherlock Holmes, in the form of the detective story—the only form that rivals the great Victorian novels in strict seriousness, as W. H. Auden and Raymond Chandler in the two best essays on the form have proposed.

13 The Gothic novelists, says Devendra Varma, "strike a union between our spiritual curiosities and our venial terrors" (*The Gothic Flame*, p. 212), and this union is another reason for that blurring together of victim and victimizer in the Gothic.

19

pursuit of shadows? In our mutual separateness? Deracinated together? Or bound in a community of individual persons, separate but not separated, capable of choosing the shadowy ideal that at however distant a curve still curves back into the whole, a manhead consubstantial at all essential angles, human and divine? The search for c~ ʳ 'y is the subject of the nineteenth-century English ʳ ,ymond Williams has said in his own study of the gᵣeat traditions.[14] The search is a matter of formal and aesthetic concern, of moral, national and sociological concern, and, since the great women and men of the great traditions were essentially, even to their own imaginations, not atheists but heretics, the search is a matter of metaphysical, even theological concern. When these concerns reached urgency, when as Leavis says of Jane Austen, "a preoccupation with certain problems that life compels on her as personal ones" (p. 7) reached literary expression, the patterns, the "machinery" of the Gothic lay ready to hand in the Shilling Shockers and in *Blackwell's Magazine,* in the poetry of Shelley and Byron and Keats and later Tennyson and Swinburne, and above all in the seminal works of classic Gothic fiction that dealt, and keep on dealing, preeminently with the metaphysical outrage of separation.

As we know, "Gothic" is a great umbrella term with urbane references historical and architectural and popular references mostly emotional. So it was when Squire Western's sister sighed to the old bear, "Oh, more than Gothic ignorance!" So it is when Robert Sherrill titles his study of Leander Perez and Orville Faubus, *Gothic Politics in the*

---

[14] *The English Novel From Dickens to Lawrence* (New York: Oxford Univ. Press, 1970). With his usual shrewd simplicity Williams probes in novels and novelists just that growing anxiety about the hard-core "unknowable" in individuals and communities (that residuum apart from those areas touched by "relationship," which is knowable) that provides the context for the vision of "Gothic" potentialities in both inner and outer life.

Deep South. Gothic is always "deep." For many of us Gothic seems simply romance going off the deep end—a series of bizarre conventions about feeling, behavior, and setting that somehow "go" in poetry but only stagger in prose. "The English Romantic novel," Robert Kiely begins (his language retreating to the more respectable term), "is, in some ways, an embarrassing subject. There is, first of all, the question of its existence."

No there isn't, there is only the question of its name. If the computer of criticism is in one of its binomial moods, then "romance" will claim the Gothic and "realism" will eschew it. In its synthetic mood, criticism will work out the manner by which the impulses of romance, clearly the urgenre, support the impulses of realism. Northrup Frye's splendid little book, *The Secular Scripture,* coins perhaps the happiest phrase for this process: realistic fiction, he suggests, often contains "kidnapped Romance, that is, romance formulas used to reflect certain ascendant religious or social ideals." Studying formal relations in the works of Austen, Charlotte Brontë, and George Eliot, Karl Kroeber sees a Hegelian rhythm—realistic fiction contravening romance, followed by a new flowering of romance, leading to a new form of realism that "incorporates new dimensions of reality explored by the immediately proceding romances."[15] If the computer of criticism is in an analytic mood, then the works I will be studying—*The Castle of Otranto, The Italian, The Monk, Frankenstein, Melmoth the Wanderer, The Confessions of a Justified Sinner, Dr. Jekyll and Mr.*

15 Northrup Frye, *The Secular Scripture* (Cambridge, Mass.: Harvard Univ. Press, 1976), p. 30; Karl Kroeber, *Styles in Fictional Structure: The Art of Jane Austen, Charlotte Brontë, and George Eliot* (Princeton: Princeton Univ. Press, 1971), p. 118. Kroeber goes on to suggest that this flowering of romance, signified especially in the works of Brontë, is one way to distinguish the realism of Eliot from that of Austen; since romance makes accessible to realism the domain of the abnormal, Eliot's novels "comprehended *within their realism* matters which would have been too 'abnormal' for Austen's realism" (my italics).

21

Hyde, and *Dracula*—will come out neatly docketted under a variety of more or less meaningful categories: Gothic, Tales of Terror, Schauer-Romantik, the supernatural, the grotesque, Love and Death in the American Novel, Dark Romanticism, or the Dark Sublime. Gothic is always "dark."

Leslie Fiedler knows its signs: "Our fiction is . . . bewilderingly and embarrassingly [there's that word again] a Gothic fiction, nonrealistic and negative, sadist and melodramatic, a literature of darkness and the grotesque in a land of light and affirmation."[16] But Fiedler on Radcliffe and *The Monk* and *Melmoth* is only repeating Lawrence on Poe. Lawrence knew where the curve of Poe's imagination originated:

> His best pieces, however, are not tales. They are more. They are ghastly stories of the human soul in its disruptive throes. Moreover, they are 'love' stories. . . . Love is the mysterious vital attraction which draws things together, closer, closer together. . . . ["The House of Usher"] is lurid and melodramatic, but it is true. It is a ghastly psychological truth of what happens in the last stages of this beloved love, which cannot be separate, cannot be isolate, cannot listen in isolation to the isolate Holy Ghost. For it is the Holy Ghost we must live by. The next era is the era of the Holy Ghost. And the Holy Ghost speaks individually inside each individual; always, forever a ghost. There is no manifestation to the general world. . . . The Ushers, brother and sister, betrayed the Holy Ghost in themselves. . . . They would love, they would merge, they would be as one thing. So they dragged each other down into death. For the Holy Ghost says you must *not* be as one thing with another being. Each must abide by itself, and correspond only within certain limits.[17]

[16] Leslie Fiedler, *Love and Death in the American Novel* (New York: Stein and Day, 1966), p. 9.

[17] Lawrence, "Edgar Allan Poe," in *Studies in Classic American Lit-*

To abide apart, yet correspond. Separate but consubstantial. Classic Gothic, the orthodox sublime, believes in correspondence, believes in love, strives against limits. It is one of the major "spines" of romance and yet it is one of the most deeply conservative of the romance genres, punishing first the community that declines to strive and then the striving being who preempts that function. Classic Gothic creates the romance world of two opposite absolutes, but the special flavor of the Gothic, as Lawrence notes, is to show not the inevitability and stamina of duality, as romance often does, but the vulnerability of it. *Pace* Levi-Strauss, the bistructured world is radically unstable: it either seeks collapse into oneness or else seeks to generate a third term to marshal itself into unity, not oneness. That is why in the Christian mystery the Trinity needs the Holy Ghost, that unseen triangulation point that makes "person" possible. As we shall see in the last essay of this book, that is what Lawrence means by the Holy Ghost, a third dimension with no manifestation to the general world that provides space to dwell in for beings who otherwise were simply points on a line infinitely collapsing. The Gothic describes the failure of its significant people to generate that triangulation point, to listen to the Holy Ghost. Romance may show the duality, the opposite absolutes, still holding apart in tension; Coleridgean romance may show the emergence, under the aegis of the primary imagination, of a third term "transcending" the paradox; but Gothic romance usually shows the merge back together.

Frankenstein, as we shall see, illustrates all these actions. At the ultimate edge of miserable hostile merging, the creature seeks to generate a third term in the duality, a woman with whom he can triangulate sufficient mental space to deal with Frankenstein. And Frankenstein tries to

erature (1924). The essay is reprinted in *D. H. Lawrence: Selected Literary Criticism*, ed. Anthony Beal (New York: Viking Press, 1966). The quoted passage is from pp. 330-331 and p. 344.

do this himself with his "sister," Elizabeth. Then, jealous and doomed, each destroys the other's triangulation point, the other's Holy Ghost. Instinctively Mary Shelley seeks this same thing in her artistic structure, creating the explorer Walton to raise and then to frustrate expectations of greater mental space within the novel. But though she can give Walton pertinence and even some complexity, she cannot give him weight enough to make that third dimension; so the novel tightens and tautens back into its destined shape, the Gothic romance, the duality snapping back into merge and annihilation. While playing fascinated with separation, the Gothic finds its opposite.

The heretics of the great tradition above all believe in the private whisper of the Holy Ghost, fight for the mental space in which to abide apart, yet cannot rid themselves of that Trinitarian dream of community, correspondence. Small wonder that many sons and daughters of the great tradition turned High Church in the twentieth century. Small wonder too that their progenitors went heretic the century before. For if the era that Lawrence initiated and symbolized was indeed the era of the Holy Ghost (as the one that preceded him is the era of the Son, the humanized god), then the one that preceeded it, that fixed the correspondences of classic Gothic, was unmistakably the era of the Father, a compelling if unsympathetic figure. Doubly fathered as priest or monk, he presides in the significant texts of early English Gothic. He started it all. We start with him.

ONE

GOTHIC FATHERS:
THE CASTLE OF OTRANTO, THE ITALIAN,
THE MONK, MELMOTH THE WANDERER

HORACE Walpole's *The Castle of Otranto* (1765) is a rather gormless tale for which Walpole claimed little, and even the claim he did make—"Terror, the author's principal engine, prevents the story from ever languishing"[1]—is not entirely true. Its merits are not in character, plot, or prose, nor as he had thought, in the dramatic structure, but in half a dozen memorable tableaux,[2] frozen moments of action, which are almost certainly lifted from Walpole's dreams, and maybe yours and mine too.

The narrative proper begins, like a primer in Gothic plot, with the father: "Manfred, Prince of Otranto, had one son and one daughter." A page later, on young Conrad's wedding day, the cry "Oh! the helmet! the helmet!" brings the family to the courtyard, where "—but what a sight for

[1] Horace Walpole, *The Castle of Otranto*, reprinted with *The Mysteries of Udolpho* and *Northanger Abbey* (New York: Holt, Rinehart and Winston, Inc., 1963), p. 4. Walpole published this preface in his own personna in the second edition; the first edition, published several months earlier, contained only the "translator's preface" in his assumed personna. Subsequent references are to this edition and will be cited by page number in the text.

[2] Gothic melodrama really does derive from *The Castle of Otranto* in this respect; most of the important Gothic romances were immediately dramatized in their entirety or contributed familiar "bits" to the wildly successful plays of this genre. A wonderfully entertaining picture of the process is Montague Summers' account of Matthew Gregory Lewis's career as a playwright; he quotes Lewis's candid admission of what "business" was borrowed from *Otranto* and what from *The Mysteries of Udolpho* or other novels for his most successful play, *The Castle Spectre*.

25

a father's eyes!—he beheld his child dashed to pieces, and almost buried under an enormous helmet, an hundred times more large than any casque ever made for human being, and shaded with a proportionable quantity of black feathers." Manfred's stupefied gazing at this portent establishes the first tableau; and the second comes pat a few pages later as, trying to become his own son, Manfred offers himself to the bereft bride, Isabella: "Heaven nor hell shall impede my designs, said Manfred, advancing again to seize the princess. At that instant the portrait of his grandfather . . . quit its panel and [descended] on the floor with a grave and melancholy air" (p. 24). The third tableau, Isabella escaping through the lower vaults of the castle, became the subject of numerous sketches and paintings in the late eighteenth century, for as Walpole says only too truly of his own prose: "Words cannot paint the horror of the princess' situation" (p. 27).

Wanting no daughter, "raving" for more sons, and intending to put away his infertile wife and beget more sons upon Isabella, Manfred meets his match, another father, in the priest Jerome. "I am sovereign here, and will allow no meddling priest to interfere," he says (p. 47), but Jerome refuses to hand over the bride: "she is where orphans and virgins are safest from the wiles and snares of this world, and nothing but a parent's authority shall take her thence." "I am her parent, and demand her," returns Manfred, leaving himself open to Jerome's unanswerable riposte: "By me art thou warned not to pursue the incestuous design on thy contracted daughter" (pp. 49-50). The property of Otranto at stake, Manfred and the real father of Isabella compromise, each to his own best advantage: each will marry the other's daughter, each hopes that his own daughter will bear no sons to his enemy and thus secure the property to him. "Thou art no lawful prince," thunders the substitute father Jerome. "It is done," responds the separated Manfred, and "as he spoke these words three drops of blood fell from the nose of Alfonso's statue" (p. 98).

This serio-comic tableau marks the third ponderous in-
tervention of Alfonso the Good, the true prince, foully
done to death by Manfred's grandfather for the lordship of
Otranto, but not before he had secretly married and begotten a daughter, who married the Count of Falconara,
who fathered the true heir Theodore and then became
Father Jerome after Theodore's disappearance. This young
"lost heir" appears at Otranto in time to be fallen in love
with by both of the girlchildren, Matilda and Isabella, who
are coveted as property by the middle-aged fathers. Thus in
this first of the classic Gothic tales the male ingenue has almost no active role, not even as an object of persecution. He
is simply the convenient receptacle of the least interesting,
most conventional sentiments; he loses his own beloved,
marries her friend as an afterthought, and after an odyssey
as sentimentally banal as Charles II's, he is only a spectator
at his own restoration, which provides the last spectacular
tableau of the tale:

> The moment Theodore appeared, the walls of the castle
> behind Manfred were thrown down by a mighty force,
> and the form of Alfonso, dilated to an immense mag-
> nitude, appeared in the centre of the ruins. "Behold in
> Theodore the true heir of Alfonso!" said the vision;
> and having pronounced those words, accompanied by a
> clap of thunder, it ascended solemnly towards heaven,
> where the clouds parting asunder, the face of St. Nicholas
> was seen; and receiving Alfonso's shade, they were soon
> swept from mortal eyes in a blaze of glory. (P. 113)

One feels impelled to start a round of applause, though
Walpole's priest-narrator informs us instead that the be-
holders fell on their faces, "acknowledging the divine will."
This narrator, it is important to note, is the first of the
holy fathers in the tale, and he may indeed have devious
clerkly motives in telling the story. In a reflex absolutely
central to English Gothic, Walpole affects to find the manuscript of this story "in the library of an ancient Catholic

family in the north of England"—that is, to the comfortable home-counties' Anglican mind, at the edge of the civilized world, where the minions of the great old religion might still dwell. Now, to the enlightened eighteenth-century mind of course, says Walpole in his "translators preface," marvelous visitations, dreams and portents, priestly tyranny, have been "exploded . . . even from romances." Two hundred and fifty years ago it was different, and "an author would not be faithful to the *manners* of the times" to omit them (p. 4).

On the other hand, Walpole offers a singular explanation for the telling of the story. Carefully deducing from stylistic evidence that the manuscript he has found dates from early sixteenth-century Italy, he theorizes:

> Letters were then in their flourishing state . . . and contributed to dispel the empire of superstition, at that time so forcibly attacked by the reformers. It is not unlikely that an artful priest might endeavor to turn their own arms on the innovators; and might avail himself of his abilities as an author to confirm the populace in their ancient errors and superstitions.

"Such a work as the following," Walpole adds solemnly, "would enslave a hundred vulgar minds beyond half the books of controversy that have been written from the days of Luther to the present hour" (pp. 3-4).

Thus in Walpole's crucial narrative conceit, the Gothic arises in "the days of Luther" as a tool of the Catholic Counter-Reformation, the priests of the old dispensation striking from beyond the grave at the new. In the 1760s, as an embattled Catholic Church suppresses the Jesuit Order under pressure from the "rational" despots of the continent, Walpole's "modern" romance restores the Jesuits to the English reader's mind.

Pursuing his scheme for material power, Isabella's father approaches a figure that, "turning slowly round, discovered to him the fleshless jaws and empty sockets of a skeleton,

wrapt in a hermit's cowl" (p. 107). In a "conflict of penitence and passion" he is recalled to his errand, which is to
work the dead Jesuit's will upon the house of Manfred according to the story's governing moral. "Yet I could wish,"
says the "translator" airily of that other living/dead priest,
the writer of the manuscript, that "he had grounded his
plan on a more useful moral than this: that the sins of the
fathers are visited on their children to the third and fourth
generation. I doubt whether in his time, any more than at
present, ambition curbed its appetite of dominion from the
dread of so remote a punishment" (p. 5).

The secret sin that works itself poisonously out into the
open, destroying at a distance of years or even generations,
is a staple of Gothic plot; it is prime evidence for a theological universe, one in which any human act, occasionally
a selfless one like Christ's sacrifice but more often a selfish
one, may call to itself a power that will magnify the act far
beyond the human scale. Time and distance supply some
of the magnification; the Gothic portrays exactly that special dread which arises from the anticipation of remote,
therefore magnified, punishment.

In terms of narrative, however, immediate punishment
is what the Gothic delivers; from the death that opens *The
Castle of Otranto* to the death that opens the novel *Jaws*,
punishment comes first—not, certainly, before the sin, but
before the revelation of the sin. In the Gothic, then, a world
that first seems rational and calm is shattered by an irrational or random punishment, which is then rerationalized
by the revelation of the generating, the original sin. And
punishment in the Gothic, we will note, is most often for
the young, while sin, the ambition for dominion, is the
province of the old. This is one hidden reason why Manfred is "mad for sons"—not only will a son secure the domain but a son will receive the promised doom. The son
must die so that the old man may live.

Or, in the last resort, the daughter must die. Manfred and
Matilda are a curious pair. As Walpole rather casually

29

creates her, Manfred's daughter is as mysterious an object of hatred to Manfred as Isabella is an object of lust. In the "conduct of the passions . . . according to probability" that Walpole feels is the central interest of his "new" kind of romance, these two passions are clearly linked. "I do not want a daughter" rages Manfred to his daughter; "I will be her parent" he insists of Isabella, his son's contracted wife. In the last pages of the book the two women and the two passions link together in a kind of murder/rape: hated by Isabella and haplessly loved by Matilda, Manfred in a fury plunges his dagger into the object of his lust and finds that he has killed the object of his hatred, his daughter. Attempting to shed "Alfonso's blood," he had "shed his own." Alfonso's revenge is complete, and his monk-substitutes are triumphant. Matilda forgives Manfred and thus locks him forever into guilt; he takes the cowl and goes into eternal penitence; woman and priest meet victorious beyond the grave, clouds parting asunder. Isabella and Theodore survive, like Shakespeare's Edgar, never to see so much nor live so intensely again.[3] Manfred and Frederick, two mighty old ones, are defeated by the still older ones, priests of the old empire of superstition. Like Marlowe's Faustus, Manfred believed hell was a fable and learns his mistake: hell is a truth, and it is wherever the sinner is. The artful priest, whom Walpole's "translator" suggests cynically contrived the whole story, has had his sadistic will with the

---

[3] It is interesting to note that the century that produced Tate's "happily-ever-after" *Lear* and Johnson's strictures on the lamentably "mixed" and "painful" Shakespeare also responded powerfully to the dark and formally rough Shakespeare as administered through the Gothic novel. Quotations from *Macbeth, Lear, Titus Andronicus,* and *Richard III* abound as headnotes in Mrs. Radcliffe's and Monk Lewis's works, for instance, and in his second preface to *The Castle of Otranto* Walpole claimed Shakespeare for his model above all in that mixture of "buffoonery and solemnity" (p. 11) which is a peculiar hallmark of the Gothic imagination and which Bram Stoker's *Dracula,* in a passage I want to advert to later, formalizes as a kind of dance between King Death and King Laugh.

Gothic antihero, the separated one, the "man of sorrows" as Manfred calls himself in echo of that ambiguous model Separated Son.

Manfred is also the skeptic, who "doubts whether Heaven notifies its will through friars" (p. 65). Here we locate the real and empathetic terror of the Gothic antihero: in the midst of his power he doubts. Heretic and would-be atheist, he yet wonders whether in fact there is not, somewhere, if not in friars, the face, the portent, the pattern of events in which he should be reading the writing of heaven. No simple savage, Manfred is usually, in the easy eighteenth-century formula Walpole uses, humane and virtuous "when his passions did not obscure his reason" (p. 31). He bears the guilty burden of the tale and shares in the secret sin, but in the midst of his obsession that his house not fall, his mortality not end, he is at least partly drawn to propagate sons on Isabella because she is distantly of Alfonso's blood. So a son of theirs might both preserve his house and restore Alfonso's: a reasonable compromise, it would seem, in any universe but the Gothic, where the powers of evil and good, "dilated to an immense magnitude," pursue their own passionate symmetries, powers made even more dreadful in their abstract emptiness by an eerie familiarity. "This can be no evil spirit," says Matilda in the most Gothic moment of all, "it is undoubtedly one of the family" (p. 41).

Again, one hardly knows how to restrain a laugh. Walpole made no serious claims to aesthetic precision in his composition but simply hoped to "[pave] a road for men of brighter talents" (p. 10). First among those talents was Ann Radcliffe, in whose novel *The Italian* (1797) we find what I take to be the richest, clearest, most morally intense evocation of the classic Gothic universe. Here we find the subtlest working out of that doubly fathered father, the sinful monk, here a family full of evil spirits, here the most elegantly crafted atmosphere of Gothic time and space. Here too is the most detailed exposition of that Gothic dynamic that Walpole saw but never reached: "terror, the author's principal engine" does its job of keeping the mind "up in a constant vicissitude of interesting passions" because Radcliffe has so beautifully orchestrated the two very different but linked terrors of the persecuted and of the persecutor.

And here, since Radcliffe has chosen the spaces of church, convent, and Inquisitorial prison to hold and increase her terrors (moated castles could never be quite as credible a domain of dilated power, not even Udolpho), here is the clearest indication of that special Gothic dichotomy, fundamentally Protestant as Porte noted, between God and the Church. Here the old institution, its ministers and appurtenances, are voluptuously painted, seen, abhorred, fought, thrown down. Religion itself remains untouched, even strengthened. And the great God rules, even as His Church is purged of its villains, its evil fathers. Yet the reader will find it difficult to distinguish the evil father from the good, since they are both—Gothic antihero and Enlightenment God—distinguished primarily for an obsessive, hidden, tyrannous, ambiguous will. Radcliffe's opening lyric about her hero, Father Schedoni, innocently exposes the terrible dilemma in terms of a simile:

> He, wrapt in clouds of mystery and silence,
> Broods o'er his passions, bodies them in deeds,
> And sends them forth on wings of Fate to others:
> Like the invisible Will that guides us,
> Unheard, unknown, unsearchable![4]

Mrs. Radcliffe is distinguished in the history of the Gothic for the invisibility of her God, the inaudibility of heaven's vengeful, signalizing thunder. No "machinery" for her ex-

[4] Ann Radcliffe, *The Italian, or, The Confessional of the Black Penitents* (London: Oxford Univ. Press, 1971). Subsequent references are to this edition and will be cited by page number in the text. This quotation appears on the title page as an epigraph.

32

cept that which human passion "bodies forth in deeds," creates or imagines for itself.

Take the first encounter with the Gothic in *The Italian*. Going with his friend Bonarmo to visit his new love Ellena, the young sentimental hero, Vivaldi, is warned two nights running not to go or he will meet his fate—warned by a person in the habit of a monk who "disappears" after the warning. In his rage Vivaldi may stigmatize the monk as a "demon [who] haunts me," but what he really believes is that the man is a rival for Ellena, and in anticipation of a flesh and blood fight he drags Bonarmo to the gloomy exposed arch that was the scene of the encounter. The scenery works mightily on the friend's sensibility; he admits that in that place and time "there is scarcely a superstition too dark for my credulity," and he proposes that the mysterious figure was "more than human" (p. 19). Vivaldi only smiles. At the same time the friend takes aim at Vivaldi's romantic superstition about a rival for the entirely chaste Ellena— "This surmise of yours is in the highest degree improbable" —and argues Vivaldi out of it.

In Chapter Two (initial exposure in Gothic is quick, though the labyrinthine penetration to the secret sins is long), the reader meets the mysterious figure and receives hints of the way in which he is both "more than human" and Vivaldi's rival. The monk Schedoni is of an unknown, in fact unsearchable, past; he eludes every inquiry. His qualities of person and mind alike exceed the human norm, rather like Frankenstein's creature's; he is too tall, too thin, his eyes too large and piercing, the lines on his face too deep and awful, and his passions, both of reserve and conciliation, of silence and argument, are extended, dilated artificially: "The elder brothers of the convent said that he had talents, but denied him learning; they applauded him for the profound subtlety which he occasionally discovered in argument, but observed that he seldom perceived truth when it lay on the surface; he could follow it through all

33

the labyrinths of disquisition, but overlooked it, when it was undisguised before him." The narrator, in a George-Eliot-like reflex, adds austerely: "In fact he cared not for truth nor sought it by bold and broad argument, but loved to exert the wily cunning of his nature in hunting it through artificial perplexities. At length, from a habit of intricacy and suspicion, his vitiated mind could receive nothing for truth, which was simple and easily comprehended" (p. 34).

It is, perhaps, a measure of the success of the Gothic impulse in the great tradition that this habit of mind, seen here as the Gothic flaw, becomes by the time of *Dracula* the state of the common intelligent mind. Faced with plain tooth marks and the drained body, the scientists in that novel seek in vain for the complicated explanation for the monstrously simple fact before them, and "the doubting of wise men" becomes the crucial ally of the "child-brain" vampire.

Father Schedoni is confessor and advisor to Vivaldi's mother, the Marchesa, in that typical Gothic plot of the old ones against the young; he is thus the right hand of Ellena's rival in the affections, or rather in the possession, of the son. The passion of pride-of-house infects both of Vivaldi's parents, certainly, but in the mother that passion is clearly dilated by infusion from another more "evil" passion, and whereas the father simply meditates the pensioning-off, or at most kidnapping, of the orphaned and portionless Ellena, both the mother and Father Schedoni image her death, leaving the husband more and more out of their meetings as they come nearer to that self-revelation. Thus, as Richardson's Lovelace noted about the fate of Clarissa after she arrived at Mrs. Sinclair's: what might have been robbery in a man's plot becomes murder when a woman enters among the conspirators.

The Marchesa retains Schedoni so that he can suggest to her the dark deeds that "body forth" her own passions but that she cannot acknowledge. He understands this perfectly, playing his role and subtly tormenting her with his understanding of the game, as in a superb scene in Vol. II, ch. 3, where the Marchesa tries for several pages to maneuver Schedoni into arguing her into having Ellena killed. Schedoni both advances and recoils from the idea, tormenting her with his delays and with his hints, and yet smoothing the way to a mutual decision and a shared guilt:

> "You, my daughter, even you, though possessed of a man's spirit, and his clear perceptions, would think that virtue bade her live, when it was only fear!"
>
> "Hah!" exclaimed the Marchesa in a low voice, "what is that you mean? You shall find I have a man's courage also."

And again the narrator steps in to make all clear: "The Marchesa wished him to lead her to the point, and he remained determined that she should lead him thither" (pp. 168-169).

In the business of the deed, Schedoni manipulates the mother expertly: "her purpose was not yet determined, according to his hope . . . [so] the sternness of his vulture eyes was softened and its lids contracted by subtlety" (p. 171). Yet even more interesting is the self-manipulation he exercises upon his own passions. In the words of the narrator: "During the warmth of this sympathy in resentment, the Marchesa and Schedoni mutually, and sincerely, lost their remembrance of the unworthy motives, by which each knew the other to be influenced, as well as that disgust which those who act together to the same bad end, can seldom escape from feeling towards their associates" (pp. 53-54).

A sentence such as the preceding, sure in construction, certain in moral judgment, yet without contempt, is scarcely possible to a Fielding, or even a Richardson but rather suggests the capacious moral intensity of a George Eliot. This intense moral judgment without contempt, this sympathetic ironic candor without superiority, this close experience of the heart's duplicity without despair, is the center of Radcliffe's narrative stance—it is also central to the narrators in the great tradition of English fiction. And the Gothic antihero, the isolato, the anathematized one, has the opposite moral center. What Walpole in his innocence, or haste, saw only as Manfred's surrender of his reason to his passion, Radcliffe pinpoints as Schedoni's "secret contempt" of the generous heart, his obsessed delight in the flaws of the human character, his willful dilation of the evil powers in himself and others—all stemming from the enraged despair of the good in which he seeks to hide his own past crimes. "Schedoni, indeed, saw only evil in human nature" (p. 52), says Radcliffe demurely in the early chapters, and proceeds for several hundred pages to show the world and human nature alternately through both her own and Schedoni's eyes.

In the long duel between Schedoni and the Marchesa for his control of her evil passions, for instance, Schedoni suffers a setback: just at the point of ordering Ellena's murder, the mother hears a requiem sung and is swayed back to human sympathy. Now, one of Radcliffe's own most characteristic and powerful techniques is to dramatize exactly how visual, aural, and tactile stimula, such as scenery, perfumes, songs, vistas, rustles, and gleams, awake and mold the sensibilities, sometimes this way, sometimes that way. And yet seen through Schedoni's eyes that very human openness becomes dangerous and hateful:

> Behold, what is women! said he—the slave of her passions, the dupe of her senses! When pride and revenge speak in her breast, she defies obstacles, and laughs at crimes! Assail but her senses, let music, for instance, touch some feeble chord of her heart, and echo to her fancy, and lo! all her perceptions change:—she shrinks from the act she had but an instant before believed meritorious, yields to some new emotion, and sinks—the victim of a sound! O, weak and contemptible being! (Pp. 177-178)

Certainly, it is an ambiguous susceptibility that we have, but Mrs. Radcliffe insists that we shut ourselves away from it at our own peril:

> Over the gloom of Schedoni, no scenery had, at any moment, power; the shape and paint of external imagery gave neither impression nor colour to his fancy. He contemned the sweet illusions, to which other spirits are liable, and which often confer a delight more exquisite, and not less innocent, than any, which deliberative reason can bestow. (P. 255)

Contracting himself away from externals into a still, hard point, Schedoni hopes to manipulate the outer world to the model of his inner world; his self-control is the most precious thing in the universe to him. No giant hand is allowed into his dreams; nothing will shake him. He is himself the giant hand. He has Ellena kidnapped and placed in a convent until he can persuade the Marchesa to compass her death: even more than the death itself, he seeks to impose his knowledge of himself as a murderer upon all human beings and to take comfort in that. And the girl "apprehended that the strong and invisible hand which governed her course, would never relinquish its grasp until it had placed her irrecoverably beyond the reach of her lover" (p. 61). Vivaldi discovers her, and they escape only to be seized and separated by the officers of the Inquisition. "With the conviction that Schedoni's was the master-hand that directed the present maneuver" (p. 188), the young man stands paralyzed while his almost-bride is taken away.

Yet if Schedoni sees no giant hand on the balcony above him, his assassin-agent Spalatro does: "The bloody hand is always before me! . . . I see it now—it is there again!—there!" (pp. 230, 232). Schedoni looks, and "nothing was visible to him" because he has cut himself off from all the external stimuli that might contemptibly sway a human being. But the agent refuses to do the deed that the Marchesa

37

has at last been brought to order, so Schedoni, drawn by the invisible hand, raises his dagger over the girl and strikes— his own portrait in miniature round Ellena's neck. She wakes, crying to the priest "Be merciful, O father!" She affirms the portrait is of her father, and "Schedoni, the stern Schedoni, wept and sighed. . . . 'Unhappy child!—Behold your more unhappy father!' . . . and drew the cowl entirely over his face" (p. 236).

To the very last pages, Radcliffe allows both reader and characters to believe that Schedoni and Ellena are father and daughter. Schedoni turns out to be the notorious Count de Marinella who, wasting his younger son's inheritance, had his brother di Bruno killed and wed his brother's widow, begetting a daughter with her, as had his brother. Shortly after, an earthquake shook down the castle, and the family scattered, each member believing all the others dead. Confronted a generation later by the beautiful girl-child who wears his portrait, Schedoni falls apart. She becomes to him, as Mathilda/Isabella was to Manfred, an object now of terror (if she were to discover his past), now of wonder (as she pleads for him to show pity to others), now of jealousy (as she wavers between concern for his and Vivaldi's well-being). The assassin Spalatro, who admitted he saw the bloody hand and who actually performed for Schedoni the fell deeds that now tear at the monk's consciousness and plunge him abruptly into paralysis—"fits of abstraction"—is now an object of horror to Schedoni. Self-hatred is displaced upon the agent; if Schedoni can kill his past self, the agent, his own "bloody hand," he believes that memory and actuality will also die.

The truth is, of course, that he can never kill that past criminal self, not only because, in Walpole's terms, the past has its own life and wants its symmetrical revenges. More terribly, like Manfred, Schedoni seeks even in his best moments not forgiveness but a compromise between his recognition of his crime and the immortal maintenance of his "house," his "consequence," the dilation of his power. Now it becomes apparent with what appropriate irony Radcliffe has called the priest-father the Confessor throughout the book. After a lifetime of manipulating others through the weaknesses they confess to him, he is now at the mercy of his own "penitent," the Marchesa, from whose bloody hand he must hide his daughter, the exposed limb of his house. In his fevered imagination the Marchesa, laden with his own displaced malice, is a stupendous figure: "Against her artful duplicity every place would be almost equally insufficient" (p. 288). His brain teems with plans for revealing part of the truth about Ellena to the Marchesa, releasing Vivaldi without incurring hostility, and like Shakespeare's Richard III, turning even disasters to account.

But the Confessor is outmaneuvered in these hopes; the wheel of irony turns another arc, and Schedoni is confronted by his own old confession, made years before in a moment of self-loathing. The seal on his guilt is set, when among the quarrelling inquisitors who have come to judge Vivaldi, wonderfully differentiated by Radcliffe in their various colors of malice, simple self-seeking, argumentative curiosity, and shrewd judiciousness, is revealed an old friend/enemy bearing witness to still another confession, that of the assassin/alter-ego, Spalatro.

Confronted, like Richard, by the ghosts of all his disaffected agents and victims, with his Buckinghams and his Clarences, Schedoni, like Shakespeare's king, goes to his end with that ultimate assertion/admission of the Gothic anti-hero—Richard loves Richard: that is, I am I—holding him firm. No last-minute hysteria for him, or Richard or Iago or even Edmund. Here Radcliffe refines importantly upon the model of Walpole's Manfred who, at the conclusion of the tale, became a monk, whether penitent or not.

Still, with that sense of subterranean authorial approval unmistakable in classic Gothic, Schedoni makes a wonderful exit:

The emotion betrayed by Schedoni, on the appearance
of the last witness, and during the delivery of the evidence, disappeared when his fate became certain; and
when the dreadful sentence of the law was pronounced, it
made no visible impression on his mind. From that moment, his firmness or his hardihood never forsook him.
(P. 364)

External stimuli are wiped out at last, and Schedoni is left
as he wanted to be, motionless mind. Fully in charge up to
the last gasp, he has the Vivaldis and his accuser, Nicola,
summoned "to attend him in his dungeon" (p. 389). There,
"the strength of his spirit contending with the feebleness
of his condition" (pp. 391-392), he forces his accomplice/ac-
cuser to vindicate and free Ellena and young Vivaldi, affirms the coming marriage as if it were he instead of Provi-
dence directing the tableaux, then dies with "a demoniacal
sound of exultation" on his lips, having secretly administered poison both to himself and to Nicola. In a grand
sweeping-up of loose questions at the end, the vain Marchesa is found to have been "dying, or as good, for many
years" (p. 375), and she expires with her own confession
made public. Ellena is discovered to be in fact the daughter of Schedoni's murdered brother, and the novel ends at
a wedding fete, "*O giorno felice!*"

In *The Italian*, Radcliffe rescues her happy day with the
aid of no supernatural machinery at all. Even the kind of
trick that made her famous—the seemingly supernatural
occurrence that is explained as natural in the end—is only
briefly toyed with. In the opening chapters, the monk who
warns Vivaldi is seen to "disappear." In the closing chapters
the same visitant "appears" in Vivaldi's locked prison cell,
and his voice floats disembodied in the Inquisitorial hall.
But it is only pages, not volumes, later before we learn for
sure what the whole tone of the book has suggested to us,
that the ultrasensitive nerves of the observer, mediating be-

tween external stimuli and internal anxiety, produce "the unearthly" every time.

This intense, this exquisite susceptibility is Radcliffe's special province of character: pursuer and pursued share it; the sentimental hero is distinguished by it, and the Gothic antihero Schedoni is characterized by his profound attempt to deny it; male and female, servant and lord possess it. Sensation bombards consciousness unmercifully in a universe with strong resemblances to Lawrence's. The Gothic antihero's consciousness grapples with its own moods and in a fury of bitterness pronounces the human condition intolerable, human nature evil, morality laughable. For him the only possible value is courage, or rather "hardihood," a good word of Radcliffe's that expresses steadfastness in the rain of contradictory emotions, the wish to be the immovable object among the irresistible forces that follow the universal curve, change the mind, and change the matter. In the eyes of his victims (which is also by the crafty convention of the Gothic the initial stance of the reader), the Gothic antihero seems to be the irresistible force, the master of plot, sweeping obstacles out of his way in the dash for power. Yet the twist inward from the terrors of the threatened community to the terrors of the monster that all good Gothic fiction makes always shows us from the antihero's standpoint a universe sweeping *him* away, sucking at his ground, his identity, his meaningfulness, his "consequence." And the dilation of his power, the solidifying of his consequence, is a struggle to hold ground, to stay in place in a cosmos that moves. The brilliant transfixing eye of the Gothic antihero is only secondarily a machine to destroy enemies; essentially it is attempting to pin the world in place. The simple lesson of the Gothic, then, is first for the Gothic antihero, with whose terrors we are always brought to identify. The lesson is that eat power, eat people, dilate your desires as you may, you cannot grow big enough to avoid being rolled away around the curve.

41

Schedoni makes a good try. Like Iago he attempts not to change when his fortune changes; he carries some of his secrets and some of his motivations with him so that even when he is rolled away, a rather disturbing blank is left. For the lesson made literal, dark, and chilling, we can look to the end of another monk, M. G. Lewis's Ambrosio. This man too has an intimation of greatness and an even more powerful sensation of instability and shrinkage; he also has —handy Gothic mechanism—an androgenous demon to taunt him with nursing unacted desires. In rage, in lust, in hate, he must flesh out each desire as its baby shape is revealed to him, and finally, ripe to bursting with hypocrisy, matricide, incest, rape, and blasphemy and huge with despair, he falls, "rolled from precipice to precipice," is broken down by rocks and picked apart by birds, dissolved by sun and air, his substance eaten by insects and washed into the sand and the sea "on the seventh day" of his decreation.[5]

The literalness of this dilation/decay picture is matched in *The Monk* (1796) by the entirely concrete descriptions of appetite and acting-out that Lewis manages. When Walpole's Frederick confronted the warning figure in *The Castle of Otranto*, it merely showed him a skeleton face, but in Lewis's inserted ballad of "Alonzo the Brave and Fair Imogene," the death's-head image is elaborated:

> The worms they crept in, and the worms they crept out,
> And sported his eyes and his temples about,
> While the spectre addressed Imogine.　　　　(P. 308)

Lewis is fond of the worm. Imprisoned beneath a convent to bear her illegitimate child, the wretched Agnes of the novel's subplot suffers the baby's death and her own slow

---

[5] M. G. Lewis, *The Monk* (New York: Grove Press, 1952), p. 420. This picture, interestingly, was expunged in the fourth edition by Lewis, and a new ending adjuring his "Haughty Lady" readers to be merciful to the sinners he depicts was substituted. Subsequent references are to this edition and will be cited by page number in the text.

starvation more than picturesquely: "Often have I at waking found my fingers ringed with the long worms which
bred in the corrupted flesh of my infant" (p. 396). In an
adjoining dungeon under the monastery, the girlchild Antonia suffers brutal rape "amidst these lonely tombs, these
images of death, these rotting, loathsome, corrupted bodies"
(p. 369) and at once becomes the object of profound disgust—Ambrosio drops her "as if he had touched a serpent"
(p. 371).

One may, of course, provide against the worm by philosophy. His sister Agnes starved and persecuted, his beloved Antonia ravished and murdered, the young Lorenzo
is laid down on a bed of sickness, but his father, one of the
indomitable old ones of Gothic fiction, is already making
plans for his son's next advantageous marriage. He knows,
Lewis quotes Shakespeare's blithe Rosalind approvingly,
that "men have died, and worms have ate them, but not
for love" (p. 381).

This adolescent daredevil calling of a spade a shovel is
the special mark of M. G. Lewis; along with it goes an entertainingly mixed diction, from the sublime—" 'Oh, let me
then die today! Let me die while I yet deserve the tears of
the virtuous. Thus will I expire!'— (She reclined her head
upon his shoulder; her golden hair poured itself over his
chest)" (p. 109)—to the ridiculous—"We were obliged to
pass by the barn, where the robbers were slaughtering our
domestics" (p. 134). There is also a prurient ellipticism—
"Heedless of her tears, cries and entreaties, he gradually
made himself master of her person, and desisted not from
his prey til he had accomplished his crime" (p. 368)—which
seems more offensive even than Mrs. Radcliffe's honest
stuffiness.[6]

One of the likeable things about *The Monk*, however, is

[6] Summers, who is in his blithe way a partisan of Monk Lewis's,
opines that Mrs. Radcliffe differs from Lewis as spiritualist from
realist: "his Paphian encounters would have curdled her very ink."
See *The Gothic Quest* (London: The Fortune Press, 1939), p. 233.

a kind of macabre sportiveness about the conventions of superstition. When the subplot lovers, Raymond and Agnes, wish to escape together from Lindenberg Castle, they make convenient use of the figure of the Bleeding Nun, whose legendary story Agnes recounts "in a tone of burlesqued gravity" (p. 152). This ghost, who walks every year with a lamp and a dagger doing penance for incest, adultery, and murder, seems a convenient disguise, and "the playful imagination of Agnes" contrives an escape plan for herself. What then is Raymond's shock to discover later that he has run off with the real Bleeding Nun in the ghostly flesh, who turns out to be another of the great old ones—"the great aunt of your grandfather" (p. 181). Raymond buries her guilty bones in the right place and gets his Agnes back again after horrid happenings. The moral is perhaps: don't make fun of your aunt or she will come out of the nearest ghost story and get you. The same advice should have restrained Agnes, whose duenna/aunt, the Baroness Lindenberg, conceives a mighty passion for the young Raymond about which the two youngsters can scarcely keep a straight face. But the mockery of carnal Aunt Rodolpha backfires just as the mockery of ghostly Aunt Beatrice had: "My love is become hatred" (p. 156) the Baroness shrills, and hounds Agnes nearly to her death.

Serious interest in *The Monk* as a Gothic novel centers on this almost farcically concrete sense of intrafamily lust and on the nightmarishly swift transmutations of love into hatred, of pride into abjection, of desire into disgust that govern this Gothic universe. The whole agony of Ambrosio, like the more subtle abstract one of Schedoni, arises from a near-Sartrean nausea at the intolerable switchability of outer forms and inner moods. Pride turns to self-hating lust, lust fastens (through the veil of piety) on the picture of the Virgin Mary in Ambrosio's room, the picture takes flesh in the beautiful boy Rosario, Rosario at close quarters becomes the ravishing Matilda, Matilda in the closest embrace of all, soul to soul, becomes a demon, and at this point

44

Ambrosio, who glutted every appetite and was everything, is suddenly food for worms and flies, and then is nothing.

The Monk is interesting for its complicated treatment of these common Gothic themes and for the surprisingly frightened review it provoked from that other lover of Gothic machinery, Samuel Taylor Coleridge.[7] In addition, Michael Sadleir put his finger on one aspect of Gothic fiction highly significant for the "serious" novels that followed when he remarked that the Gothic was "as much the expression of a deep subversive impulse as . . . the French Revolution."[8] And Montague Summers enjoyed testily countering: "A revolution in literature, a revolt against a set and sapless classicism . . . is a very different thing from a social Revolution. . . . The great Gothic novelists abhorred and denounced political revolution. . . . The Romanticist is not a Revolutionary; he is rather a reactionary."[9] And the truth is that despite some de Sade-like moments, even the schauer-romantik or adolescent daredevil branch of English classic Gothic fiction is surprisingly circumspect in its revolutionary impulse. After all, the point of the splendid overthrow of monkish tyranny that animates the early Gothic is surely that in the English mind it *has been overthrown*. In fact, part of the appeal of the Gothic great old man is that he has defied external tyranny and set up his own heart to rule, whether like Manfred in defiance of institutional power or like Schedoni and Ambrosio in hypocritical wielding of it. Lewis can quote Cowper's paean to "thine altar, sacred Liberty" (p. 333) as his climax approaches, but like Cowper and the other Romantics it is order that he really seeks: natural order, organic growth, and judicial pruning.

And since it is necessarily the Gothic antihero's liberty

---

[7] Coleridge published his appalled reaction ("And this—from a legislator of the land!") in the *Critical Review* of February 1797.

[8] "The Northanger Novels," English Association Pamphlet, no. 68 (London: Oxford Univ. Press, 1927), p. 4.

[9] *The Gothic Quest*, pp. 398, 399, 404.

that is to be pruned, and since no sentimental young hero ever quite matches him in this kind of romance, it is left to the community to do that job, or more specifically, to the institution. It ought to be no surprise to anyone, then, that after revelling in the liberty of the mind-freed monk and in the delicious tyranny of prioresses and inquisitors, both Mrs. Radcliffe and Lewis turn in the end to the Inquisition for the establishment of order: it is a judicious president of the Inquisition who reforms his unruly members and brings Schedoni down; it is a courageous nun with the archers of the Inquisition at her back who brings down Lewis's tyrant prioress and eventually Ambrosio with whom she is in league. The remaining nuns go happily into other more orderly convents, saved from popular fury by the officers of the Inquisition under the local duke, to whom they "felt a proper sense of gratitude" (p. 378). It is from the safety of the Inquisitorial prison that Ambrosio flees to the demon who finally destroys him.

No, as a social impulse it is not revolution that the Gothic celebrates, not even reform, but riot. The general community is present in early Gothic mostly in the form of hand-wringing, wise-cracking servants, their function as chorus to yearn for an end to turmoil and the restoration of the proper heir and the *giorno felice*. In *The Monk*, the community is a credulous mob with the same lightning shifts of mood as the hero. In Lewis's climactic scene, the nuns holding Agnes prisoner leave the convent of St. Clare in an elegant procession complete with choruses, floats, and tableaux. "St. Genevieve" surrounded by "merry devils" who try to distract the saint from her office is the biggest crowd pleaser. Lorenzo accuses the prioress, and the carnival laughter changes instantly to rage in behalf of the persecuted daughter of the Church. The local duke threatens them with the Inquisitorial archers, and they fall silent. The reforming nun adds her accusation, and the crowd rushes her to the highest throne in the procession, demanding not so much an explanation as a sensational tale, which

46

she gives them, "a tale, whose circumstances will freeze every honest soul with horror" (p. 339). The honest souls below, not frozen, drag the prioress from her guards and beat her to death ("til the body became," Lewis delights to add, "no more than a mass of flesh, unsightly, shapeless, and disgusting" [p. 344]) and then riot through the district, destroying the convent, killing both innocent and guilty nuns, and even killing each other in their blind fury.

While that obsessed love which turns to objectless hatred pursues its communal path in the midnight streets and courtyards above, a linking action occurs in the tunnels and tombs below the convent, as Ambrosio pursues Antonia first with blandishments, then with threats: love turns to fear and disgust, rape leads to murder, and murder leads the Monk finally to self-destruction. Rather than be killed by the community, which Ambrosio holds in a measure responsible for the whole terrible sequence because of its original pride-inducing worship of his eloquence and personal magnetism, "a reverence that approached idolatry" (p. 402), he chooses, in classic Gothic fashion, to go to hell by himself.

Meanwhile the community, linked as it always is to the Gothic antihero, performs on him, in concert with the elements, its own decreation:

> For some days the whole city was employed in discussing the subject. Gradually it ceased to be the topic of conversation. Other adventures arose whose novelty engaged universal attention; and Ambrosio was soon forgotten as totally as if he had never existed. (P. 417)

Thus the man who separated himself from his family to pursue his private dilation is drawn back irresistibly, though unknowingly, to murder his mother, rape and murder his sister, and through those crimes to destroy himself. The man who separated himself from the community to become its idol provokes the community into a general destruction, which brings him down. He gets what he wanted, and he

47

is frozen forever in hell, in self-hatred, while the universe, matter and mind, curves on.

Matching Lewis's procession-riot in Gothic import, though exceeding it both in philosophical subtlety and in gore and terror, is the spectacular riot toward the end of the Spaniard's tale in C. R. Maturin's *Melmoth the Wanderer* (1820). Again the scene is Madrid; a spectacular procession, "the most solemn and superb ever witnessed," winds through the streets partly as an entertainment and partly as a direct expression of ecclesiastical authoritarian power, statues and crosses towering over accompanying monks and soldiers. Again the community packs itself together to watch, in an unconscious demonstration of its counterpower:

> I wondered how the procession could ever make its way through such a wedged and impenetrable mass. At last, I could distinguish a motion like that of a distant power, giving a kind of indefinite impulse to the vast body that rolled and blackened beneath me, like the ocean under the first and far felt agitations of the storm. The crowd rocked and reeled, but did not seem to give way an inch.

Again the mood of worship seizes the crowd:

> Then I saw the multitude at a vast distance give way at once. Then came on the stream of the procession, rushing, like a magnificent river, between two banks of human bodies, who kept a regular and strict distance, as if they had been ramparts of stone,—the banners, and crucifixes, and tapers, appearing like the crests of foam on advancing billows, sometimes rising, sometimes sinking.

Again one of the worshipped, an official of the Church, is accused of crime, and the mood of the people changes to murder. Neither the intangible might of spiritual condemnation nor the swords of the military trying to keep order

48

can prevent the death, the literal effacement of the proud
monk:

> They dashed a mangled lump of flesh right against the
> door of the house where I was. With his tongue hang-
> ing from his lacerated mouth, like that of a baited bull;
> with one eye torn from the socket, and dangling on his
> bloody cheek; with a fracture in every limb, and a wound
> for every pore, he still howled for "life—life—life—
> mercy!" till a stone, aimed by some pitying hand, struck
> him down. He fell, trodden in one moment into san-
> guine and discoloured mud by a thousand feet.[10]

But there are several important differences. Lewis's
crowd, separated from the reasonable figures through whose
eyes the narration is proceeding, goes on to wreck everything, feeling itself sheer power, becoming in its turn the
tyrant authority. But Maturin's crowd sweeps up all by-
standers, including the reasonable narrator, in a complex
rhythm of ecstatic identification first with tyrannic cruelty—
"I echoed the wild shouts of the multitude with a kind of
savage instinct"—and then with cruelty's object—"then I
echoed the screams of the thing that seemed no longer to
live, but still could scream; and I screamed aloud and
wildly for life—life—and mercy!" There is, for the moment, no one apart from this crowd—not in the tale nor
outside it. Maturin's skill in rendering the awful scene completes on the reader's own level the crucial moral and social point the Spaniard makes at last: "The drama of terror
has the irresistible power of converting its audience into its
victims."[11]

10 C. R. Maturin, *Melmoth the Wanderer* (Lincoln, Neb.: Univ. of
Nebraska Press, 1961), pp. 194-196. Subsequent references are to this
edition and will be cited by page number in the text.

11 In a fine short study entitled *Horror and the Paradox of Cruelty*
(Middletown, Conn.: Wesleyan Univ. Press, 1969), Philip P. Hallie
remarks on this special fascination of the drama of cruelty for the
observers, who feel "an impulse to make those energies part of our-

Another difference: Lewis's murderous crowd, blundering about, discloses, if just too late, the individual villainy of Ambrosio and directly brings about the capture of the guilty and the release of the innocent. Maturin's crowd, in keeping with the incomparably darker view of humanity and fate that animates *Melmoth the Wanderer*, spies the innocent Spaniard, Monçada, in his hysterical fit of identification with its victim. They had thought him dead, but now instead of being mercifully decreated and forgotten, he is re-created: the story "was now repeated by a thousand mouths" (p. 199), and Monçada escapes the resulting dragnet of the Inquisition only by a hair.

And a final difference. Lewis's prioress is a tyrant-mother guilty of her children's death, but the victim monk in Maturin's crowd was an intemperate son, a parricide. And this, in a thoroughly black world made livid here and there by the austere curses and destroying laughter of the greatest of the great old ones, Melmoth the Wanderer, is ultimate crime. For in this universe the old men hold fast to their wealth, their power, their obsessive purposes, their lives, with a monstrous passion that bids fair to suck the whole planet dry. The end of such a passion, as they understand full well, is that the universe simply slides away out of their grasp, and they, like the lovers they mock and victimize, will be destroyed, leaving nothing in the world of the novel but pitiless withering irony.

Melmoth is both the finest and most representative example of classic English Gothic and a deeply impressive novel in its own right. Like Richardson's *Clarissa*, it marshals its great length and its repetitiveness somehow in its favor to achieve a narrative of harrowing intensity. Tale succeeds tale, story unfolds inside story, each slanting in-

---

selves, its victims. In the midst of our terror there is an impulse for self-surrender . . . this ambivalence of the victim toward [the] victimizer. This yearning does not light up the darkness; here love is indeed blind; this yearning is full of terror and the darkness of the understanding. It is the Noche Oscura of St. John of the Cross" (p. 12).

exorably into the same scene, set in madhouse or monastery, prison or refuge, public feast and solitary wedding, and deathbeds from seventeenth-century Madrid to nineteenth-century Dublin, where malice contends against innocence and power against love. Here one's strengths and one's weaknesses equally bring desolation, and one's human understanding and even one's natural affections are recognized as brittle, artificial defenses against emptiness and despair. Here at the very end of the mind's dodges and the heart's resources, "community" becomes the urge to pollute the world, "diminish . . . misery by dividing it, and, like the spider, feel relieved of the poison that swells, and would burst, by instilling a drop of it into every insect that toils, agonizes, and perishes in [my] net—*like you!*" (p. 90).

Here at the point to which either deep thought or deep feeling brings every man and woman, where the only escape is by way of the iron butterfly of imagination renewing every day the hope of escape, waits Melmoth the Wanderer, with his unspeakable bargain, with its "incommunicable" condition. As the tales move to this point in the hearing of the reader's friend, young John Melmoth, he interrupts the narrator with shocks of recognition and is rebuked: "Have patience, and you will find we are all beads strung on the same string. Why should we jar against each other? our union is indissoluble" (p. 229).

Our indissoluble union is the identity of spectator with victim that Monçada experiences at the riot, defined earlier and ironically by the parricide monk:

> It is actually possible to become *amateurs in suffering.* I have heard of men who have travelled into countries where horrible executions were to be daily witnessed, for the sake of that excitement which the sight of suffering never fails to give, from the spectacle of a tragedy, or an *auto da fe* [*sic*], down to the writhings of the meanest reptile upon whom you can inflict torture, and feel that torture is the result of your own power. It is a species of feeling of which we never can divest ourselves. (P. 160)

51

It is the union of tales, author, and reader, which Maturin unwisely tries to break in a disclaiming footnote: "As, by a mode of criticism equally false and unjust, the worst sentiments of my worst characters, . . . have been represented as *my own*, I must here trespass so far on the patience of the reader as to assure him, that the sentiments ascribed to the stranger are diametrically opposite to mine, and that I have purposely put them into the mouth of an agent of the enemy of mankind" (p. 233).

Maturin is ingenuous here. Melmoth is a complicated character, the apotheosis of the figure seen in Milton's Satan and in classic Gothic, with significant genes from the Romantic poets—the self-dramatizing misanthropy of Byron's narrators, the crushed rage of Shelley's speakers in the face of the tremendous pageant of human stupidity and cruelty. His early life and the circumstances of his bargain with "the enemy of mankind" are shrouded in mist; we know only that this elder brother of an Irish Cromwellian,[12] stricken with a virulant form of that "curiosity" which is the peculiar eighteenth-century name for hubris, disappeared to the Continent in the early 1600s and is reported at scenes of despair and death over many lands for the next two hundred years. And since every line, every story and substory of the novel demonstrates that the enemy of man is man, we have to conclude, without even the ambiguity that surrounded Lewis's demonic Matilda, that Melmoth is his own enemy. As for the rest of the race whom he appears to persecute, the truth is that each visited soul *calls* Melmoth to himself or herself; he is the visible form of that desolating self-hatred, that withering loathing of life, which fascinates the heart and hypnotizes the mind.

For most of his visitations, Melmoth has only to dramatize the real answers to the rhetorical questions preachers ask at funerals:

12 We note again this near conflation of the Catholic and Protestant counterreformations: the Cromwellian Melmoths have moderated back into the Anglican John of the novel's frame, but the elder brother is still in direct league with the devil.

"Why hast thou, Oh God! snatched him from us?" And a deep and hollow voice from among the congregation answered: "Because he deserved his fate." . . . "What," proceded the preacher, pointing to the corse, "what hath laid thee there, servant of God?" "Pride, ignorance, and fear," answered the same voice. (P. 28)

Like the deceased servant of God, Father Olavide, who sought in "forbidden studies" the actual presence of "the evil one" and dropped dead at the sight of Melmoth, these victims summon Melmoth as the final form of their own pride and malice.

But to those whose tales form the basis of the novel, he comes summoned not by their surrender but by their struggles against what he represents and has surrendered to. The Englishman Stanton, also a man of "curiosity," is imprisoned in a madhouse by a young relative who covets his fortune. Neither the fight not to become what he sees around him nor the effort to relax into it avails him; he sees before him an eternity of torment, always on the threshold of release into madness but never quite across it. His fellow madmen are sunk in the satisfying logic of new worlds created by their "ruling passions" of religion and politics, or old worlds created out of one totally preemptive memory, like the woman who constantly relives the night her family burned before her eyes in the great fire of London. The Spaniard Monçada is imprisoned in a monastery by parents who conceived him before they were married and wish literally to sacrifice him for their sins. Like Stanton in the madhouse, he is surrounded by all the most despicable human ruling passions in all the most fantastic shapes, people who have adapted to their prisons by creating obsessed little worlds in which the most trivial breaches of decorum or the most minor debates over rules become profoundly significant *coupes de théâtres*, as Monçada phrases it. Like Stanton, he alternately rages against and tries to submit to the intolerable, can do neither, and lives in a frenzy that makes him wine to Melmoth's peculiar thirst. And like Stanton, Monçada refuses the bargain that Melmoth offers, but falls victim to him in another sense: both men, countries and generations apart, take the mysterious knowing stranger for *their* ruling passion, hang his portrait around their necks, and seek him far and wide.

The world Maturin creates in the first two tales is the familiar Gothic space inhabited only by victims and tyrants, rendered perhaps more intensely here than anywhere else in classic Gothic. The iron bars mocking the sweet air, the enclosing walls of prisons, the highly charged gestures of nature ("the first flash of the lightning broad and red as the banners of an assaulting army . . . shatter to atoms the remains of a Roman tower; the rifted stones rolled down the hill" [p. 23]) and of man ("It was on the fourth night that I heard the shriek of the wretched female;—her lover, in the agony of hunger, had fastened his teeth in her shoulder" [p. 165]), build a wonderfully disturbing rhythm of awful powers clutching, of narrow escapes that lead to still worse imprisonments, of helping hands reaching out only to be chopped off.

In the third tale of the Indian, however, a new strain enters the music—love, or more particularly, women's love. And whereas before the novel showed Melmoth trying to bring all the destructive passions, fear, rage, jealousy, to a final "natural" conclusion in damnation, here we see him trying the same thing with love. For this enterprise he goes to an island girl, whose solitary harmony with nature and separation from human society have made her incapable of evil; in joy and wonder, she accepts the stranger as she accepts herself, the flowers, and the trees, as simply another beautiful thing that grows on the island. Laying hold of this joyful givenness, Melmoth proceeds, by artful use of his presence and absence, by alternate cajolery and argumentation, by the brilliant re-creation in his own person of the tree of the knowledge of good and evil, to raise in Immalee/ Isadora that ecstatic and terrible love that is the most doomful madness of all:

To love . . . is to live in a world of the heart's own
creation—all whose forms and colours are as brilliant
as they are deceptive and unreal. . . . [Lovers] have but
two eras in their delicious but visionary existence.—
presence-absence. These are the substitutes for all the
distinctions of nature and society. The world to them
contains but one individual. . . . To love is to live in an
existence of perpetual contradictions—to feel that absence is insupportable, and yet be doomed to experience
the presence of the object as almost equally so . . . to be
eloquent in his absence and dumb in his presence . . . to
feel that our existence is so absorbed in his, that we have
lost all consciousness but of his presence . . . to *be* only
because *he is,* and to have no other use of being but to
devote it to him, while our humiliation increases in proportion to our devotedness. (Pp. 278-279)

Even after she is restored to lost family and community
Immalee/Isadora admits in shame and triumph that she
loves this love. And after the declaration, Melmoth re-
nounces her forever and "disappears" in a glorious demonstration that the true nature of love is an inevitable cycle
of obsession, betrayal, madness, and extinction.

Two subtales within this one, both heard by Isadora's
father as warnings for her safety (one is from Melmoth
himself) alter but do not really counter for the reader
Melmoth's dictum that love is doom. The Walberg branch
of the family of Guzman is brought down to starvation by
old Guzman's dying malice and pride and the Church's
avarice: yes, their mutual love allowed them to survive for
a long time with the intolerable, but the distraught husband had already fantasized and half carried out the murder of his father and his children when the authorities burst
in with the news of another will and coming wealth. Elinor
Mortimer tried honorably to uproot from her heart her
love for John Sandal after he deserted her, as he tried to
forget that the woman he had wanted to marry was secretly

his sister: yes, both survive intact and try to turn their aching hearts to other objects or to religion, but by the time that they are in each other's arms again, John has lost his mind as the result of his mother's having confessed she lied to him about a secret relationship between himself and Elinor in order to keep him for herself.

In all of these cases, the Gothic vendetta of the old against the usurping young is carried through to mutual destruction. The young achieve at best the triumph of a momentary foothold of trust and loyalty outside the world of terror and pain that the malice of the old has created out of the young person's screaming sensibility—a temporary edge of sanity from which to balance that terrible reality against a fragile but steadfast intuition of faith, hope, and charity. On that intuition, staring all of their contradictory experiences in the face, not resolving the contradiction, they perish. So it is with Immalee/Isadora, her family victims of Melmoth's wrath, Melmoth's own child mysteriously dead at her breast, breathing her last in the prison of the Inquisition where she has been brought as bait to trap Melmoth. Although she has strength enough to reach up out of her obsession in the conventional way— "Oh, that I had loved none but God—how profound would have been my peace"—when the priest invites her to direct her thoughts to the hope of paradise, her last words, italicized by Maturin to increase the *frisson*, show the obsession still preempting all but the edge of consciousness: "Paradise! *Will he be there!*" (p. 405).

So it is too with Melmoth himself, though in reverse. He was ordered out from the bloody ruined banquet hall of Immalee's family: "Go, cursing and to curse," and he responded fiercely, "I go conquering and to conquer" (p. 397). And it is true that in the universe Maturin creates, Melmoth seems to conquer; the whole planet, its time and its space, seems to offer no lasting home to the gentle and innocent and loving but only to the proud passionate souls, burning with malice and huge with the wielding of pre-

56

ternatural power, whose dilation Melmoth is. Yet in terms of Melmoth's own peculiar bargain and his eventual fate, he is clearly not the conqueror. The awful condition upon which he was to offer deliverance from the world's victimization to Stanton, Monçada, Walberg, Elinor, and Immalee was to change destinies with himself—each of these, and all those whom he tempted over the nations and the generations, refused.

Does this mean he is defeated? From one point of view, yes. The clergyman Maturin offers us the suggestion that the sound human heart, even pushed to the desperate limit of torment, will not change places with its tormentor. Is this because, ultimately pushed, it can reach that established though precarious edge of moral autonomy where it can choose love and community instead of power and isolation? Perhaps. Or is it because it can see in the burning eyes of the powerful tormenting Melmoth and hear in his hideous laugh a pain and terror that exceeds its own, and therefore prudently chooses to stay in the frying pan rather than leap into the fire? From this latter point of view, Melmoth is again the classic eighteenth-century Gothic antihero, so caught up in his cynical exploitation of power, so paralyzingly dilated with ego, that his cynical wisdom is its own obsession and he is his greatest victim; his is the fate of Ambrosio, to be dragged from his chamber up to the top of a high mountain, to fall and be smashed to pieces on the crags and washed to oblivion in the "engulphing ocean."

Perhaps. Yet Maturin is strangely ambiguous about Melmoth's end. Are those cries of supplication or cries of blasphemy that issue from the Wanderer's chamber on the last night, John Melmoth wonders. Is death, the ending of his fruitless 150-year quest for another like himself, something he desires or fears? He announces to young Melmoth and Monçada that he is "about to resign that existence" (p. 407), but in the Wanderer's dream he shrieks to arrest the hand of the giant clock that approaches the end of his span. Waking, he asks to be alone for the last hours of his mortal existence, "if indeed they are to be the last" (p. 411). When the chamber is found empty, Monçada and young Melmoth follow a trail to the top of a rock, "a kind of track as if a person had dragged, or been dragged, . . . through it" (p. 412). And though they find on the crag below the handkerchief Melmoth had worn, no trace of the man himself is found.

In this ambiguity there is room for another theory closer to the heart of the Gothic: in a thousand years Melmoth would not willingly resign his mortal existence; his eternal defeat in that chosen quest for another like himself is the term of his existence, and he has chosen it knowingly so that he can stay forever in mortality, a fixed hard choice-point for men as long as there are men. No Gothic antihero wants to find another like himself; Melmoth has made himself such a living horror that no one could choose to be like him. He has made himself a still point in a turning universe, has arranged according to the very nature of the human heart to live forever—O Gothic heaven!—because every single time he offers his existence to another, offers to turn over his allotment in the natural way to a would-be child of his, that child will choose instead to die and return to him his horrible existence. Once he almost slips, is almost drawn into the universal curve of love, death, and change, lets slip a morsel of his being, and Immalee bears him a daughter. The infant is with her on her penultimate night, and so is Melmoth. Hours later Immalee has refused the great exchange, and the child is dead; the next night she dies herself. And Melmoth lives, even past the end of the novel, I would say, proof, in eighteenth-century terms, "of a truth . . . echoed by every human heart in the habitable world: . . . *no one, to gain that world, would lose his own soul*" (p. 409). But proof in nineteenth-century terms, as we shall see, that life, pure roaring amoral energy as Melmoth has made himself, does not resign itself unless it is harnessed by a specific morality and is indeed practically unkillable.

Yet there is a special fear that goes with that unkillability, that life past mortal or rather moral span, that life past death. It is a very modern fear, now that our lives are subject to artificial prolongation—a fear dramatized not so much in the novel as in the film versions of *Frankenstein*, a fear unforgetably imaged at the end of the life-preserving nineteenth century in the figure of Dracula and hinted at all over the world of Melmoth the Wanderer: the fear of automatism. Thus Monçada describes the special horror of conventual immurement in a dialogue with a priest already sunk into thinghood:

> "But your regularity in religious exercises—"
> *"Did you never hear a bell toll?"*
> "But your voice was always the loudest and most distinct in the choir."
> "Did you never hear an organ played?" (P. 86)

Thus he describes his own sinking: "No automaton, constructed on the most exquisite principles of mechanism, and obeying those principles with a puntuality almost miraculous, could leave the artist less room for complaint or disappointment, than I did" (p. 76). And thus even more frighteningly does he describe to young Melmoth the inner mechanism of an earlier heroic scene:

> Melmoth then changed the subject, to thank him . . . for the preservation of his life.
> "Senhor," said the Spaniard, "spare me; if your life was no dearer to you than mine, it would not be worth thanks."
> "Yet you made the most strenuous exertions to save it," said Melmoth.
> "That was instinct," said the Spaniard.
> "But you also struggled to save mine," said Melmoth.
> "That was instinct too, at the moment," said the Spaniard. (P. 53)

Even the tools of heresy can turn orthodox, of course. And to remind the English how some religions closer to

home promote automatism even without the aid of convents and Inquisitorial powers, Maturin gives us in the first
tale the picture of the "puritanical weaver who had been
driven mad by a single sermon from the celebrated Hugh
Peters, and was sent to the madhouse as full of election and
reprobation as he could hold,—and fuller . . . [who] regu-
larly repeated over the *five points* while daylight lasted"
(p. 37). In the final tale he offers the acceptably sane life of
Elinor Mortimer's puritan aunt:

> She rose at a fixed hour,—at a fixed hour she prayed,—at
> a fixed hour she dined,—at a fixed hour received the god-
> ly friends who visited her . . .—at a fixed hour she prayed
> again, and then retired,—yet she prayed without unc-
> tion, and fed without appetite, and retired to rest without
> the least inclination to sleep. Her life was mere mecha-
> nism, but the machine was so well wound up, that it ap-
> peared to have some quiet consciousness and sullen satis-
> faction in its movements. (P. 363)

We think here again of Brontë's image of the heretic, com-
posing her spontaneous and painful narrative as an alternative to the genuinely soothing but frighteningly automatic
and solipsistic counting of beads in the convent cell. That
part of the self which responds to some other force than
personal will, that part open to demonic or heavenly possession, to the shaping primary imagination, is alternately
the terror and the hope of men in these novels. Orthodoxy
counsels greater openness to these forces; atheism counsels
their expulsion. The heretic narrates from the point where
personal will and impersonal force compete to enlarge their
domains in the mind.

This heaviest fear of all, the fear of automatism, is clearly present to Melmoth the Wanderer, the fear that even
"that ghastly and derisive smile" of self-mockery may now
be simply automatic, like the victims' rejection of his bargain, like his eternal offering of it, and like his eternal in-

effectual dream of closure. For Melmoth, for the automaton, no closure is possible. Or rather—supreme horror—the closure was coextensive with the quest, and all is helpless repetition, the sins and the punishment of the Gothic father circling forever through one being.

GOTHIC BROTHERS: *FRANKENSTEIN,*
THE MEMOIRS AND CONFESSIONS
OF A JUSTIFIED SINNER,
DR. JEKYLL AND MR. HYDE, DRACULA

In the eighteenth century the place of separation is the monastery, and the tyrannizing force is passion, or superstition. When Mary Shelley comes to write *Frankenstein* in 1816, the place of separation, though it is a "tower" like Schedoni/Marinelli's, is now a laboratory, and the tyrannizing force is reason. But the structure is essentially the same, and so is the conflation of monk and priest in the identity of the separated one. Victor Frankenstein raises his hands over the mortal scraps on his table and calls down into them the ideal.

In the ordinary celebration of this mystery, there is always a space between the altar and the chapel; the priest is both dangerously separated from the community and together with it. But it makes *all* the difference in the circling story of Victor Frankenstein that there is no community present at his Mass—not even an altar boy and certainly not the "Igor" of popular fancy. The priest is separated but together, son and brother to the congregation that calls him father, child to the power he calls upon, brother to the person who emerges in the mortal scraps from and with and to the father. Without the presence of the community somewhere behind, this dynamic is lost, and a terrible, simple, doomful transference occurs in the would-be priest: you choose to play God, and the deity points out that the position is already occupied.

He who separates himself as completely as Victor Frankenstein did from the curve of the community, from the marrying-begetting, giving-over of life to the new generation, dying in his turn—he is by that wish a murderer, and in the Gothic he gets, horribly, what he wishes for. It is an economical universe: if he wants immortality, all the life in the world, Victor is doomed to take it away from others. It is one thing to take life away from his mother; in the natural order he may do that, if his son may take it away from him in turn. But utterly fixed in outrage and guilt when he looks upon the death of his mother, Victor expects to keep death at bay by reversing her example, by withholding life from his own child, who would take it away. It is a mistake to be too far misled by Victor's unselfish wish to become "the father of a new race of beings." Like Walpole's Manfred, who calls in sly desperation for "more sons" when the family sin strikes his son dead, he is not so spontaneously generous with life as he seems.

We must look instead to these fathers' attitudes towards their daughters, objects of horror and lust, custodians of life barred from the fathers' control by the oldest of patriarchal taboos. Manfred doesn't want his daughter, and he finally kills her; Frankenstein looks at his daughter/creature lying unanimated on the table, recognizes that she, unpredictable and uncontrollable, will take both the son/creature and the new race out of his power, and destroys her.[1] With Schedoni it was his brother, his brother's wife, and almost his daughter that were destroyed; with Ambrosio it was his mother and sister, living their share of the familial life and by accident or design, by agent or by hand, killed and emptied of it so that the preempting father could live, could forsake

[1] There are several arresting accounts of *Frankenstein* as representing its author's female vision of birth trauma, of which Ellen Moers' is the most persuasive (*Literary Women* [Garden City, N.Y.: Doubleday, 1976], pp. 90-100). My own interest in the Gothic as descriptive of criminal preemptions makes me prefer Robert Kiely's notion that a hidden feminism leads Mary to punish Frankenstein for seeking "to combine the role of both parents in one, to eliminate the need for woman in the creative act." See *The Romantic Novel in England* (Cambridge, Mass.: Harvard Univ. Press, 1972), p. 164.

his real nature as son/brother, could avoid his Trinitarian choice to curve his lifeshare back to the Father or pass it on to a son.

Victor Frankenstein is a compendium of all these Gothic dooms and mysteries. From childhood he knew himself "the idol" of an aged father and a young mother whose special tenderness to him sprang from "the deep consciousness of what they owed towards the being to which they had given life."[2] When he was five he was "given" an adopted sister, Elizabeth Lavenza: "My mother had said playfully, 'it was a pretty present for my Victor.' . . . I, with childish seriousness, interpreted her words literally." In school he was "indifferent . . . to my schoolfellows in general," but he selected one friend, Henry Clerval, whose interest in "the moral relations of things"—politics, culture, social interactions—complemented Victor's own lack of interest in these things and left him free to pursue that "curiosity" about the "hidden laws of nature" that is among the "earliest sensations" he can remember.

Perhaps his deepest sensual memory is the outrage he felt at the death of his mother. Death, "that most irreparable evil," seems to his questing mind the key to the significant secret of life: "To examine the causes of life we must first have recourse to death" (p. 311). Anatomy is "not sufficient" recourse; the boy spends "days and nights in vaults and charnel houses" (p. 312). In the grisly study of worm and waste, of rot and decay, he is checked by no natural or supernatural repugnance, having had a thoroughly republican pragmatic education: "My father had taken the greatest precautions that my mind should be impressed with no supernatural horrors" (p. 311). Neither is he checked by that fellow-feeling with human life, both human and natu-

[2] Mary Shelley, *Frankenstein, or The Modern Prometheus* (1818; reprinted in *Three Gothic Novels* [Harmondsworth, Middlesex: Penguin Books, 1968]), p. 291. Subsequent references are to this edition and will be cited by page number in the text. Quotations in this paragraph can be found on pp. 293-296.

ral, by which Radcliffe and the Romantic poets dramatize the harmonic universal curve: "My eyes were insensible to the charms of nature. And the same feelings which made me neglect the scenes around me caused me also to forget those friends . . . whom I had not seen for so long a time" (p. 315). Cut off, self-separated, he "lost all soul or sensation but for one pursuit" whose goal, the benevolent and disinterested creation of life, seems from the start linked with a sinister dilation of himself: "A new species would bless me as its creator and source. . . . No father could claim the gratitude of his child so completely as I should deserve theirs" (p. 314). Even the wish to so increase his consequence constitutes a profound separation, so that in Victor's words, "I shunned my fellow creatures as if I had been guilty of a crime" (p. 317).

When on that "dreary night of November" the conception is birthed, love turns shockingly, without warning, to hatred, as it is wont to do in the Gothic: "I had desired it with an ardour that far exceeded moderation, but now that I had finished, the beauty of the dream had vanished, and breathless horror and disgust filled my heart" (p. 318). He rejects and abandons his desire, his eight-foot-high dilation of himself. And the creation and rejection together bring on the novel's most significant dream: Victor is embracing Elizabeth—she is a corpse—the corpse is his dead mother— "and I saw the grave worms crawling in the folds of the flannel" (p. 319). A Freudian might see in the whole progress of Frankenstein via the dream a wish to join his dead mother in the grave; but as we've seen, the Gothic adds an extra dimension, a profound resentment of the sources of one's being, especially the female sources, stemming from the desire to be one's own source—and goal. Thinking that he has sought life in the embrace of death, Victor has in fact been seeking death in the embrace of life. And his creature/son, his hold on immortality, his dilated self, too gigantic to be overturned in the going-out of time, has this same nightmare in his makeup. Insofar as he is Frankenstein's avatar, the creature proceeds with dreamlike thoroughness to cut off all those whom Frankenstein cut off from his affections while he fed his obsession: his brother, his friends Justine and Clerval, eventually and indirectly his father, and of course preeminently, his "more than sister," his almost-wife, Elizabeth.

Insofar as he is his own being, first Adam and then Cain and finally Satan, the creature reenacts the whole hopeless cycle. He cannot stand the state of separation. He knows he is the son, but his deep resentments make full recommunion impossible. Since his memory constantly torments him with Frankenstein's rejection and with Frankenstein's ultimate responsibility for his being, and since he looks like what he is, the separated one perversely joined together, he can deceive no one, make no compromise or accommodation.

Nor can Frankenstein. Like Prospero he finally acknowledges this thing of darkness his, even acknowledges this thing of darkness him: "my own vampire, my own spirit let loose from the grave and forced to destroy all that was dear to me" (p. 339). But he cannot bring himself outside himself, to share his power, to actualize woman on any level: "Alas! to me the idea of the immediate union with my Elizabeth was one of horror and dismay. . . . Could I enter into a festival with this deadly weight yet hanging around my neck?" he mourns, ambiguously clutching his albatross (p. 420). As it has always been in the Gothic, the drama is inexorably between himself and himself, since he wants to keep himself fixed and immortal, yield no atom of his being back to death. This drama, which in figures like Ambrosio and Schedoni went under the name of hypocrisy in eighteenth-century Gothic, enters the nineteenth century as schizophrenia, the actual detachment of multipersonalities. In nineteenth-century Gothic the fragment of self that escapes and must be reabsorbed is not recognized as child, as it was in Walpole and Radcliffe, but as brother, as it is in Hogg's *The Memoirs and Confessions of a Justified Sin-*

66

ner and Stevenson's *Dr. Jekyll and Mr. Hyde.* Mary Shelley's book, which dramatizes both a kind of hypocrisy and a kind of schizophrenia in Victor's consciousness, both a father-child and a brother-self relationship in the two central figures, stands right at the tipping point in Gothic presentation of this dilemma.

Consciously, both beings know they are in a battle for the one available quantum of existence, "bound by ties only dissoluble by the annihilation of one of us" (p. 363). It is above all Frankenstein who seeks to annihilate the creature, to take back his life. But the creature's indestructible dilated self, even in the accomplishment of pursuits and torments upon his creator that double his own agony, keeps him alive at all costs out of a powerful sense that he cannot sustain existence alone, that alone, despite his size, he is not quite real, cannot stand his ground. Locked together in a race to the North Pole, the one steady state on the compass, the two pass and sight and lose each other in a fury of malice and thwarted love. The father has looked upon himself, and that look has begotten a son; the son has looked upon the father, and that look which was, as both recognize, naturally holy and creative, is now an Unholy Ghost of utter destruction, decreation, the last term in the series of Mary Shelley's atheistic trinity.

That Unholy Ghost is the real pursuer of both beings into the ice. Frankenstein dies, hounded. Looking at the corpse, the son in this trinity keens in the Miltonic biblical cadence that marks all their exchanges: "In his murder my crimes are consummated; the miserable series of my being is wound to its close" (p. 492). "My work is nearly complete," he repeats to Frankenstein's friend, the explorer Walton: "Neither yours nor any man's death is needed to consummate the series of my being and accomplish that which must be done, but it requires my own. Do not think that I shall be slow to perform this sacrifice" (p. 495).

This has a familiar holy ring, but we should remember that *Paradise Lost* impressed the creature not as a heroic

67

sacrifice-story but as the story of a God "warring with his creatures" (Book II). And indeed the reader of Milton's epic learns about two trinities. One is holy, with an arguably Arian twist to its picture of a gaudily subservient not very separated or choice-agonized Son and a Spirit that "came forth spontaneous" to create the world at the moment when the Father most shone in the Son. Another is unholy, remarkably imaged in Book II as Satan, Sin, and Death. In this incestuous trinity, the just-rebelling Satan looked upon himself, and that look, that self-perception, half narcissistic love, half candid disgust, burst from the Father as a daughter, Sin, not Son. The two curved back toward each other again in stark narcissism, and that mutuality emerged as Death: Death, repeating the narcissism that is always half love, half hate ("though more, it seems/ inflam'd with lust than rage"), revisited the daughter and produced the fearful hellhounds who also endlessly repeat the enraged lust. This trinity's dramatic climax comes when Death and Satan meet at the gates of hell, Father and Unholy Ghost ready to slay one another until the mediating word, Sin, convinces each to turn his hate and hunger outward, upon creation. At the end of the encounter, fighting has turned to fawning, and Death, the final inevitable term in the series of Satan's being, the Unholy Ghost, spirit of decreation, emerges through the great gate to breathe upon the new earth his invitation to return to eldest night and chaos, where all movement is either purposeless strife or blind rigidity.

No wonder Victor Frankenstein shrinks at the last moment from the animation of his daughter, the next term in what has now turned into an unholy series of his being. No wonder that the creature, looking upon that destroying father, shifts permanently to that unholy series, turned in a moment from Christ to Sin. He binds Frankenstein permanently to himself, as Sin did Satan, by the murder of his wife, the closing off of any positive or normal further terms of his being, and by the constant saving of his creator's life,

1. "The great old one" descends frighteningly upon the young in this illustration of one of the significant motifs of eighteenth-century Gothic. The drawing by John Masey Wright portrays some of the major characters in Horace Walpole's *The Castle of Otranto*; the old man descending from the portrait is the once-wronged Alfonso the Good.

2. In this illustration from Anne Radcliffe's *The Italian*, the monk
Schedoni breaks up the marriage of the young hero and heroine, separating them and intending their deaths. Behind him looms the crucifix which he thinks gives him power, but which in fact is an icon of
the eighteenth-century Gothic scene before it, the destruction of the
young by the "father."

3. Milton's *Paradise Lost* and Michelangelo's "Creation" clearly figure
in the artist's image of the awakening of Frankenstein's creature, as the
scientist flees from his unholy attempt to make life out of death. The
doppelgänger similarity between Victor and his monster is marked.

S·G·Hulme Beaman

4. One of the primary images in nineteenth-century Gothic works is embodied in this illustration of the creation of Mr. Hyde by the scientist Jekyll. Again the similarity between the "monster" and the human creator whose dark side he expresses is marked.

supplying him with food as Sin does Satan during his progress to the final frozen rest. The two persons, first and second terms of the trinity, alternately holy and unholy on
that long progress, lock regards, lock wills, seek to materialize a third person. Will it be the Holy or the Unholy Ghost?
Something in the serenity and even nobility of the ending
of the novel seems to promise the former, the creative spirit,
brooding over northern waters and keeping alive in the explorer Walton and his men somehow *both* prudence and
aspiration. Perhaps. But the content of the wish, the Word's
word at the end, seems unequivocally decreation, the in-
voking of the reign of night and chaos. On his self-made
funeral pyre the creature expects that "light, feeling and
sense will pass away, [and] my ashes will be swept into the
sea by the winds. . . . the very remembrance of us both will
speedily vanish" (p. 496).

Decreation—the pulling apart, laying asleep, washing
away of body, soul, and consciousness—is a Gothic anti-
mystery vividly dramatized in novel after novel, one that
rules more strongly than the creation mystery, the awakening moment. The exquisite, the unbearable "awakeness" that
characterizes the citizens of the Gothic world, that makes
them see and hear the ghosts that we do not, gives way in
the central citizen, the Gothic antihero, to a recognition,
willing or unwilling, of decreation, the falling asleep.

Frankenstein is a deeply complex and somewhat ambiguous palimpsest of analogies that play more or less heavily
at different times. It will not do to regard Victor Frankenstein simply as mad scientist as do historians of the science
fiction phase of Gothic, for he also has crucial roles to play
as cloistered monk, as flawed God, as antihusband. And
now critics who come to look more closely at the author of
this remarkable novel are recognizing in Victor Frankenstein too a variation on the Shelleyan doomed seeker, an
Alastor who refuses all comfort in the community, vile
stuporous mass that it is, to seek his vision of ideal beauty
with such passion that the actual loving figure of the In-

dian maiden beside him becomes the illusion and the abstract illusion becomes the reality. Or on another level, Frankenstein seems like the poet of "Epipsychidion," a man who seeks as a lover not an autonomous human being but his imagined double self, that "soul fled out of my soul" which he dreams of taking apart from the world into a tower on an island where he and his recovered soul will melt back together again in a creation (love) that sounds more like a decreation, first of the other being, then of the single soul:

> In one another's substance finding food, . . .
> One hope within two wills, one will beneath
> Two overshadowing minds, one life, one death,
> One Heaven, one Hell, one immortality,
> And one annihilation.

(Ll. 580, 584-587)

These are Shelleyan decreation poems, written in the same span that saw the great creation, or rather resurrection myth, of "Prometheus Unbound." *Frankenstein* was published in 1816, and it partakes of the same ecstatic despair before the old aesthetic paradox: the poet sets out to create an image of beauty and instead looses into the world, soul of my soul, an image of death. The poet masters himself in the arduous making of the poem, but the poem, once free, is masterless. And vulnerable. Critics in the world may turn on the poem and attempt to kill it as (let us say) "a loose baggy monster." Or the poem may turn harsh and tear human nature, and in the general emotional conflagration, poet and poems may lock together in a miserable destroying bond that leaves no room for the living woman, who is the daughter of William Godwin and Mary Wollstonecraft after all, and hence no anxious bourgeoise, but who would still quite like to be a wife.

If Frankenstein as creator is of changing import, alternately Shelleyan resurrector and Miltonic Nobodaddy, even more so is the creature. Automaton and artwork, son and brother, alter ego to Frankenstein not as black is to white but as mirror is to man, or imagination is to the whole being, the creature matches Frankenstein in his progress from Adam to Satan, from Abel to Cain. In their stature, their capacity to think and feel more intensely than the community, in the profound sense of original grace and gift that attends them and the equally profound intuition they both have of secret and original sin and burden, both beings are the Gothic antihero as Manfred described himself, the man of sorrows.

Yet behind that phrase in the Western Christian heritage stands another figure, of whom the Gothic antihero is not a blasphemy but an appropriation. He too is a Son pursued and killed by the Father; yet as in the case of Manfred it is not so much the Son who must be annihilated but the sin that the Son harbors. In the Christian vision of this second Adam, the Father's Son remakes himself out of the sins of men, constructs a new being, as Frankenstein did, from the limbs and organs of criminals and vagrants. The creature, both apart from and together with his father, recognizes his dependence and struggles against it, knowing that his father's will curves toward his death. At the end, the creature decides to fulfill that will. He sets off to construct his funeral pyre partly to end his personal torment and to leave a world made cold by the absence of his creator but also to fulfill the last wish of Frankenstein, which was that the creature, whose relationship to the human community if not to Frankenstein himself is now unambiguous hatred, remove that threat to the community: "Thou didst seek my extinction, that I might not cause greater wretchedness. I shall . . . consume to ashes this miserable frame, that its remains may afford no light to any curious and unhallowed wretch who would create such another as I have been" (p. 496).

Thus at the end, the creature leaves unsolved in himself the two great paradoxes of the novel. The community of feeling beings is so linked that when he causes wretchedness to Frankenstein whom he knows or even to Justine

71

whom he knows not, he feels wretchedness, and when they cause him misery, no exertion of will or reason, not even the anticipation of his own remorse, can keep him from returning misery to them—he is "the slave . . . of an impulse which I detested yet could not disobey" (p. 493). Yet both creature and creator, because they cannot disobey the impulse that irresistibly feeds their life into the community, also cannot resist the contrary impulse to go apart, to seek truths where community is not, to do their greatest endeavors where men are not.

This is Frankenstein at the beginning, holding his little community of family and friends in stasis and at a distance while he pursues his object. And thus he is even at the end. In his pursuit/flight with the creature in the Arctic, he has been succoured by the explorer, Walton, who also has as his object the conquest of the farthest material secrets. Like his creature after him, Frankenstein tells his tale as a warning to all who would travel too far out of the will and the touch of community, and he looks forward to his death as the seal on that warning. Yet when the men of Walton's ship vote to turn back from the dangerous ice and gales, Frankenstein harangues them to continue, to "believe these vast mountains of ice are molehills which will vanish before the resolutions of men" (p. 486). The impulse to move out of community into the void, to compel the community to submit to his desire if he can, or to go on without the others if he must, is alive in *Frankenstein* to the very end. And beyond. Embodying that impulse, the creature sets off into the north wastes in the novel's last sentence—not wearily or reluctantly but rather "springing" from the ship. He intends, it is true, to go to extinction, or if to a life after death, to a place tranquil and unquesting where "my spirit will sleep in peace, or if it thinks, it will not surely think thus" (p. 497). Yet the novel does not show his extinction anymore than Maturin shows Melmoth's, and succeeding generations of the community, responding unerringly through their own artists to Mary Shelley's real message,

have brought him back to seek friends, to be repulsed, to kill
and be killed and remain unkillable.

So it is essentially with the other masterpieces of nineteenth-century English Gothic, with those unkillable energies liberated as the protagonists' brothers or masters or
lovers in the psychodrama of Hogg's *The Private Memoirs
and Confessions of a Justified Sinner* (1824), Stevenson's
Dr. Jekyll and Mr. Hyde (1886), and above all, with those
dilating desires never relinquished but held demonically in
classic Gothic style by the single isolated being, Maturin's
Melmoth or Bram Stoker's Dracula.[3]

The two former novels are linked with *Frankenstein* in
their sense of the exemplary destruction of a *soi disant*
privileged and questing being. In Hogg's fable, which is
wonderfully illuminated in the manner of Scott with Scottish superstition and Scottish caustic peasant wit, the protagonist is Robert Wringhim, whose sense of Calvinist election, like Frankenstein's sense of intellectual election,
inflates his soul until it can no longer be held in one case.
The elegant young gentleman he meets and attaches himself
to, whose countenance shifts sometimes into a dreadful
familiarity with his own, who feeds all his egoistic, finally
homicidal and then suicidal desires, is taken by Robert
first as the incognito Czar of Russia, and then, rather flatter-
ingly, as the devil himself. While hateful and even dire acts

---

3 This is the case too with those other much studied masterpieces
of Victorian Gothic, *Wuthering Heights* and *The Turn of the Screw*.
James has characteristically drawn the red herrings of sexual per-
version and pure "evil" across the path as possible explanations for
the persistence of his ghosts (or alternatively, of his hallucinating
governess), but Brontë's story is clearer and starker. Energy, human
power—especially power divided against itself as Cathy's is—cannot
be entirely eliminated. If there are plenty of characters like Brontë's
Lockwood or James's narrator who cannot imagine unquiet sleepers in
the graves, there are many, like Nelly or Mrs. Grose, who can, and
others, like Heathcliff and the governess, who must and whose imagination is therefore a participation in that power.

that he doesn't remember doing are reported of Robert, the young man Gil-Martin becomes the most vivid thing in his life, next to his hatred of his brother, George Colway. George is the legitimate son of Lord and Lady Dalcastle, and Robert, though he thinks himself the second Dalcastle son, merely adopted, "elected" by the Rev. Wringhim, knows at some level that he is Wringhim's and Lady Dalcastle's illegitimate son, another Gothic child intolerably double-fathered, both spiritually and materially, by one powerful obsessed old man. The duality that results in the pressured psyche, the simultaneous conviction of sin and of election planted in his infancy and heightened by the paradoxes of an inflexible Scottish Calvinism, is another nineteenth-century Protestant variation on the eighteenth-century Catholic hypocritical monk. Here he is transformed into the mad-canting Presbyterian of two hundred years before. Hogg's novel, published the year prior to the repeal of the Anti-Catholic Test Acts, thus obliquely restores to the English reader a kind of prejudicial fear that he is on the conscious level discarding. The story is still comfortably distant in time, but the material space and the supernatural cast of mind are altering. Victor Frankenstein conceived his first creature in Switzerland, but he went to northern Scotland to build the second; Robert Wringhim meets his embodied hatred, guile, and misery outside Edinburgh. The Gothic is coming closer.

The man Robert meets on the road after his election tells him, in phrases that might have come from either Frankenstein's creature or Milton's Satan: "We are all subjected to two distinct natures in the same person. I myself have suffered grievously in that way. The spirit that now directs my energies is not that with which I was endowed at my creation . . . and, since my conversion, my misery has been extreme."[4] Anguish, the Gothic tells us over and over, is even

4 James Hogg, *The Private Memoirs and Confessions of a Justified Sinner* (New York: W. W. Norton, 1970), p. 174. Subsequent references are to this edition and will be cited by page number in the text.

a greater dilator of the ego than joy. Frankenstein's creature could not resist the competition even at his creator's death-bed—"Blasted as thou wert, my agony was still superior to thine" (p. 496)—and in Robert the old religious conviction that greater misery is the ticket to greater glory is fed by competition with his mysterious young friend, "that mighty potentate of misery." The consequence of such dilation is that one loses the boundaries of one's palpable being, an experience rendered memorably by Hogg in Robert's narration of his "strange distemper":

> I generally conceived myself to be two people. When I lay in bed, I deemed there were two of us in it; when I sat up I always beheld another person, and always in the same position from the place where I sat or stood, which was about three paces off me towards my left side. . . . this occasioned a confusion in all my words and ideas that utterly astounded my friends, who all declared that, instead of being deranged in my intellect, they had never heard my conversation manifest so much energy or sublimity of conception; but, for all that, over the singular delusion that I was two persons my reasoning faculties had no power. The most perverse part of it was that I rarely conceived *myself* to be any of the two persons. I thought for the most part that my companion was one of them, and my brother the other; and I found that, to be obliged to speak and answer in the character of another man, was a most awkward business in the long run. (Pp. 139-140)

My brother the other. The inner struggle between his two selves, his healthy brother and his loved monarch of misery, is soon over. Led by his companion, Robert goes forth to explore and act out all the dreadful possibilities of elective Christianity, challenging the gigantic mercy that is, epistemologically, more than equal to the fullness of puny human crime. The progression is from filicide, to matricide, to suicide. It cannot be halted by the increasing intuition, given by his constant mental pain, that damnation or destruction are his goal, since pain and wretchedness are now the index to heavenly glory as well as damnation. And it cannot be halted, more significantly, since crime in the devil's dictionary, or de Sade's or Raskolnikov's, is the measure of a man's freedom. As Frankenstein's knowing and despairing creature cleaves to the evil that "is become my good," Robert Wringhim hesitates before the darkness that he assures himself must be light—and Gil-Martin rouses the community to burn his house: "So fare it with everyone who puts his hand to the great work of man's restoration to freedom, and draweth back, contemning the light that is within him!" (p. 206).

In the tale that Gil-Martin (or Satan, or Robert himself) tells of being Czar Peter honing his character in preparation for the great work of freeing his serfs, Hogg is playing ironically with revolution—playing ironically but conservatively, as Lewis did. His respect and love for the Scottish community is of course much greater than was Lewis's for his Spaniards. But he has Lewis's eye for the transmutation of community, into party, into mob. His picture of an Edinburgh evening turned into a bloodbath between the prelatic and covenanter parties as a cover for the special crime meditated by brother upon brother is less gory than Lewis's mob scene, less elevated and philosophical than Maturin's, but it is defter, more detailed and credible in its rendering of political and religious high spirits melding into antagonism, being turned aside by circumstances and then gathering force again to turn upon itself:

A mob is like a spring tide in an eastern storm, that retires only to return with more overwhelming fury. . . . Finally it turned out that a few gentlemen, two-thirds of whom were strenuous Whigs themselves, had joined in mauling the whole Whig population of Edinburgh. The investigation disclosed nothing the effect of which was not ludicrous. (P. 30)

76

A credulous people, with the spirit of factional and then general murder easily raised in them, is of course one of the most useful of Gothic terror-conventions. The convention's function is twofold: symbolically to enact on the community level the transformation from benevolence to malice and from inactive to active, focused ego that takes place in the Gothic antihero's soul; practically to block him off from all escape from his personal demon once he has fully chosen his obsessed solitary path. In Hogg's *Memoirs*, a mob drives Wringhim from his murdered brother's domain of Dalcastle when they discover, through Gil-Martin's agency, the bodies of Wringhim's mother and sweetheart. Totally alone, pursued as a murderer, he flees to hiding and is ultimately ejected from every refuge. Escaping from one suddenly unsafe hideaway, he entangles himself in a room-size weaver's loom, rendering a superb image of the trapped soul trying to evade the universal harmony: "My feet had slipped down through the double warpings of a web, and not being able to reach the ground with them (there being a small pit below) I rode upon a number of yielding threads . . . I was utterly powerless" (p. 195). He calls out to the family for rescue, and is evicted from the house.

Escaping from a similar situation, he darts through a stable and is battered from wall to wall by the terrified animals. Driven from his third and final refuge with a poor family over the English border as the result of a tumult of execrations from the outside, Robert is no longer sure whether it is demons or the alerted community pursuing him. "Friend," he urges the landlord, "no Christian would turn out a fellow creature . . . in the midst of such a commotion of the villagers" (p. 210). But when he is turned out, his perceptions change: "I was momently surrounded by a number of hideous fiends, who gnashed on me with their teeth, and clenched their crimson paws in my face. . . . They all had monstrous shapes" (p. 211).

This is the community monsterized in the despairing imagination of the separated one. Yet after all, the com-

77

munity—especially the wider commuity of friendship around the more dangerous intensities of the family—is the source of those gentle affections, that humorous criticism, that deep wordless wisdom, which proposes the proper size for a man's spirit. Profoundly ambiguous in its capacity to set boundaries, to make demands, to establish "home" and "norm," to reconstitute itself endlessly without ultimate reference to particular souls, the community in the Gothic is alternately the tool and the master of the solitary spirit, alternately the cast-off shell of his dilating ego and its crushing vise. At the end, engaged with his demon on the road to suicide, Robert Wringhim writes his story in a long narrative that trails off in a series of letters, Bunyan-like, to the Christian reader. These last scenes are one of Hogg's triumphs: the wretched isolato addresses the community in the certainty that he is its exemplar, but whether of steadfast persecuted elected virtue or of duped and damned criminality he scarcely knows. He scarcely knows either to whom he writes—to God, to himself, to an equally beset reader whom he tearfully wishes "a happier destiny than has been allotted to me" (p. 213), to a "reflecting reader" who should "judge . . . to what I am now reduced" (p. 216), or to the interfering narrow-minded skeptic, nemesis of all Gothic antiheroes, to whom he directs his final crabbed words: "I will now seal up my little book, and conceal it, and cursed be he who trieth to alter or amend" (p. 217).

The Private Memoirs and Confessions of a Justified Sinner shares with Frankenstein and with Dr. Jekyll and Mr. Hyde a triple Chinese box narrative strategy that also dramatizes the message of involvement between the community and the isolated schizophrenic soul. No longer are the reasonable editor and the horrid story separated by great time and distance, as was The Castle of Otranto from its editor, as was the story of Schedoni the Confessor from the shocked English tourists who ask for the tale in Radcliffe's preface. Mary Shelley's Walton is on the interface between the reader and the man Frankenstein, whom he meets exploring. Walton feels some of Frankenstein's centrifugal drive, but he feels the community-link even more strongly. After listening to Frankenstein's story and then his account of the creature's story, Walton returns to England with his frightened crew, mourning the death of that beautiful spirit, keeping it alive in his own muted way.

In rather the same way Hogg's editor, a sedentary Edinburgh advocate addicted to the "ingenious fancies" of *Blackwood's Magazine*, notices an account there by one James Hogg describing the finding of the perfectly preserved corpse of a legendary suicide, and visits the grave again with Hogg. On the body he finds the *Memoirs* and publishes them, along with a prefatory section on such facts of the case as are ascertainable from other documents and from historical inference. Evidence shows that at the very last minute Wringhim and the community made one last gesture of mutuality and security: the justified sinner changes clothes with a shepherd on the Scottish hills (clearly Hogg's reference to himself, the Ettrick shepherd), and in that garb "was made welcome in every house." Yet his despair and pride attract the demons back, and he comes out from the community a last time to end his life. The editor adds a conclusion in which he confesses "that I do not comprehend the writer's drift" (p. 229). Like Walpole's Anglican editor musing on the wily priest who wrote *The Castle of Otranto* to entrap a superstitious people, Hogg's liberal editor approves the Calvinist *Memoirs*, "a bold theme for an allegory, and would have suited that age well," and then goes on to propose a tentative explanation for the undoubted suicide that should give pause to all prospective authors: "[He] wrote and wrote about a deluded creature, till he arrived at that height of madness that he believed himself the very object whom he had been all along describing" (p. 230).

That authors and readers are themselves that terrible object being described, is made perfectly clear in Stevenson's *Dr. Jekyll and Mr. Hyde.* Here too we start out in company with reasonable hearers and tellers and move slowly toward the secret sin or sorrow at the heart; not until two-thirds of the way through this short novel (as in *Frankenstein* and the *Memoirs*) do we finally get "Henry Jekyll's Full Statement of the Case." First we meet Utterson the lawyer, whose restrained doubleness is evident in the first paragraph: "lean, long, dusty, dreary and yet somehow loveable . . . drank gin when he was alone, to mortify a taste for vintages; and though he enjoyed the theater, had not crossed the door of one for twenty years."[5] There is already something sinister in this description. Like the town of Auchtermuchty in Hogg's fable, which grew "so rigidly righteous [with] preaching, praying, argumentation, and catechising . . . till the deils in the farrest nooks o' Hell were alarmed, and moved to commotion" (*Memoirs,* p. 180), this overbearing austerity seems to be asking for a horrid visitation.

Fortunately, tolerance of other men's pleasures, or perhaps a vicarious enjoyment of them, keeps Utterson in balance. The reader is less surprised than the town to see the dull and stony lawyer in constant company with "the well-known man about town, Mr. Richard Enfield" (p. 5). From Enfield, Utterson hears of the man Hyde, who in Enfield's sight knocked over and trampled upon a child by accident but without remorse. Two kinds of duality in the incident still haunt Enfield: the "black, sneering coolness" in the man of violence, and more, the hot frightening rage in himself and in the doctor who was called for the child: "He was the usual cut and dry apothecary . . . with a strong Edinburg accent, and about as emotional as a bagpipe." But in the doctor's face as he looks on Hyde, Enfield saw the twin of his own feeling, "sick and white with a desire to kill him." But the men transpose the homicidal desire into

5 Robert Louis Stevenson, *The Strange Case of Dr. Jekyll and Mr. Hyde* (New York: Bantam Books, 1967). Subsequent references are to this edition and will be cited by page number in the text.

a more acceptable key, threatening Hyde with the ruin of his character and procuring money from him for the injured child. Interestingly, the women onlookers cannot transpose their hatred: "We were keeping the women off him as best we could, for they were as wild as harpies."

Since the check given by Hyde was signed by Utterson's friend Jekyll, the lawyer is drawn into the case by curiosity. Yet clearly his friend is not the sole reason why his "imagination was engaged, or rather enslaved," why he decides at last, "if he be Mr. Hyde. . . . I shall be Mr. Seek" (p. 15). Utterson cannot shake the recurrent image in his dreams of a child brutally crushed at every cross street in London by a figure "which had no face by which he might know it. . . . or one that baffled him and melted before his eyes" (p. 14). His search for Hyde indicates the terror that Hyde's face might be his own. As he comes closer to the secret, preferring at first the conventional possibility that the murderous Hyde is blackmailing his respected friend Jekyll for some youthful pecadillo, Utterson sits brooding on his own past, "groping in all the corners of memory, lest by chance some Jack-in-the-box of an old iniquity should leap to light there" (p. 20).

The first narrative of which Utterson is the center gives way to a second, "Dr. Lanyon's narrative," and another reasonable mind is drawn into the terror of that jack-in-the-box. Lanyon was a colleague of Jekyll's until the man's experiments got "too fanciful" for him; a "rosy man" and a genial, he suffers a shock when he understands the case of Jekyll, which brings about his own death. It is Lanyon whom Jekyll contacts in horror and despair when, sitting quietly in Regents Park, "the animal within me licking the chops of memory; the spiritual side a little drowsed" (p. 95), the change to Hyde occurs without drugs, without warning, without will. Once again a heresy adopted to free the mind from orthodoxy has become an automatism. Since Jekyll as Hyde cannot enter his laboratory for the antidote, he has Lanyon do it. And when Lanyon witnesses the transformation, his own life is "shaken to its roots; sleep has left me; the deadliest terror sits by me at all hours of the day and night" (p. 77). The abstract thought of the jack-in-the-box as memory devastates Utterson; the physical presence of it kills Lanyon: "I feel that my days are numbered and that I must die," he says, dying, one might almost say, before his own jack can pounce.

As for Jekyll himself, whose full statement is enclosed along with Lanyon's narrative in a posthumous letter to Utterson, the earliest statement of his dilemma shows how far the Gothic antihero has come from the eighteenth-century hypocrite. Unlike Frankenstein and contrary to later cinematic portraits of him, Jekyll has known his doubleness perfectly well all his life. He contrives the drug not in ignorance or even in escapist fear but virtually in celebration of it. He feels an attachment to, even a kind of respect for, both the "impatient gaiety of disposition" that fuels his hidden life of sensual pleasure and the "imperious desire to carry my head high" and excel in all the respectable arts:

> Though so profound a double-dealer, I was in no sense a hypocrite; both sides of me were in dead earnest: I was no more myself when I laid aside restraint and plunged in shame, than when I labored, in the eye of day, at the furtherance of knowledge and the relief of sorrow and suffering. (P. 79)

He speculates that disassociated, each of these dead earnest selves might reach its own natural peace, even natural beauty, free from the twists and taunts of the other.

Interestingly, he is also struck during his legitimate scientific inquiries by the "trembling immateriality, the mistlike transience, of the seemingly so solid body in which we walk" (p. 80). His chemical is designed to unlock the molecular bondings, body and soul, that constitute "the fortress of identity" and to express the real nature of man's spirit, atomic like his material being, "a mere polity of multifarious, incongruous and independent denizens" (p. 79).

Thinking like Frankenstein and even Robert Wringhim that he can control "my brother the other," he liberates Edward Hyde. Unlike Frankenstein, he feels no repugnance but rather "a leap of welcome" to the new countenance in the glass, which is, though ugly and "deformed," not large and frightening at first but smaller, younger, and "happier in body" (pp. 82-83). Jekyll is proud, and he celebrates his new feeling.

But he celebrates too soon. The hoped-for balance of pure spiritual excellence and pure sensual freedom never occurs. Since virtue had to "slumber," Jekyll says, and selfishness to predominate even to undertake such an experiment, the spiritual side of him is fatally weak at the outset. Far from perfecting itself as the Hyde emanation is perfecting itself, the entity knowing itself to be Henry Jekyll, laboring in the eye of day for the furtherance of knowledge and the relief of suffering, remains a "polity" of conflicting aspirations, while Hyde quickly gains the strength and purity of his amoral single nature.

In the despairing statement written just before his death, Jekyll is bound to call Hyde pure evil, his life of pleasure pure shame, and Hyde's hold on the wiser self the hold of passion over reason. But it seems clear that the real hold of Hyde over Jekyll at the start is simply his youth, his liberty, those sensations "incredibly sweet," that "more generous tide of blood," the "light step and leaping impulses" (pp. 90-91) that make Hyde Jekyll's barrier against mortality. Hyde is in this sense Jekyll's son, and beneath the allegory of high spirits running ungoverned and amoral from crime to crime, of ego dilating past all boundaries of reasonable control or even reasonable self-protection, runs the old Gothic battle between the old man (Jekyll is in his fifties) and the young one for possession of the single quantum of being. In the Gothic we are familiar with the terrible figure

83

of the mummy, dead dust once living, returning to demand life. Here, in a remarkable passage reaching the deepest springs of horror, Stevenson dramatizes the attack of the not yet living dust, the usurping next generation:

> He thought of Hyde, for all his energy of life, as of something not only hellish but inorganic. This was the shocking thing; that the slime of the pit seemed to utter cries and voices; that the amorphous dust gesticulated and sinned; that what was dead and had no shape, should usurp the offices of life. And this again, that that insurgent horror was knit to him closer than a wife, closer than an eye; lay caged in his flesh, where he heard it mutter and felt it struggle to be born; and at every hour of weakness, and in the confidence of slumber, prevailed against him and deposed him out of life. (Pp. 100-101)[6]

In the last hours of this mutual life, when Jekyll has taken the last of the "impure" accidental compound that was his only access back to Jekyll from the victorious Hyde, Jekyll recognizes as Hyde's essence the "raging energies of life," a "wonderful" love of life, in fact "an abject and passionate attachment to it," and finds it in his heart to pity Hyde, knowing as he does how tenuous, how laughably sorrowfully minute is a person's hold on those energies. Profoundly dramatized here as it was in *Melmoth* is the peculiar powerful Gothic equation, the being that can will to die is human but the entity that cannot admit death into its will is monstrous.

In a fury of hatred, condemned not to kill his "father" Jekyll because he is his hyde-out, Hyde destroys the letters

[6] Since Jekyll is the single parent of this child, we again note an evasion of woman and sex in the birth-myth. In contrast to cinematic elaboration of Hyde's sex life, Stevenson's fable has no women in it, except for the short opening scene where Hyde uncaringly tramples a girlchild and is berated for it by some vengeful women. Women and sex make a dramatic return to the Gothic birth-myth in *Dracula*.

and the portrait of Jekyll's father—almost the last scene that Jekyll is able to record in his own character. When the community bursts into the laboratory to corner "the murderer" of Henry Jekyll, they hear Hyde's animal scream and find his body "still twitching" on the floor, the "cords of his face still moving," though "life was quite gone" (pp. 61-62). Utterson, in his innocence, looking at the crushed phial and smelling poison, thinks Hyde in his coward murderer's soul a "self-destroyer." Innocent but still "aspiring," Jekyll hoped in his final lines that Hyde would "find the courage" to release himself and defy the gallows. But Hyde absolutely cannot will death to himself. It seems more likely that a returning final flash of Jekyll, not as "goodness" or "reason" but as one ambiguously, outrageously valued term in that old aching polity of life and death that is man, committed murder on Hyde through his own suicide.

This nineteenth-century nightmare of the polity within fuses with the eighteenth-century fear of automatism in that remarkable novel *Dracula* (1897). Gothic authorship seems dominated by outsiders, Irishmen, Scotsmen, and women, and Irishman Bram Stoker's novel has interesting affinities with Maturin's *Melmoth*, not to mention with Oscar Wilde. A background of heavy Catholic symbolism framing a foreground of deeply sensual blasphemies makes *Dracula* a novel of high Victorian decadence, like a Moreau painting. White Mass meets Black Mass, Holy Communion replaces Unholy Communion. More powerful even than the crucifix in *Dracula* is the sacred wafer. Rolled, kneaded, and stuck in the cracks of the tombs (" 'I have za dispensation,' Van Helsing announces solemnly"), it keeps out the undead; flourished, it cows him; traced round the endangered, it makes a ring of safety; laid to the forehead of a woman in communion with the vampire, it burns in her the scar by which she recognizes herself as "unclean." When mild-mannered Anglican advocate Jonathan Harker rides alone into "the horseshoe of the Carpathians . . . the centre of some sort of imaginative whirlpool,"[7] he hangs grimly onto an enlightened business-as-usual attitude that will serve him ill with his client. As scientist Dr. John Seward notes down meticulously the consumption of flies, spiders, and cats by his zoophagous patient, Renfield, he maintains the reasonable separation of work from life, of science from emotion, long past the time when a connection between the events in the asylum and events outside it would have saved lives. The *via media* is not equal to the extremity of evil power contained in the novel's universe: older, harsher magic is needed. The great old religion alone is adequate, and the old man from Amsterdam, Abraham Van Helsing, scientist and mystic, comes to England with what seems a whole cartful of the sacred wafer, the life-giving flesh of the Master—comes to do battle with the blood-giving as well as blood-drinking anti-Master.

And yet, despite the aura of magic, it is again important to note that the powers that blight and blast each other in the novel are created by Stoker as preternatural, not really supernatural powers. As with *Melmoth* and *The Italian*, or even with *The Monk* and *Frankenstein*, the real question of powers "beyond" is begged. There may be a demon, there may be an almighty God offended by hasty tampering with His universe, there may be a Prince of Darkness with whom to bargain one's soul, but the experience of the novels suggests that Ambrosio, Schedoni, and Victor, Melmoth and Dracula are only trying to claim in innocent greed powers that are or, as in the story of Eden, once were, the real prerogatives of man: greater strength, greater penetration, more swiftness. And more life.

The special symmetry of *Dracula* results from the two ways in which the two "companies" of humans—Dracula and his victims, Van Helsing and his allies—attempt to claim and exercise these preternatural powers. Very simply,

[7] Bram Stoker, *Dracula* (New York: Dell, 1965), p. 8.

Dracula's is the way of the isolato, the obsessed alone, and Van Helsing's is the way of community. "We have on our side power of combination—a power denied to the vampire kind," says Van Helsing (p. 266); "my bountiful wine-press" (p. 319) is the relationship between Dracula and his company. Both men, Dracula and Van Helsing, can call others to give them their lives. Yet Dracula takes the whole and leaves only a shell, "my creatures, to do my bidding" (p. 340), while Van Helsing takes only a part, and his "creatures" can naturally restore their full power. Dracula drains his companions and passes on; that is why in the suggestively barren landscape of Castle Dracula, he plans his long and difficult journey to populous London, ripe with Englishmen in masses "like the multitude of standing corn" (p. 354): it is an instinct of survival.

But confronted several nights running with Lucy Westenra who is dying from fresh blood loss, Van Helsing watches intently over the transfusion mechanism as each of her three young lovers gives a share and stops short of weakening the donor. Van Helsing's instinct for survival is to combine strengths: Arthur Holmwood's money, Seward's science, Harker's experience, Quincy Morris's Rooseveltian vigor. When he makes the mistake of isolating one from the company—when an impulse of "chivalry" excludes Mina Harker from the tactical conferences—Dracula strikes through the lone woman. In Dracula's company, no living being is tolerated by the vampire. When Harker comes to Castle Dracula, he finds that the Count himself has been his maid, cook, and driver. And of all Dracula's countless victim-consorts, only three remain in the castle, two who are sisters or daughters, with coloring, eyes, and "high aquiline noses, like the Count" (p. 47), and another fair woman, perhaps a wife, whose tomb is large and high "as if made to one much beloved" (p. 408).

Thus Dracula makes no new blood and will perish after he has drained the world, whereas Van Helsing and the others produce new blood even while sharing it, and Mina

Harker, who must be saved at all costs by the others, makes a child, a new maker of blood. Immortality with the Van Helsing community is horizontal: life spreads, holds, and increases. With Dracula, as it is always with the Gothic antihero, the great old man, immortality is vertical, a great stream pouring down that one must contrive to entirely swallow, although getting and keeping life on these terms is more like climbing a ladder that is itself constantly descending. Like Ambrosio, Melmoth, and the others, Dracula is unable to bear the changing world, the curving universe, his own curve out of the familiar phases of life where he led armies and ruled peoples. His fight to drain the world is really a fight to stay in one solid place. And since the universe does curve and move, he is bound to lose, dead or undead.

He knows he can delay death, however, by returning again and again to the blood. Of all the facts in the King-Vampire's history—the Szeckely patriotism, the familiar Gothic family intensity of betrayal, loyalty, and ambition, the rumored recourse to secret instruction in forbidden schools—the most significant is surely the connection between bloodfury on the battlefield and the acquiring of preternatural power, immortality, the staving off of death. "He must indeed have been that Voivode Dracula who won his name against the Turk," Van Helsing concludes after study, and the mighty "Little Dragon" himself has already described to Harker his bloodfury: "who in a later age again and again brought his forces over the great river into Turkey-land, who, when he was beaten back, came again, and again, though he had to come alone from the bloody field where his troops were being slaughtered, since he knew that he alone could ultimately triumph!" (p. 39). Here, it seems, was the root of the evil, the need to triumph alone, the staving off of one's own death by substituting thousands of others. From dealing in cannon fodder to vampirism seems a short logical step.[8]

[8] Dracula goes on to sneer at "mushroom growths" like the Haps-

In this sense of obsessive return to blood, of obsessive repetition of habit, Dracula himself is the greatest of automatons, and his victim/company are mindless drinking machines fettered by those dozens of rules—can't cross flowing water, can't enter a house unless invited, must come when the King calls, can't use your powers in the afternoon, can't travel without your coffin of home ground[9]—that make an undead's life scarcely worth living. The rhetoric of the opposing company is all of "freeing" the vampires out of the "slavery" of life into the peace of death, of restoring natural bodily death and natural spiritual continuity to those whose bodies are still unnaturally living while their spirits have been unnaturally swallowed, put out, preempted by the dark other. The vampire undead are in this sense like the zombie undead, taken over, taken away. Thus her friends are comforted by the belief that Lucy Westenra is "not there" in that "thing" that seeks to entrap and kill children, that smiles wantonly and voluptuously at her fiancé from beyond the grave. Thus they are able to patronize and pity even Dracula—to watch for that expression of peace on his face between the malice of the undead life and the moment of complete dissolution.

In another equally important sense, though, the vampires as Stoker presents them are not chained but freed, not taken over but let out into that polity of life and life, and of life

burgs and Romanoffs "who can never reach real greatness because the warlike days are over. Blood is too precious a thing in these days of dishonorable peace" (p. 39). One cannot but suppose that the echo of Draculoid laughter may have been part of the inspiration behind that world essay in bloodspending whose premonitions could be felt as early as 1897. In Stoker's novel, however, it is Belgium that saves England.

9 Van Helsing has a wonderfully "orthodox," that is, anti-Manichean (though disturbing) reason for this famous vampire habit: "There have been from the loins of [Dracula's ur-ancestor] great men and good women, and their graves make sacred the earth where alone this foulness can dwell. For it is not the least of its terrors that this evil thing is rooted deep in all good, in soil barren of holy memories it cannot rest" (p. 269).

and death, that Stevenson talked of.[10] Lucy is not Trilby but Jekyll/Hyde. But where the dual life liberated in Jekyll —and in Dracula for that matter—was a youth-coveting, domination-bent, power-seeking energy, only peripherally sexual, the new entity liberated in the woman is pure driving sexuality. In their daylight lives, Lucy and Mina are perfect Victorian women, although underlying Lucy's virtue is a certain childlike and faintly sinister love of flirtation (surely an invitation to vampires?) and behind Mina's wifely submission lies both a hint of matriarchal amusement at the behavior of the boys about her and a suggestion of a Jane Eyre-like attraction for the weakness of Jonathan after his first encounter with Dracula. To their men they are love goddesses, full of sweetness and light: Jonathan makes notes of Transylvanian recipes to send his fiancée, while Lucy's three lovers, the scientist, the lord, and the American (in a caricatured class of his own) come in to lay their proposals before her one by one like little boys in a May Crowning procession. But Lucy's mysterious "illness" makes her lips redder as well as whiter in a strange rhythm of death and beauty, and a new personality begins to emerge in her as death comes closer: "Arthur! Oh, my love . . . kiss me!" (p. 181), she urges. We discover what liberated that personality when Mina discloses the double nature of Dracula's attack —first he takes, and then, more horribly, he gives:

> He placed his reeking lips upon my throat! . . . I felt my strength fading away, and I was in a half-swoon. . . . With that he pulled open his shirt, and with his long sharp nails opened a vein in his breast. When the blood began to spirt out, he took my hands in one of his, holding them tight, and with the other seized my neck and

10 This is the notion that Anne Rice explores in the recent, interesting *Interview with the Vampire* (New York: Ballantine, 1976), the old tempting proposition that the killer obtains special knowledge and special sensitivity to life, and the vampire, whose life *is* death, has supreme comprehension and sensitivity.

pressed my mouth to the wound, so that I must either suffocate or swallow some of the—oh, my God! my God! what have I done? (P. 319)

It is significant that she blames herself for her actions, as women have been taught to do. It is suggestive too that Mina's husband is asleep on the bed beside her as Dracula and Mina enact this voluptuous baptism, this dark intercourse. Jonathan, who alone of the males in the story has felt the vampire's kiss from Dracula's sister/consort, has admitted, as Mina later also admits, that "part of the poison" is that you don't want to resist it. Jonathan decides in despair that if Mina slides over the edge into the undead life, he will accept that kiss from her and follow his wife into that sexual darkness, even though both lose their souls.

As a teacher of decorum and etiquette, Mina feels even more deeply than Lucy, who was only a pupil, the horror of this new preying personality, both in its automatic slavery to a single impulse and in the special uncleanness of that impulse. Like Jekyll, she cannot refuse the awful potion, but she can, with the help of friends, guard against its being offered again. Like Jekyll, she approaches the point where the potion will no longer be needed nor the antipotion be of use, the point just before death where the undead life clicks into place and goes seeking its own circle of victim/consorts. Like Jekyll she would kill that other life, but her will is not her own; that is, her will is divided.

There is a curious emphasis, almost Jesuitical in its complexity, on the will of the "innocent" partner in the evil act. The vampire cannot simply go about the world devouring: he or she must be "invited" across the threshold in some indirect way; the victim must somehow be "seeking" the encounter. When Harker stands in the doorway of Castle Dracula, the Count makes a point of standing still until the Englishman crosses into the castle on his own, and Harker is deliberately exploring forbidden rooms in the castle when the vampire women materialize for their deadly kiss. The flirtatious Lucy walks out to meet Dracula in a half-trance, and only Van Helsing's inexplicable violence pulls Arthur back from his willing embrace of the new Lucy. Renfield, the half-sane patient who seeks the more abundant life by swallowing particles of it in flies, spiders, and cats, waits eagerly in an oddly sexual froth for the vampire to show him "The Way": "The bride-maidens rejoice the eyes that wait the coming of the bride; but when the bride draweth nigh, then the maidens shine not to the eyes that are filled" (p. 116). Harker's bitter lament that many vampires were willingly created because they welcomed or followed loved ones testifies to Bram Stoker's high Victorian sensitivity to original sin, for those pockets of invitation to the known evil, those bubbles of curiosity about the unknown forbidden, those wayward gleams of antiprogress in the heavy fabric of Victorian will.

It is, of course, Dracula's own wish to emigrate to England, the center of the new clean logical progressive world, from his home in the Carpathian horseshoe, the center of all the old superstitions of man. Yet the novel opens, as do many of the most important twentieth-century Gothic works, with the penetration of old mysterious lands and races by the new confident willful civilization, and clearly it is this willful penetration, read as invitation, that really triggers the awful visitations of the old powers and races upon the young. In its modulated form as "wierd tales" and then science fiction, this penetration-with-counterattack became the spine of Gothic fiction in a century of imperialism and world war. This makes particularly interesting the novel's conception of Dracula's power (the "old power") as pure solitary ego, as a dilated willpower in opposition to the "power of combination" of community or of thought. Dracula is in Van Helsing's terms a "child-brain." That is why he can finally be defeated; because like a child he repeats himself.

And that is why he *must* be defeated. For now that he has come into the new world, "what more may he not do

when the greater world of thought is open to him" (p. 355).
Already Dracula has learned one crucial and dangerous
way to use and pervert the power of combination: if at the
outset the women in the castle were only in their small way
rivals with him for their common prey and Jonathan
Harker was just thoughtlessly left behind alive when the
great purpose of the London trip came to climax in the
child-brain, later both Lucy and Mina are deliberately attacked primarily as a means of drawing the men into
Dracula's power and only secondarily for the "wine" they
themselves provide him. Jonathan lay beside Mina on
Dracula's first entrance, and a child-brain would have ban-
queted on both. But Jonathan is already in combination
with the other men, and his subornation would be a warning to them, whereas the isolated Mina might have been
made an accessory and a lure had Dracula been able to resist
the vanity of another conquest in the zoophagous Renfield,
who gave the game away. Dracula, however, is unmoved
even after Renfield's warning: his world contains no serious
enemies, only food and the vermin, rats, wolves, and humans
whom he can control by sheer strength of will.

This sort of vanity, always the weak spot of the masters
of will, brings Dracula down. Though he literally cannot
think of defeat, he retires from the bloody field as he did
centuries before, across the river to his life-giving home
earth, to recruit strength for the return, again and again.
Community research and shrewd analysis have revealed this
pattern to his opponents; they follow and then anticipate
him, triumphing by the breadth of a sunray.

Dracula is almost unique in classic Gothic for the equality of the battle. It is no longer a drama of heaven against
one usurping human will as in *The Castle of Otranto*, nor
of conflicting wills inside a family, as in *Melmoth the
Wanderer*, or inside a single self, as in *Frankenstein* or *Dr.
Jekyll and Mr. Hyde*, but of conflicting wills inside the
species. The "haunted castle" is the whole planet, and the

beat of special and dangerous mystery on one continent calls forth its answer from another. In this, *Dracula* is influenced by another form of the Gothic that has modulated through Godwin's *Caleb Williams* and the Dickens/Wilkie Collins axis into the nineteenth-century detective story. The black genius always has his opposing white king, the Napoleon of crime has his violin-playing, cocaine-sniffing Wellington, the one equally as eccentric and frightening to quotidian humanity as the other. Like his opposite, Van Helsing is an outsider, old/young, with bushy eyebrows and an iron will. He too has a gourmet's eye for a nourishing human spirit: "Now, as he took in [Arthur's] stalwart proportions and recognised the strong young manhood which seemed to emanate from him, his eyes gleamed" (p. 137). And if Dracula's humor is macabre—"First, a little refreshment to reward my exertions" (p. 318)—Van Helsing's more than matches it:

> "Well, for the life of me, Professor," [Seward] said. "I can't see anything to laugh at in all that. . . . But even if the burial service was comic, what about poor Art and his trouble? Why, his heart was simply breaking."
> "Just so. Said he not that the transfusion of his blood to her veins had made her truly his bride?"
> "Yes, and it was a sweet and comforting idea for him."
> "Quite so. But there was a difficulty, friend John. If so that, then what about the others? Ho, ho! Then this so sweet maid is a polyandrist, and me, with my poor wife dead to me, but alive by Church's law, though no wits, all gone—even I, who am faithful husband to this now-no-wife, am bigamist." (P. 197)

He shares with Dracula too the ultimate knowledge of the secret continuity of human life: it is one living organism, one mystical body. They are together in this knowledge, apart from the community. Quotidian humanity, irregularly emancipated, fitfully enlightened, now to "believe not even what they see" (p. 355), will never believe this ultimate revelation about the human soul, not even though the demonstration of it compiled in *Dracula* is deliberately full of modern media, shorthand journals, newspaper clippings, phonograph memos, medical records.

Still, one distinction between the black king and the white king matters supremely. For Dracula his own willful survival is paramount, a circle that "goes on ever widening, as the ripples from a stone thrown in the water" (p. 239), until it can encompass the whole living pond. For Van Helsing the living pond is all. In order to defeat the voiding ring that threatens to devour it, he will focus inward on his own kind of ring—"Then, without a word we all knelt down together, and, all holding hands, swore to be true to each other" (p. 330)—to make a hard rock against which Dracula's spreading circle will break. And then he will return his life doubled to the pond.

PART II

THE GOTHIC HERITAGE

ONE wants to maintain some discretion in applying the Gothic measure to works of fiction. Few novels are entirely without that apparatus of suspense, hidden violence, ritual obsession, mysterious pursuits, and secret sins that we want to call Gothic. In his scrutiny of the ordinary paths of human behavior, the most "realistic" novelist must take into account the spiritually hypersensitive person, the bizarre event, the extreme feeling that outpaces its objective correlative. Gissing's Mr. Biffin writes "Mr. Bailey, Grocer," that scrupulously unfantastical ideal of a realistic novel, and it immediately becomes the focus of melodramatic flames, heroical rescue, poignant suicide; in New Grub Street or Parnassus, art irresistibly works a dramatic reversal upon the ordinary.

When the great traditions of English fiction took shape in the eighteenth century, the philosophers were debating the conditions of the sublime and the beautiful. Perhaps the most memorable of the treatises, Edmund Burke's "Inquiry into Our Ideas Concerning the Sublime and the Beautiful," argues not only that terror, the source of the sublime, "is productive of the strongest emotion that the mind is capable of feeling" but also that the sublime is the root of, in a manner encircles, the beautiful, for it is present in every direction of "magnitude" and "extension" from the very great to the very small, from the shape that hews to "the right line" to the shape that shows the sharpest deviation from the right line. Beauty, smooth, polished and, at its best, only subtly deviating from the perfect line, seems a secondary quality of the sublime, an artful playing with the given. And rather in line with this idea, the popular writers of the time were establishing the Gothic romance as the fundamental condition and desire of the mass mind, establishing it in prose as they had in Elizabethan and Jacobean drama, the first great age of public literary life between Marlowe and Ford.

As Fielding invents, so he claims, the new form, the novel, in which the narrator is to free himself, visibly, from old conditions and set up his very own new designs, he takes special pains to warn against the tired use of "the marvelous." And Richardson tries hard, in footnotes and above all through the pen of Clarissa, to resist viewing the human world as the demon-angel duel to which the obsession of Lovelace and the swell of events are reducing it. But the prime condition cannot be easily evaded: Fielding's conjurer-narrator in *Tom Jones* admits he intends to use the marvelous himself when necessary, and Richardson's editor concludes *Clarissa* with a leap into the consolations of the old supernatural vision and a claim to having been about the business of the marvelous all along: "[the author imagined] he could steal in, as may be said, and investigate the great doctrines of Christianity under the fashionable guise of an amusement."

The "heretic narrators" of eighteenth- and nineteenth-century fiction were inheritors of this volatile condition, this dangerous machinery, that in its own genres continued vigorous. At the same time they were self-conscious innovators; they came in from the courts and convents and rocky crags to the city streets and parlors and eventually to the offices and workrooms. Some wore motley (though, as with Thackeray, the lineaments of melancholy man were visible beneath); if they brought gods into their fictions on a machine, a wind would surely blow aside the cardboard to reveal pulleys and hairy legs. These self-styled homely entertainers were far from frivolous, but at the same time their works do not display that "high seriousness," that intense meditation on the moral life of the individual and the spiritual predicament and future of the community—a meditation evident especially in a dominating narrative voice but also in the paradigm of their plots—that Leavis has proposed is the hallmark of the great tradition of English fiction.

So described, Leavis's classic tradition, running from Richardson and Fanny Burney through Austen, George Eliot, James, Conrad, and Lawrence, constitutes a coherent category that includes many great works of prose fiction, and excludes some. Out of Leavis's dismissals, one can surely construct two other great traditions, one of artists he calls often interesting but trivial—regionalists and minor philosophers, such as Fielding, Thackeray, Hardy, "the ruck of Gaskells and Trollopes and Merediths"[1]—and a second of supposed near-misses, inspired writers or even geniuses who just miss "greatness" through not feeling or displaying "the creative writer's interest in literature" (p. 5), the "profounder responsibility as a creative artist" (p. 19) that is evident above all in a concern for form. These artists produce works that, though "astonishing," are basically "a kind of sport" (p. 27); according to Leavis, Scott, Dickens, and the Brontës fit into this category.

Rankings on the scale of "greatness" aside, this critical habit of describing family patterns throws up valuable and fascinating gestalts. It may be noticed that the list of Leavis's "trivial" writers includes mostly Englishmen, while the "great" tradition seems to have been made by those outsiders, women and foreigners, whom we earlier proposed also dominate the Gothic. It may also be noticed that the "near-misses" comprise those writers whose debt to the Gothic inheritance has been most clearly marked by readers in their own time and ours,[2] and it is for this reason that my look at these latter half-way heretics will be brief.

[1] F. R. Leavis, *The Great Tradition* (New York: New York Univ. Press, 1969), p. 15. Subsequent references are to this edition and will be cited by page number in the text.

[2] Although of course one may take issue with the way in which that connection with the Gothic is assessed. There is a tendency, for in-

Scott, Dickens, and Charlotte Brontë seem alike in one important biographical fact: an early obsession with romantic and supernatural adventure tales from both oral and written sources established in each writer that crucial respect for the mysterious intensities of experience, the exalted or perverse cavities of personality that illuminates all of their respective works, even though these works were written from the conscious base of a profound acquaintance with the quotidian life of their time and place. These authors are clearly engaged in that "rehabilitation of the extra-rational" that Robert B. Heilman notes was "the historical office of the Gothic." Linking these writers too is their puzzled exasperation with critics who cannot see ordinary life by this "light," and, crucially, this exasperation, this implied warning that those who refuse to recognize this light not only do themselves and the authors a disservice but may even be part of the great social problem, makes its way characteristically into their narrative stance. "Indeed, the most romantic parts of this narrative are precisely those which have a foundation in fact," Scott insist in a postscript to *Waverley*, at the start of an immense body of fiction that draws much of its power from the author's reiterated claim to having witnessed the very documents

stance, toward off-hand remarks about a new mature comic "undercutting" of the Gothic (cf. Robert B. Heilman, "Brontë's 'New' Gothic," in *The Victorian Novel: Modern Essays in Criticism*, ed. Ian Watt [New York: Oxford Univ. Press, 1971]) and the humorous or farcical use of the Gothic (cf. Mario Praz on Scott's contribution to the process by which "Romanticism turned bourgeois" in *The Hero in Eclipse in Victorian Fiction* [London: Oxford University Press, 1956], as though there were no self-conscious "mixing" of the solemn and the burlesque in the Walpole-Radcliffe tradition, no macabre humor warped into the essential character of a Melmoth or Dracula, as if there were no more morally serious or adventurous use of the Gothic in Scott and Austen than making the world safe for the bourgeois. What readers and critics did clearly perceive about Scott, Dickens, and the Brontës was stated perhaps most memorably by Humphry House when he remarked that "the floor of consciousness has been lowered" (see his essay, "The Macabre Dickens," reprinted in *The Victorian Novel*, ed. Watt, p. 40).

and events (or similar ones), the very scenes and characters that his reader is even then chalking up to the author's fevered imagination. "There is sometimes an odd disposition in this country to dispute as improbable in fiction what are the commonest experiences in fact," Dickens mourns in the postscript to *Our Mutual Friend*, which was written at the end of a long career characterized by the frustrated but faithful rendering of the apparently crazed, possibly demonic progress of public institutions into sloth and private follies into crime. Dickens creates a world, like Carlyle's, like Maturin's, governed by a terrifying ironic Walpolean justice, although the world scintillates beautifully, here and there, about the loving and the candid. Charlotte Brontë, whose career closed too soon for her to acquire quite the wide exposure of a Scott or a Dickens to either the demonic possibilities in public life or to the foolhardy atheism of comfortable readers, dramatizes brilliantly in *Jane Eyre* and *Villette* the enraging predicament of the soul that sees deeply and speaks extremely in a society that affects to take its romance and its facts in separate doses. In *Jane Eyre*, the exchange in Chapter Four between Jane and her hatefully commonsensical Aunt Reed is a classic expression of the exasperation of the "sane" who cannot bear to hear the truths of the passionate:

> "People think you a good woman, but you are bad, hardhearted. *You* are deceitful!"
>
> "Jane . . . what is the matter with you? Why do you tremble so violently? Would you like to drink some water?"
>
> "I'll let everybody at Lowood know what you are, and what you have done."
>
> "Jane, you don't understand these things; children must be corrected for their faults!"
>
> "Deceit is not my fault!"
>
> "But you are passionate, Jane. . . . now retire to the nursery—there's a dear—and lie down a little."

Close to their passion, certain of their experience of the "improbable," factual in their apprehension of the numinous, yet full of Anglican anxiety about the pits of "superstition" and of adult emphasis on the felicities of control, Scott, Dickens, and Brontë each create a personal shape for the artistic expression of Gothic intensities and possibilities, surrounded, not "undercut," by the responsibilities of rational doubt and personal originality. Austen, Eliot, and Lawrence are separated from Scott, Dickens, and Brontë, as Leavis wants to suggest, by the self-consciousness of the former about artistic form and by their special anxiety about where history is taking the community (Austen), the race (Eliot), and the species (Lawrence). But Scott, Dickens, and Brontë have their individual formal selves to find too; none of them, deeply affected as they were, wanted simply to reproduce the tales of Yorkshire and border shepherds, or the episodes from Spenser and Gil Blas or the Arabian Nights and Walpole.

Scott briefly considered doing so. In the 1829 "General Preface" to the Waverley novels, he records how he moved from collecting and recording to editing and embellishing border songs and then to writing his own long songs; from writing fragments of a tale of chivalry in prose, "which was to be in the style of the Castle of Otranto, with plenty of Border characters, and supernatural incident," to writing an early section of a tale about Scotland "determined to give another turn to the style of the work" to embarking on the Waverley series. The stance he adopted of a "willing listener" to those contending parties, those fractious singers and preachers who believed they had seen God, enabled him, his protagonists, and his readers to participate imaginatively in the supernatural or preternatural atmosphere that the visionary lives in.[3] We can respond alike to the

---

[3] Scott's intimacy with his national heritage provided a mass of Gothic materials, some already notched with peasant humor, some not, much of it catalogued in Coleman O. Parsons' *Witchcraft and Demonology in Scott's Fiction* (Edinburgh: Oliver and Boyd, Ltd., 1964).

druidical vengeance of the "witch" Ulrica in *Ivanhoe* or to the god-demons who speak out of the mouths of *Old Mortality's* covenanters, to the momentary, supernatural dire presence of incest in *The Antiquary* or to murder in *Rob Roy*, to the guilty ancestral legends that play themselves forcibly out in the modern families of the *Bride of Lammermoor* or *Redgauntlet*. The narrative sophistication engendered by the stories within stories, the apparatus of footnotes, and the judicial tolerance of the teller of the tale, inclines us to think like those wavering Waverley heroes and yet to feel with them that psychic embarrassment before the more purposeful visionaries and overreachers. Thus the dream-visions that overtake Frank Osbaldistone and Francis Lovel when their debating minds are asleep gain from the great stress each man has to use at waking to restore the rational balance.

Above all, this stance of the willing listener enables us to feel the almost literal "unearthliness" of Scott's version of the classic Gothic antihero, the one who has separated himself in pride of person or family or despair from the community and its ordinary moral anchors: the monk Templar Brian de Bois Gilbert, the prophet-demon John Burley, the deformed and sublimely Melmothian Black Dwarf, the ruined Robertson/Stanton of *The Heart of Midlothian* who turned, after his anathematizing crime, like Walpole's Manfred, to wearing a secret hair shirt and monk's beads, the kidnapper Edward Redgauntlet with his familial devil's hoof printed on his forehead.

The latter should serve as a good brief example of Scott's handling of that "matter of Otranto" that he inherited to use with a different "turn to the style." Structurally interesting for its combination of epistolary, autobiographical, and omniscient narrative devices, *Redgauntlet* thematically centers around two Gothic "tales": one a supernatural fiction told "as a lesson" to the passive pondering hero, Darsie Lattimer, by the not so blind fiddler, Wandering Willie, and the second a compound of fact and legend,

"that fancy which creates what it sees,"[4] related to him by
the current head of the house of Redgauntlet in explanation of, in persuasive celebration of, the "fatality" that
marks his race.

As with a number of the Waverley heroes, the inner dilemma of Darsie Lattimer is a Hamletian one—the discovery of himself as his father's son and the temptation to
be instead his uncle's son—although in Scott the father's
ghost proposes policy and accommodation while the living
uncle proposes fatality and violence. Darsie's Redgauntlet
father married an Englishwoman and as a result began to
think moderately on things Whig and Jacobite after being
"out" with his brother Scot "in '45." That brother, a self-
proclaimed man of sorrows like Manfred, sold his freedom
of reflection to the devil of Scott's real, choice-ridden, world,
"Destiny, the manager of this strange drama" (p. 235) and
is living the legendary fate of his family by fighting constantly on the losing side of civil broil. Legend holds this
fate to have been the reward of the first haughty Redgauntlet's curse upon his son for setting up an opposing will, a
curse fulfilled by the father's half-accidental slaying of the
son by a blow that branded him and all the descendants
with a horseshoe indentation on the forehead—the devil's
mark. And Wandering Willie's tale recounts how a later
Redgauntlet hated his son enough to write a deed in hell
after his death to confound the son's plans, although
Willie's grandfather followed the dead man down to the
pit to get the deed:

> And there was as much singing of profane sangs, and
> birling of red wine, and speaking blasphemy and scul-
> duddry, as had ever been in Redgauntlet Castle when it
> was at the blithest. . . . But their smiles were fearfully
> contorted from time to time; and their laughter passed

[4] Quotations from Walter Scott's *Redgauntlet* (1824) are from the
Everyman Edition (London: Dent, 1970) and will hereafter be cited
by page number in the text. This phrase occurs on p. 234.

into such wild sounds, as made my gudesire's very nails grow blue, and chilled the marrow in his banes. (P. 124)

The tone of Willie's narrative places it somewhere between parable and tall tale; similarly, as the sombre Edward Redgauntlet tells his family legend, his own sense requires him to preface many a supernatural or hideous detail with a perfunctory "it is said that. . . ." Yet it is exactly the uncle's will to submit to that legendary devil-image for both his own emotional satisfaction and for the power it gives him over the credulous (and momentarily, even over the temperate) that represents acute danger to Darsie Lattimer. For the elder Redgauntlet had long before sought to kidnap his nephew and force him into the chain of Redgauntlet violence; finding him now at the crux of the last desperate Jacobite plot, he means to force or seduce him into leading an uprising, and rather than have his coconspirators discover the new Redgauntlet to have broken from the image of the great old ones, he threatens to kill him.

Thus, over and over in Scott, the Gothic occurs only superficially as parody or whimsical peasant tale, more deeply as an accurate description of a kind of behavior, a way of seeing the world, that seems not only possible but often, in flashes, even desirable when personal choice making seems tedious and obscure and reasonable compromise hollow and ignoble. *Redgauntlet*'s Darsie, like *Old Mortality*'s Morton, berates himself for the inner restraint against heroic behavior that often translates into the apparently abject, and like Morton, he is astounded to discover that the powerful men of the world regard him as a potentially dangerous, even magically decisive figure. Vigorously arguing with his uncle, Darsie sees in a mirror his uncle's devil-mark on his own forehead, and though, on the whole, he chooses against that self and that world, the thrill of guilty identification, the flash of forbidden pleasure, is clear.

So it is with Scott, who was not sorry to find himself descended from the bloody rieving border Scotts of two centuries before or in imagination from the reputed "wizard" Michael Scot, not sorry to muffle his own middle-class identity in the one that came, gratifyingly and with justice, to his editorial persona, the "Wizard of the North." Unmistakable as was his commitment to the new world and the new turn of style, his instinctive place was on the border between the world view governed by fate, destiny, and the hero who derived his preternatural power from an alliance with the ambiguous deep forces beyond the mundane, and the world view governed by choice and compromise, though lit by flashes of the old intuitions.

Dickens started out as a borderer too, but his faith in the civilizing, compromising world was subject to greater shocks than was Scott's, and his imagination enlarged his doubts. The interpolated Gothic tales of the *Pickwick Papers* became the fundamental condition of his exploration of the darkening present as Scott's interpolated legends were his warning about a permanent possibility in the makeup of man.[5] Dickens's eye for the literally monstrous shapes in the ordinary scene is supreme: the remorseless machines of *Hard Times,* the train-monster of *Dombey and Son,* the strangling bureaucracies of *Little Dorrit, Bleak House*'s noxious slum where the Red Death waits to join the masque outside. He tries the historical novel twice: in the manner of Monk Lewis and Maturin, the mobs of *Barnaby Rudge* and *A Tale of Two Cities* reflect the Englishman's unshakeable conviction that mass action always ascends to riot, and in this company the purposeful disciplined Porteous mob of

[5] Edmund Wilson's seminal essay on "The Two Scrooges" (first published in *The Wound and the Bow: Seven Studies in Literature* [New York: Oxford Univ. Press, 1947]) makes this observation at its opening and continues to pick out important Gothic plot paradigms in the novels up to its final section on *The Mystery of Edwin Drood,* whose "subject is the subject of Poe's William Wilson, the subject of Dr. Jekyll and Mr. Hyde, the subject of Dorian Gray."

The Heart of Midlothian stands out as a romantic fancy of Scott's (it is, however, Scott insists, documented).

But Dickens's genius is most apparent in his exploration of the Gothic potentiality of character, and here again the determining factor is the vision of the world either as fated or as conducive to choice. Dickens's world is harsher than Scott's: it takes a powerful faith to believe in choice. *Oliver Twist*'s Nancy, refusing the charity of Brownlow after she has betrayed Bill Sikes' plot to kidnap Oliver, can see no way back but to "such a home as I have raised for myself with the work of my whole life." When *Bleak House*'s young Richard Carstone feels himself fated to be a Jarndyce, he enters upon the long suicide characteristic of his house; when Esther Summerson works her way through and out of the identity of abandoned bastard, guilty of her mother's crimes, and entrusts her faith and identity to the intuitions of love that challenge death all through her story, she is viewed as a heroine. The same applies to Arthur Clennam, who suffers gladly the literal collapse of his house that he may be, at last, the man he chooses to be, without the powerful personality of his putative mother and father or the weaknesses of his real parents.

Crucial to Dickens's examination of character is a profound sensitivity to the Gothic projections that guilt without repentance and remorse without hope throw upon the screen of the everyday. The very first tale in *Pickwick Papers*, containing "nothing of the marvellous . . . or even uncommon," says its "dismal" narrator, concerns a wretch on his deathbed who, after a long course of beating and starving his wife, sees her eyes staring at him waking and sleeping and is convinced that she has all along been an evil spirit cunningly planning his deeper damnation: "A devil! No woman could have borne what she has." Bill Sikes too sees Nancy's eyes after he has murdered her, is shaken from his desperate perch, and hangs himself. In the chapter entitled "Conclusion of the Enterprise," Jonas Chuzzlewit, fired with pride and dread after his murder of Tigg-Montague, splits under the pressure, becomes "his own ghost and phantom, and was at once the haunting spirit and the haunted man." In a brilliant passage in *Our Mutual Friend,* Dickens has us participate in this kind of projection, this hallucination, as the murderous, repressed, and tormented Bradley Headstone pursues his quarry-tormentor Eugene Wrayburn in the "Scouts Out" chapter: "Looking more like the hunted and not the hunter . . . he went by them in the dark, like a haggard head suspended in the air; so completely did the force of his expression cancel his figure."

Dickens uses both what I have been calling the classic eighteenth-century plot—the young struggling in the power of the great old ones—and the nineteenth-century plot— the alien brother within. The second tale of *Pickwick* records the efforts of a son to match the evil cruelty of his father; in the final confrontation the old man strikes the final blow, the son responds, snarling "Father—devil!" but his arm falls powerless because it is his father; the old man howls in fury, and his own passion kills him. The battle of the god/fathers and mothers for the spirit of the future, of Fagin and Murdstone, old Tom Jarndyce and old Paul Dombey, whose scarcely explicable hatred of his daughter parallels Manfred's, of Cleopatra Granger and Miss Havisham, goes on in Dickens as it did in *The Castle of Otranto.*[6]

In this area, the characteristic movement is to a child-narrator, for whom the world really is Gothic, full of powerful barely invisible forces, figures, and motives. They see giants, demons, and madonnas; they feel unspeakably sub-

---

[6] In his *Dickens: From Pickwick to Dombey* (London: Chatto and Windus, 1965), Stephen Marcus titles his excellent chapter on *Barnaby Rudge* "Sons and Fathers" and proposes that the novel, in its account of persecuting fathers, "prodigal parents," poses the question "whether there may not exist . . . certain relationships of conflict, injustice and suffering which are not susceptible to reconciliation" (p. 88). Later in the chapter his remark that Sir John Chester "remains untouched by time [by] denying manhood to his sons" reminds one forcibly of Melmoth.

lime possibilities for destruction and love around them. The whole creation is animate to them: young Paul Dombey can hear the message of the waves; young Lizzie Hexam can read the pictures in the fire; Jenny Wren and Esther Summerson learn manners and even morals from their dolls. And most clearly Gothic of all are the boychildren, Oliver, David, and Pip, who come to a first knowledge of themselves, as Pip does in the remarkable opening scene of *Great Expectations*, as "a small bundle of shivers" separated from land, sea, and river precisely by that bundle's power to *fear* all these other things. Pip discovers that "memorable raw afternoon" at the grave of his father not only that a visibly hideous giant may "start up from among the graves" and call for his heart and liver as food but that, more terribly, there is another invisible power still more horrible behind that giant, "a young man hid with me, in comparison with which young man I am a Angel" who has "a secret way peculiar to himself, of getting at a boy, and at his heart, and at his liver," from whom all attempts to hide will be "in wain." As a young man, Pip learns to understand that pitiful giant, his rages and his hungers, but as the narrative progresses towards its various éclaircissements, one obscure patch, one ghostly figure beside and behind Pip and Magwitch remains unreconciled to reasonable understanding. The young man Compeyson, hidden wrecker of many lives, remains a secret and "peculiar" terror to the very end, when he and Magwitch go fighting into the water together and only Magwitch returns. We have no clear knowledge of his death; he continues for the reader as he was for Magwitch and Pip, Miss Havisham and Estella, that eater of hearts who is all of our shadows.

Increasingly it is this shadow, this brother, the double, that fascinates Dickens: Magwitch/Compeyson, Bradley Headstone/Rogue Riderhood, Carker/old Dombey, the pure deadly evil spirit clutching and feeding its passion upon the human corruptible soul until the only nobility left in the victim sibling is the will to destroy the incubus,

at the price even of its own life. At the last moment, Magwitch disengages himself from his revenge, and survives; old
Dombey, who might have madly pursued his incubus into
the path of the train, is saved by Carker's cowardice, or perhaps "some touch of tenderness and remorse" caused Carker
to back away from the man he had been spiritually grap-
pling with for years.

But Bradley Headstone, willfully taking Lizzie Hexam
as his doom and Eugene Wrayburn as his incubus, struggles,
as Dickens profoundly discerns, not away from but towards
his corruption and his crime. Like Victor Frankenstein,
like Robert Wringhim, like Dr. Jekyll, he loves his tormenting wicked other for sanctioning the unbridling of his
darkest passions. The same dark motive stirs in Eugene:
the incubus strikes alike at the heavily repressed man and
the lightly drifting one. In the chapter called "Tracking the
Bird of Prey," restless and guilty during the pursuit of the
supposed criminal Gaffer Hexam, Eugene proposes half
seriously to his friend: "Next time (with a view to our
peace of mind) we'll commit the crime instead of taking
the criminal." Eugene moves toward the seduction of Lizzie
as Bradley moves toward the murder of Eugene: Lizzie tries
to resist her part in the first crime, but Eugene practically
invites the second. Passion's overreach and Lizzie's strength
make the murder only an assault, and intimate contact with
love and death rouses Eugene from his sleepwalk into crime.
But Bradley has acquired, has fatally accepted and enlisted,
a new and deadlier incubus in Rogue Riderhood, who unlike Eugene has come out of his little death in the river with
a new sense of his evil immortality. Bradley's intuition to
disguise himself as Riderhood to commit the murder is not
really a cunning stratagem but rather an admission of identity. It is also a covert invocation of that mutual murder/
suicide paradigm that alone, as we have seen in the Gothic,
relieves the intolerable pressure of passion and criminal
freedom that the human spirit ungoverned by community
ties seeks.

That paradigm occurs for both men in the chapter entitled "What was Caught in the Traps that were set." "I'll drain you dry . . . . you can't get rid of me. . . . this is a dry game," Riderhood asserts as Bradley makes one futile bid for separation from his vampire. Then, accepting what he has sought, Bradley makes himself the vampire—"I'll hold you living and I'll hold you dead"—and goes down into the water with his victim. In the penultimate chapter of *Dombey and Son*, Cousin Feenix's words surely describe the sensation with which one comes away from the scene in *Our Mutual Friend* and from the Dickens world itself—that dislocation from safe harbor, that perfect at-seaness amid a flood of strange phenomena of which we ourselves, together with our faculty of perception, are the strangest: "And in regard to the changes of human life, and the extraordinary manner in which we are perpetually conducting ourselves, all I can say is, with my friend Shakespeare—man who wasn't for an age but for all time—that it's like the shadow of a dream."

A brave fidelity to that shadow of a dream marks Charlotte Brontë's works too. Although her dreamers, at great cost, struggle awake and bend powerful minds to the understanding of dreams, the discriminating of the solitary dream from the communally shared "real"—the shadow of the dream—remains; tyrannical reason never totally draws the discriminating line. Unlike Scott and Dickens, who because of the circumstances of their lives, and perhaps their sex, possessed an intense social daylight in which to assess and mold their dream lives, Brontë's social situation afforded her many days as solitary and demonic as the night. *"I am not like you,"* Charlotte has to emphasize again and again to her friend Ellen Nussey: "If you knew my thoughts, the dreams that absorb me, and the fiery imagination that at times eats me up, and makes me feel society, as it is, wretchedly insipid, you would pity, and I dare say despise me."[7] Eternity and

<hr>

[7] Mrs. Gaskell reports this in her *Life of Charlotte Brontë* (1857; reprint ed., Harmondsworth, Middlesex: Penguin Books, 1975), p. 161.

duty, those two ideas quintessentially sublime if not always beautiful to the mind's eye, gave her minimal anchorage in the storms of despair and anger that periodically flattened the spirit, sometimes in the presence of those objective correlatives death, illness, failure, sometimes in anticipation or memory of these. Sometimes, as she powerfully describes it in *Villette*, the awful visitation simply came of its own: "Death challenged me to engage his unknown terrors. When I tried to pray I could only utter these words—'From my youth up thy terrors have I suffered with a troubled mind.'"[8]

Yet terrors fascinate, are even, obscurely, holy. Emily Brontë's early Gondal poem uses the voice of that power to describe the Gothic approach to the "awful time": "Dost thou not feel upon thy soul/ A flood of strange sensations roll,/ Forerunners of a sterner power,/ Heralds of me?" After the awful time, grinding as it is, *Villette*'s Lucy Snowe rather pities "those whom mental pain stuns instead of rousing"; after that experience, "a composite feeling of blended strength and pain wound itself wirily around my heart," and the spirit feels stirrings of preternatural capacities (p. 209). One such visitation leaves Lucy wishing, half believing, "that I had wings and could ascend the gale, spread and repose my pinions on its strength, career in its course, sweep where it swept" (p. 142); after another, "the pang of waking snatched me out of bed like a hand with a giant's grip" (p. 209). A final awful time drives her out into Villette's festival streets where she discovers what appears to be the truth about a courtship between her more-than-friend M. Paul and the mysterious Justine. No longer shrinking from this pain, she "gathered it to me with a sort of rage of haste" (p. 427), and in the power of her rage, she encounters on her return to her own bed the phantom

8 Charlotte Brontë, *Villette* (1853; reprint ed., New York: Dutton, 1972), p. 143. Subsequent references are to this edition and will be cited by page number in the text.

nun who has been making ghostly appearances throughout
the narrative:

> I was not overcome. . . . I defied spectra. In a moment,
> without exclamation, I had rushed on the haunted
> couch. . . . I tore her up—the incubus! I held her on
> high—the goblin! I shook her loose—the mystery! And
> down she fell—down all around me—down in shreds
> and fragments—and I trod upon her. (P. 429)

This is a true battle of giants, as real a destruction of the
deadly by the life-affirming as Alfonso the Good's of
Manfred's house, Van Helsing's of Dracula's, as real as if
the phantom were not simply the stuffed simulacrum that
Ginevra Fanshawe left as a hoax before eloping with the
man who had used the nun-disguise as a trysting device.[9] In
Jane Eyre, when Richard Mason shrank from the madwoman, he raised her demonic power. "You should not have
yielded; you should have grappled with her at once," says
Rochester in Chapter 20, and he proves his point in the
next encounter. Whatever the unmistakable identification
of Jane Eyre with her fiend-rival "Grace Poole," of Lucy
with the ghost-rival "nun" of the Pensionnat de Demoi-
selles, it is not to be compressed into the daylight terms of
the scientist John Graham Bretton: "This is all a matter
of the nerves, I see. . . . a case of spectral illusion: I fear,
following on and resulting from long-continued mental
conflict" (p. 227). When, considering this possibility, Lucy
asks about a cure, Dr. John tells her to cultivate happiness
and a cheerful mind, and Lucy muses with proper scorn,
"What does such advice mean? Happiness is not a potato,
to be planted in mould and tilled with manure."

9 Thus, the relationship between this scene and its predecessor in
Radcliffe's *The Mysteries of Udolpho*, where the heroine approaches
the phantom but drops the veil in terror before she can see it is a
waxen dummy, is not parody nor imitation but transformation—a
re-Gothicizing.

No such natural, such vegetable, life is available or finally desirable for Charlotte Brontë's dreamers. "Forerunners of a sterner power" open their eyes and ears to the preternatural that is their real heritage. The mastering by direct wrestle of the phantom who is not exactly unreal describes in pure Gothic terms the wrestle between the *two passions*, reason (or control or duty) and imagination (or passion), on which Brontë's characters and plots are molded. The force of these wrestling angels fills the air with voices: "Jane! Jane!" she hears Rochester calling in agony three counties away; "Go to London," say the voices in the aurora borealis to Lucy Snowe. And it fills the night with visions: a dream of an endangered infant or child-self haunts Jane on the nights preceeding her ill-fated wedding day, and later she dreams of some fearful hostile spirit who tears her veil in half. Although the latter turns out to have been no dream, the former points to the deeper difficulty in her relationship with Rochester. Similarly, an "avenging dream" terrifies Lucy Snowe: "Methought the well loved dead, who had loved me well in life, met me elsewhere, alienated" (p. 143). And to the last, writing her "heretic narrative" as a kind of alternative to the more slothful imaginings of the dedicated nun, Lucy cannot assert that the "chain of communication" by which, as Rochester had said in *Jane Eyre*, a pain in one heart can cause another to bleed though separated by counties or the wide sea itself, still operates, unalienated, across the gulf of death. Among the many meanings in *Villette*'s enigmatic farewell after M. Paul's shipwreck, the admonition "leave sunny imaginations hope. Let it be theirs to conceive the delight of joy born fresh again out of great terror . . . the wondrous reprieve from dread. . . . Let them picture union" (p. 451) surely hints at the shadow of that dream of the alienated well-loved dead. Facing that ultimate question, that root dread, Brontë's heretic narrative candidly addresses both the reader and itself: "Here pause: pause at once. There is enough said." Here is neither evasion nor reconciliation, nor, really, the "undercutting" of the faiths available for reconciliation. But anything that comforts the spirit after that pause, she rightly notes, is kindled by that "sunny imagination" which is Brontë's word for grace.

Scott's, Dickens's, Brontë's strategy of embracing the Gothic presentation of dread by way of the mouths and eyes of children, eccentrics, and primitives seems coherent with (and perhaps contributed to) a certain sunny imagination of our own century, which views fear and guilt as products of unresolved childish conflicts that, when touched to that philosopher's stone, adult reality, may be resolved and their "unnatural" fallout of dread eliminated. The position of Scott, Dickens, and Brontë in the adolescents' corner of the library for a good part of the century is perhaps connected with this fancy. Yet a strong movement in psychology is proposing to stand that fancy on its head, is suggesting that the child's straightforward perception of the "overwhelmingness," to use Ernest Becker's word, of creation, is after all the clearest truth we have, that anxiety is the truest response to this truth, that adult behavior is a slippery, dangerous, not ignoble layering of denial/transformation strategies that, together with these truths, provide for survival. In his important account of this movement, *The Denial of Death*,[10] Becker argues for the Brontëan pause for recognition before the strategies are chosen: "Reality and fear go together naturally" (p. 17), "guilt is not a result of infantile fantasy but of self-conscious adult reality" (p. 261), "repression is not falsification of the world,

10 Ernest Becker, *The Denial of Death* (New York: Macmillan, 1973). Treading a line between the morbidness of Freud, who hated "helplessness" more than anything in the world (p. 115) and was therefore doomed to a fight he couldn't win, and the sanguineness of Norman O. Brown's return to Eros, Becker's book, as he says, "has as a major aim the closure of psychoanalysis on religion" (p. xiv) through a study of Otto Rank, Kierkegaard, and other philosophers of the "numinous," which Devendra Varma argues *is* "the Gothic flame." Subsequent references are to this edition and will be cited by page number in the text.

it is truth—the only truth man can know because he cannot experience everything" (p. 265), these supposedly "morbid-minded" qualities are not temperamental dysfunctions but on the contrary "functions of real overwhelmingness, the stark majesty of objects in the child's world. If we, as adults, are well dulled and armored against all this, we have only to read poets such as Thomas Traherne, Sylvia Plath, or R. L. Stevenson, who haven't blunted their receptors to raw experience" (p. 262).

This classic appeal to the poets like Cousin Feenix's "friend Shakespeare," whose denial strategies cover the "truth" so faithfully as to suggest its shape with perfect fidelity, brings us back to the Gothic, whose business first and last is with the fact of overwhelmingness and with the strategies that men design to admit, uphold, and live in the presence of—not instead of or against—the truth. What distinguishes Scott, Dickens, and the Brontës—and one may surely add James and Conrad to this list—is the quality and sheer persistence of their efforts to explore and validate overwhelmingness. Their protagonists, Lambert Strether and Lord Jim, Isabel Archer and Lucy Snowe, David Copperfield and Edward Waverley, bear to the gaze of the "armored" adult observer, and to themselves as well, the unmistakable mark of the "fool," the capacity to be overwhelmed. What further unites Austen, Eliot, and Lawrence, I will argue in succeeding chapters, is the special understanding of how *much* this fact matters, for the individual, the race, even the species of man—that the deep truth of life is overwhelming, that it cannot be managed or fully assimilated. They are united too in their perception of the *uses* of anxiety and dread as a way of recognizing and admitting the fact of overwhelmingness. These novelists display a sense (which Becker says was shared by early Darwinians) that fear has "a high survival value" for the race but that fear of death undefended by strategies of denial paralyzes development. There are a number of such strategies—myth systems that offer models for heroic behavior or mortal systems that reduce death from the petrifying inevitable to a human choice available to the rightly formed conscience and the tutored will.

Bram Stoker graphically portrayed this paralysis and the near-failure of the conventional myth systems in *Dracula*, whose Gothic antihero is, in his pervasiveness and power, "King Death." But the proper human response to this failure, according to that novel, seems to be a kind of rhythm between honorable terror and a more complex re-action that the magus Van Helsing calls "King Laugh":

> That laughter who knock at your door and say, "May I come in?" is not the true laughter. No! he is a king, and he come when and how he like. He ask no person; he choose no time of suitability. He say, "I am here." . . . it is a strange world, a sad world, a world full of miseries, and woes, and troubles; and yet when King Laugh come he make them all dance to the tune he play. Bleeding hearts, and dry bones of the churchyard, and tears that burn as they fall—all dance together to the music he make with that smileless mouth of him. Ah, we men and women are like ropes drawn tight with strain that pull us different ways. Then tears come; and like the rain on the ropes, they brace us up, until perhaps the strain become too great, and we break. But King Laugh he come like the sunshine, and he ease off the strain again; and we bear to go on with our labour, what it may be. (Pp. 196-197)

Nietzsche's magus Zarathustra refers to this response as the Song of the Midnight Bell, this note that can only be reached through terror, this standing up with overwhelm-ingness, this sweeping out with it until one is without op-position to it and finally this return to it refreshed. This, I proposed, was the vision of the "forces of good" in *Dracula*, whose alliance with the blood of life enables them to coexist with, finally to outlast, King Death, though for any of the individuals, the end of that adventure is certainly to return

that blood of life and that victory to the general pool, perhaps we may say, at the behest of King Laugh, the Grace
Poole. This seems also Becker's vision: "Who knows what
form the forward momentum of life will take in the time
ahead and what use it will make of our anguished searching.
The most that any one of us can seem to do is to fashion
something—an object or ourselves—and drop it into the
confusion, make an offering of it, so to speak, to the life
force" (p. 285).

The forms that the forward momentum of narrative has
taken over the past two hundred years are reflected in this
language, these visions. From the relative simplicities of the
Gothic romance and pursuit stories and the obscure verities
of the worshippers of King Laugh, to the race anxieties
explored in the complications of historical and "science
fiction" Gothic, to the great traditions whose latitude is
"formal realism," the shape with which all these forms must
reckon is King Death. What use Austen, Eliot, and Lawrence make of this shape and of the Gothic machines on
which he customarily rides into fiction is the study of the
following essays.

THREE

JANE AUSTEN: THE ANXIETIES
OF COMMON LIFE

OUT of Walter Scott came a bad tradition; out of Jane
Austen came a good one. So said Leavis. But their contemporaries saw it a bit differently. In Scott a bad old tradition continued somewhat redeemed;[1] in Austen a decisive
break with that tradition produced "the modern novel."
What was broken at last, so they thought, was above all that
Gothic "machinery" in which the Greek and the Elizabethan stage had delighted, which Fielding and Richardson
had mocked, and which had held the imagination of the
novel-reading public, especially the female one, for half a
century.[2]

[1] As recently as 1972, Andrew Hook was seeing Scott as the rescuer
of the novel from traditions squalidly Gothic—and female: "Scott's
triumph became a triumph for the form he wrote in. The novel
gained a new authority and prestige, and even more important perhaps,
a new masculinity. After Scott the novel was no longer in danger of
becoming the preserve of the woman writer and the woman reader.
Instead it became the appropriate form for writers' richest and deepest
imaginative explorations of human experience." "Instead"? See the
introduction to *Waverley* (Harmondsworth, Middlesex: Penguin Books,
1972), p. 10.

[2] In *Tom Jones*, Fielding mourns the machines of Homer, "his gods
coming on trivial errands," and allows to the modern writer only the
ghost machine: "But of these I would advise an author to be extremely sparing. These are indeed like arsenic and dangerous drugs in
physic, to be used with utmost caution." Indeed, Fielding's antimachine,
antimarvelous position leads him in the end to the antireal conclusion,
"It is no excuse for a poet who relates what is incredible, that the thing
related is really matter of fact" (ch. 1, bk. 8). Similarly, Richardson
wrote a friend that "An excellent Physician was so good as to give me
a plan to break Legs and Arms and to fire Mansion Houses to create
Distresses. . . . But I hate so much the French Marvellous and all

The concept of machinery and the ascribed aesthetic Ludditism of Jane Austen are crucial to the understanding of the English novel, especially as Eliot and Lawrence developed it. Formally, machinery is the outward and visible sign of an invisible power—mind in material motion. In the Oxford English Dictionary, between descriptions of the theatrical machine (almost pure materiality) and the political machine (almost pure power) is a definition of the literary machine: "a contrivance for the sake of effect, a supernatural agency or personage introduced into a poem; the interposition of one of these." A literary machine conveys power and carries and demands effect—or more precisely, affect. It is a convention, that is, a contrivance, separately visible within the contrivance of the literary object for its greater audacity of design, separately visible within the affect of the literary object for its more insistent and focused call to emotion.

Essential to the idea of the literary machine is this sense of its "interposition": it is a surprise, an anomaly in the created world, it knocks it about, or is knocked about in it. The scale is, of course, arbitrary. In Homer's world Athena is the machine that carries the convention of the "godlike," the "otherworldly"; in Swift's world it is Gulliver, a machine wherever he goes. To the humanists, all agents or manifestations of the numinous, the fated, or the supernatural were machines, needed machines. They were the potent, vanishing reality, god in the machine, on the machine, *as* the machine: it was difficult to separate the reality from the manifested form and the form from the motion by which it was manifested. To the neoclassical critics, the ancients were the machinery, the not quite dead, not quite natural, not quite ghosts of the house of fiction. Giant forms of Homer and Virgil and the "old romancers" lay shattered

unnatural Machinery, and have so often been disgusted with that sort of Management" (letter to Stephen Duck, 1741; quoted in *Selected Letters of Samuel Richardson*, ed. John Carroll [Oxford: Clarendon Press, 1964], pp. 51-52).

in the courtyards of poets, their ghosts seeking new machines to ride on. As Patricia Merivale has noted, Poe's raven perching on the bust of Pallas represents a Gothic contradiction or overcoming of the classical world, terror "riding" on wisdom and beauty; yes, but it also represents the ghost of that world of guilt and terror that was defeated by classicism, represents a permanent world of mystery in which the classical artifact not the melodramatic bird, is the "interloper."[3]

Walpole, the father of Gothic, speaks loftily of the ancients in his preface to *The Castle of Otranto*, but the anxiety of influence is strong: "The actions, sentiments, conversations of the heroes and heroines of ancient days were as unnatural as the machines employed to put them in motion."

Walpole's remark reminds us that the notion of "machinery"—to the Newtonian eighteenth-century critical mind, the unnatural in motion—spreads from its locus in plot to encompass character and even sentiment. By the end of the century, one had to include a fourth machine, a fourth carrier of mysterious powers perfected above all by Radcliffe—setting. Jane Austen inherited her machines as Walpole had inherited his and Shakespeare and Homer theirs: *they are machines precisely because they were inherited*; in the hands of living artists, the conventions insist on retaining some of the undead life of the past. This tincture of alien life often resists even the greatest artists' efforts —showing a mordant rictus or a whimsical grin against even the most powerful creative wills, congealing rocklike in the flow so that even the profoundest originality shows a little froth around it.

This wrestle of authors with literary machinery is fascinating wherever one finds it, but I am especially drawn to that section of the game that followed the ascendancy and paralleled the development of the Gothic novel in England.

[3] Patricia Merivale, "The Raven and the Bust of Pallas: Classical Artifacts and the Gothic Tale," *PMLA* 89 (October 1974): pp. 960-966.

For it was Gothic machinery that the nineteenth-century novelists inherited and attempts at conversion went on furiously at the turn of the century. Out of the basic Gothic motions and machines, William Godwin began the fashioning of the detective story, Mary Shelley the science fiction tale (in *The Lost Man*, that is, not *Frankenstein*, which is pure Gothic), and Walter Scott the historical romance. And Byron instituted Byronism and Wordsworth natural supernaturalism. Dickens and Bulwer and the Brontës rode the Gothic machinery brilliantly with almost no opposition to it. And Jane Austen, whose sense and sensibility were the finest of all, sat down to deal with the Gothic by way of the loving subversions of parody and achieved, between *Northanger Abbey* and *Emma*, not a subversion nor a conversion but a real transformation of the machinery, a true and original grasping of her inheritance.

Parody, after all, as George Levine remarked in a penetrating essay on *Northanger Abbey*, is a dangerous game for a novelist: "novels, by and large, cannot remain parodies exclusively, as *Joseph Andrews* or *Don Quixote* demonstrated."[4] The impulse of parody is *too* mechanical to be sustained; either the parody will cease to govern the life of the novel, as in *Joseph Andrews*, or the convention being parodied will reassert its genuine life, as in *Don Quixote*, or as in Austen's parody of the Gothic, where, as Levine concludes of successful parody in general, "both sides of the opposition implicit in parody are attractive and remain so, whichever one seems to be getting the upper hand in a given moment of literary and cultural history" (p. 345).

This inheritance, taken up in parody, is not, cannot be, entirely spent in parody. If it is a living inheritance, it remains as material for, even as a kind of foundation of, Austen's worlds of fiction. The distance between *The Mysteries*

---

[4] George Levine, "Translating the Monstrous: *Northanger Abbey*," *Nineteenth Century Fiction* 30 (December 1975): 335-350. Subsequent references are to this edition and will be cited by page number in the text.

of *Udolpho* and *Northanger Abbey* can be quite small or even nonexistent for an artist. It is a staple of Gothic tales to argue that transformation processes can be bewilderingly self-activated, or self-reversing. From the Gothic point of view, form, like feeling, shows a disquieting facility for switching into its opposite and back again. As C. L. Pitt remarked in a funny satire on *The Age* (1810), simply by "scratching out a few terms and inserting others," one may make "a novel out of a romance, or a romance out of a novel."[5]

Pitt's comic transformation formula, which he proposed "may, like machinery in factories, greatly facilitate the progress" of the art of fiction, contains several charming and workable propositions about how to use the Gothic inheritance. According to Pitt, in order to make a novel out of a romance:

Where you find:—
A castle . . . . put An house
A giant . . . . A father
A knight . . . . . A gentleman without
                                        whiskers

A lady who is the heroine .   Need not be changed,
                                        being versatile

The formula also contains at least one proposition that is not only workable, but profound:

Where you find:—
A midnight murder . . . put A marriage[6]

We shall return to this proposition with emphasis in the next two essays.

---

[5] E. F. Bleiler records Pitt's recipe for novels in his introduction to *Three Gothic Novels* (New York: Dover Press, 1966), p. 4. The recipe was a footnote to Pitt's *The Age: A Poem, Moral, Political, and Metaphysical, with Illustrative Annotations* (London, 1810).

[6] From Pitt's *The Age*, in Bleiler, *Three Gothic Novels*, p. 4.

The process of transformation—the true reworking of the inheritance that links Austen's experimental parody and her richest novel—is visible especially in her use of five major machines, five conventional carriers of power: *The Mysteries of Udolpho* itself, the programmatic Gothic setting, the isolated and tyrannical villain, the ruined church, and the overimaginative heroine. What makes these machines Gothic and Austen's handling of them, after all, Gothic, is again that they are energized by dread—designed for the candid facing and managing of this emotion. The turning point of *Emma*, as of *Northanger Abbey*, is not the dispelling or undercutting of dread but its recognition: "The anxieties of common life began soon to succeed to the alarms of romance."[7] Thus, in the form of Radcliffe's *The Mysteries of Udolpho*, the total machinery of the Gothic is "interposited" into the given machine of *Northanger Abbey*'s common life, not to be mocked but to raise that machine to its real importance. In both *Northanger Abbey* and *Emma*, the result is not to make romance ridiculous but to make common anxiety "serious" or "high" (to use two Leavisite words). And this elevation is the heart and purpose of the novel as Austen, Eliot, and Lawrence write it.

Udolpho *at Northanger*

Austen has a famous and misunderstood paragraph in *Northanger Abbey* that seems to disqualify England itself as a programmatic setting for the Gothic, seems to lightly repudiate the book and the author at the center of her parody. Apparently recovering, Emma-wise, from the "humiliation" of her mistaking General Tilney for a murderer, Catherine remonstrates with herself in the narrator's voice:

[7] Quotations from Jane Austen's novels are taken from the standard editions of her works by R. W. Chapman (London: Oxford Univ. Press, 1933). This phrase occurs in volume V (in which *Northanger Abbey* and *Persuasion* appear together) on p. 201. Subsequent references are to this edition and will be cited by volume and page number in the text.

Charming as were all Mrs. Radcliffe's works, and charming even as were the works of all her imitators, it was not in them perhaps that human nature, at least in the midland counties of England, was to be looked for. Of the Alps and Pyrenees, with their pine forests and their vices, they might give a faithful delineation, and Italy, Switzerland, and the South of France might be as fruitful in horrors as they were there represented. Catherine dared not doubt beyond her own country, and even of that, if hard pressed, would have yielded the northern and western extremities. But in the central part of England there was surely some security for the existence even of a wife not beloved, in the laws of the land, and the manners of the age. (V, 200)

Several important elements seem to make this passage a complex admission rather than rejection of the Gothic. First, Catherine has just had the worst fright of her young life in discovering that the master of Northanger Abbey did not, like Radcliffe's villain, seek to murder his wife, and that his son, whom Catherine loves, knows she had thought he did. This self-scolding is a way both of calming her nerves and of punishing herself; this ferocious application of the scourge of reason has the effect, carefully underscored by Austen's sly humor, of boxing the soul even further into its claustrophobic fortress of security, the central part of England, its laws and its manners. Clutching these props, Catherine is ready for the greatest hurt of all, when the master, discovering she is not after all an heiress, boots her out of the abbey with no money nor guidance home, as part of an edict that would have wiped her out of both his and his children's lives as cleanly as the workings of poison. General Tilney possesses neither law nor manners—only, like Radcliffe's Montoni, a nasty temper and an overweening desire to keep his property and his family absolutely at his own disposal.

Another point to be noted is Catherine's fervent dismissal

of Radcliffe's knowledge of human nature. After the passage quoted, Catherine goes on to take comfort in the mixed character of the English as opposed to the unmixed evil or good in Radcliffean, or Pyrenean, Gothic. As careful readers of *The Mysteries of Udolpho* know, this is a truly adolescent reading of Radcliffe. As Catherine comes to see, General Tilney is totally unamiable; his character is not even enlivened by the valor, wit, and sorrow of Montoni. On the other hand, the character of Radcliffe's young gallant, Valancourt, is as variegated as Austen's Henry, and her Emily is a model for Catherine in the most important respect of all: hers is a rational, principled mind battling from start to finish with its own shadow side—"causeless terror" embedded in the mind, Austen calls it; "superstition" is Radcliffe's word. Only the villain, from the worst of motives, encourages the heroine to erase that recognition of the shadow: "I recommend it to you to retire to your chamber, and to endeavour to adopt a more rational conduct, than that of yielding to fancies, and to a sensibility, which, to call it by the gentlest name, is only a weakness," urges Montoni plausibly.[8] Significantly, Emily's father has a slightly wider perspective: "I would not annihilate your feelings, my child, I would only teach you to command them; for whatever may be the evils resulting from a too susceptible heart, nothing can be hoped from an insensible one; that, on the other hand, is all vice—vice, of which the deformity is not softened, or the effect consoled for by any semblance or possibility of good" (p. 20).

If this apparent clear division of character is complicated by the fact that one's father harbors as destructive a mystery as does Udolpho, so that many critics recognize in Radcliffe's father/uncle a doppelgänger, no less is true of this figure in Jane Austen's major works. The father in *Sense and Sensibility* dies leaving Elinor and Marianne Dashwood vul-

---

[8] Ann Radcliffe, *The Mysteries of Udolpho* (1794: reprint ed., London: Oxford Univ. Press, 1970), p. 230. Subsequent references are to this edition and will be cited by page number in the text.

nerable to villains in his own family, as does Emily's father. And Austen's live fathers—the sarcastic and ineffectual Mr. Bennet of *Pride and Prejudice*, the affable but selfish Sir Thomas Price of *Mansfield Park*, *Emma*'s delicate and tyrannical Mr. Woodhouse, *Persuasion*'s vain and obtuse Sir Walter Elliot—are as willful and threatening to their daughters' happiness as Montoni is to his niece.

The point is that in her attack of reasonable sensibility, whatever Catherine may deny to *The Mysteries of Udolpho* and whatever complexities of Radcliffe's sense of human nature Austen may establish in the end, Austen has in fact spent the first section of *Northanger Abbey* establishing an appreciation of that charming book as the touchstone of good character. Seventeen-year-old Catherine Morland has two suitors in her first days as a young lady "out" in Bath: John Thorpe hasn't read *Udolpho* and wouldn't read *any* novel written by a woman; on the other hand, Henry Tilney's well-informed and flexible mind includes a shivery two days' engagement with *The Mysteries of Udolpho*—"my hair standing on end the whole time" (V, 106). Catherine makes two female friends there, both of whom have read *Udolpho*. But Isabella Thorpe's reading has been facile and witless; her wide knowledge of "horrid" books has been lifted from conversations with her friends, on which unstable information she bases her shrill conviction that *Sir Charles Grandison* is also a "horrid" book. And while Eleanor Tilney will join Catherine against Henry's gay mockery —"Let us leave him to meditate over our faults in the utmost propriety of diction, while we praise Udolpho in whatever terms we like best" (V, 108)—she also has room for the study of history.

Their discussion of history is significant to the uses of *The Mysteries of Udolpho* as a machine, a real carrier of power from outside the novel's world. Both young women recognize that "invention" is at the core of historical writing as well as novel writing, and they wonder why history is nevertheless so dull. Catherine naively hits the nail on the head: "The men all so good for nothing, and hardly any women at all—it is very tiresome" (V, 108). This observation, we may recall, describes many of the central works in the Gothic as well, for it is Radcliffe, not Walpole or Lewis or Byron, who makes the Gothic available to the great novelists of the nineteenth century because she subtly treats both the terrors of the antihero, the "good for nothing" man, and those of the victim, the woman—both the intensities of male aggressive will and of female resistant reason. Even "invention" fares best when it balances those two interests, otherwise, as Eleanor muses, the historian will "display imagination without raising interest" (V, 109). At once more forbearing and more discriminating, she is willing to take the dull and true with the false, invented, and interesting; she is able both to distinguish them and to harmonize them, resisting Catherine's youthful wish to avoid the merely true and intelligent but also resisting the educated Henry's drift toward mockery of the freshly imaginative.

What we see in the discussions surrounding *The Mysteries of Udolpho* in the first volume of *Northanger Abbey* is Austen's placement of the novel itself in the significant landscape of common life. And her choice of *Udolpho* as the machine for that plan is careful synecdoche. Richardson's *Sir Charles Grandison* is in there too, on the periphery, and so is Fanny Burney's *Cecilia*, and John Thorpe thinks nothing really good has been written since *Tom Jones*. But these are not, candidly, "the novel" as the ordinary person sees it. Not yet. And if one is going to argue for the necessary arousal and cleansing and refining of the sensible imagination, of the inventive heart, as Jane Austen is going to do in all of her work, and for the utility, even the centrality, of the novel in that enterprise, then, wryly and lovingly, *The Mysteries of Udolpho* is your proper machine.

The distance between that novel and *Northanger Abbey* is closer, the relationship more subtle, the felt bond more important than we may think. Not quite a parodist, almost an imitator, Austen is in fact an heiress of Radcliffe. And whereas we must not exaggerate when claiming special qualities in the artistic relationships between authors of one sex as opposed to the other (although there are surely tart moments in *Northanger Abbey* where one could swear the anxiety of influence adds an edge), this female heirship has a startling quality of mutuality one might almost call love. "Alas! if the heroine of one novel be not patronized by the heroine of another, from whom can she expect protection and regard?" the narrator of *Northanger Abbey* asks and, segueing from heroine to novelist, continues, "Let us not desert one another; we are an injured body" (V, 37). Pursued by the dark elders of the press, the reviewers ("Let us leave it to the Reviewers to abuse [us]"), cut and undercut by their henchmen, the abridgers ("And while the activities of the nine-hundredth abridgers of the History of England, or of the man who collects and publishes in a volume some dozen lines of Milton, Pope and Prior, are eulogized by a thousand pens . . . there seems almost a general wish of decrying the capacity of the novelist"), betrayed by that faithless young hero, the reader (" 'I am no novel reader—I seldom look into novels—it is really very well for a novel'—such is the common cant"), the novelist/heroine yet stands her ground: " 'Oh! it is only a novel!' . . . . or, in short, only some work in which the greatest powers of the mind are displayed, in which the most thorough knowledge of human nature, the happiest delineation of its varieties, the liveliest effusions of wit and humour are conveyed to the world in the best chosen language" (V, 38).[9]

If the machinery of *Udolpho* is on one level meant to represent the novel and its special width of sensitivity and to act as a discriminating touchstone of character, it is on

[9] Austen's most recent biographer reminds us that this passage comes out of the 1816 period of the novel's revision, not its original youthful composition: "This is no unpublished novelist speaking." See Jane Aiken Hodge, *Only A Novel: The Double Life of Jane Austen* (London: Hodder and Stoughton, 1972), p. 178.

another more strictly mechanical level meant to provide a shadow plot, an analogous action, a prophetic foreshadowing of the progress of Austen's own novel. Here the machine seems to creak noisily—the shadow doesn't glide, it clumps. Radcliffe's men and women are near-aristocrats, the fortunes and properties at stake are huge ones, the secret sins run to · adultery and murder and the passions to "phrenzy," the landscapes of the mind are as foreign ("she suffered all the delirium of Italian love" [p. 656], "she was going . . . to endure, beyond the hope of succour, whatever punishment revenge, and that Italian revenge, might dictate" [p. 225]) as the physical landscape:

> Emily could not restrain her transport as she looked over the pine forests of the mountains upon the vast plains, that, enriched with woods, towns, blushing vines, and plantations of almonds, palms and olives, stretched along, till their various colours melted in distance into one harmonious hue, that seemed to unite earth with heaven. (P. 28)[10]

In Radcliffe's tale, Emily de St. Aubert's protecting father is dead, and she has sent her young lover away to the dissipations of Paris; she is in the farthest room in the most inaccessible castle in the wildest mountains in the most foreign country (to her Provençal/English mind) in the world. As protector against her stupid and brutal suitor, Count Morano, she has only the fearsome Montoni, who "had invention equal to the conception and talents [equal] to the execution of any project" (p. 240) and whose project in inviting her to Udolpho is to terrify her into marrying that same stupid and brutal henchman, or, more darkly to

---

[10] Austen's characters suffer "transports" in the countryside as well—one thinks of Emma's swell of the heart upon beholding Donwell Abbey: "English verdure, English comfort, English culture." But her landscapes are emphatically *not* united with heaven, and the transports have to do with the distinctions rather than the mergings of features in the scene.

Emily's suspicious mind, to murder his wife and marry Emily himself. Like Frankenstein's creature, such a plot is eight feet tall in a six-footer's world. And some of its parts are awry too. In Austen's novel, unlike Emily's father, Catherine's father is alive, though absent, and Henry Tilney's disappearances are for distances of only a few miles; the fearsome General Tilney (how the Englished 'ey' tames the villainous Italian 'i'!), misled by Catherine's stupid and brutal suitor John Thorpe, purposes to marry Catherine to her young lover, his son, or more darkly to Catherine's suspicious mind, to provide the Abbey with a new mistress to gloss over the fact that he has already murdered his own wife. Emily suffers terrors such as a Catherine can only wish for: the progress of her "distress,"[11] from innocent enjoyment of life, to puzzled wonder, to sensitive apprehension, to "this exhaustion of suspence" (p. 319), to horrible but mistaken certainty is classic and satisfying, whereas Catherine's is so deceptively smooth that she keeps forgetting her terrors.

Catherine has only one distress that Emily lacks—but it is the one that counts for everything in the world of common anxieties. Again and again Radcliffe's heroine notes (protests almost too much, one might say) that although "superstition" may invade her mind, and passion even at times shake it, the final mind-unhinging scourge of *remorse* is avoided. She had sent away young Valancourt from her dangerous proximity, and so, "whatever her future sorrows could be, she was, at least, free from self-reproach" (p. 240). Presentiments of doom assail her at Udolpho, but she resists rash action, "for whatever I may be reserved, let me, at least, avoid self-reproach" (p. 251). It is in this context that the coincidence of Radcliffe's heroines always being

---

11 "Distress" is almost a technical term in the fiction of the time, as George Sherburn remarks; it is the dramatization, usually by way of melodramatic materials, of the building-up and the releasing of pent-up emotions. See the introduction to the Riverside edition of *Clarissa* (Boston: Houghton-Mifflin, 1962), p. vi.

clothed when accosted can be viewed as something more than mere comedy or prudery. When Emily is visited after 2 A.M. by Count Morano and she springs from the bed "in the dress which surely a kind of prophetic apprehension had prevented her on this night, from throwing aside" (p. 261), Radcliffe is adding a final twist of embellishment to that character whose inner stability is utterly dependent upon "the consciousness of having deserved praise, instead of censure" (p. 270). Imprisoned, abandoned, deceived, terrified, Emily stands up to fate and Montoni because "the luxury of conscious worth" makes her proof against the real terrors, against the guilt that is always the province of the Gothic hero-villain.

That luxury is hers because on her own she never takes a wrong step or makes a wrong decision, always listens to the right premonitions even in the matter of undressing, and always discards the wrong ones, even in the matter of escaping. When the passionate but "phrenzied" Morano offers to help her escape from the hated Montoni and she chooses instead to remain under Montoni's "protection," we see her meet the crisis that "ruined" and almost maddened Richardson's Clarissa. Morano is as entertainingly ironic on the subject of Montoni's "protection" as Lovelace is about Mr. Harlowe's. And so he should be. But Emily meets his satire not with prudery or ignorant hauteur but with a just understanding of the situation that comes too late to the gloriously self-reproaching Clarissa; Montoni's conduct convinces her that "I should not be placed beyond the reach of oppression, as long as I remained in your power" (p. 264).

As Andrew Wright remarks, Emily is an amazingly credible and "coherent" heroine. What makes her credible is the range and solidity of her experiences; what makes her coherent, keeps her together, is this unfailing steely-principled, self-enhancing avoidance of anything that could bring self-reproach. For, far more than passion or even ego-giganticism, remorse is the mind-killer in the Gothic world:

it is a complicated part of Clarissa's death,[12] and it causes the final "unsettling of the intellects" in Laurentini di Udolpho, whose unbridled sexual passion started the novel's machinery. And it is likewise the ruin of Montoni and Schedoni and all the other fascinating villains who can neither control nor forgive themselves their appetites. Self-reproach is the distinguishing mark for many of Jane Austen's important heroines too. Catherine, Elizabeth Bennet, and Emma are all the reverse of Emily, since they make false steps almost immediately; they go the journey not of the Gothic heroine but of the Gothic antihero, struggling against self-hate, trying to cut that destructive emotion down to size.

In this struggle for a healthy perspective on one's terrors, the setting is extremely important. Though *The Mysteries of Udolpho* has in fact several important settings, its mystery and its continuing impact on the public mind as a machine (an easily understood convention carrying special power) resides in its titular setting. Mario Praz has talked about the sense in the Gothic of endless sliding visual perspectives, staircases and corridors melting away from the eye into nowhere, long vistas that sweep formidably in upon the eye or vertiginously away from it. And we have seen how thoroughly the Gothic depends upon the substitution of the isolated Gothic setting—tower or mountain, mad-house, labyrinth, laboratory—for the flat communal normal setting. The sense is always of a kind of lifting up, lifting away, to a perspective where all the kingdoms of earth are visible—in miniature—a perspective in which one must inflate one's own ego to a size sufficient to justify the minuteness of everything else, to overcome the dizzying recognition of oneself as also motelike. In that contest an important part of the Gothic setting is the region of *approach* to

---

[12] Austen's last heroine, Anne Elliot, bears the closest resemblance to Richardson's characters in this respect. It is not, in any simple sense, "patience" that these characters display but rather a tense withholding of oneself from action.

the place of mystery, the area in which the land begins to change, or seems to begin to change.

This playing with perspective demonstrates the extreme instability of the material world as perceived and hints at the more terrifying instability of the material world as it exists in itself, so that at the heart of the machinery of Gothic setting is the intuition that living amid the bewildering and apparently hostile changes in the external world is not simply a matter of new recognitions—things that seemed to be A are in fact B—but a matter of continuous reperception of a world always in motion—things that are A are also B, or will soon be. In such a world, repeatability, even the repetition of sin, seems an anchor, and conventions, even the machines of terror, are comforting—or would be, if they always delivered what they promised. What distinguishes Radcliffe's Gothic set machines is that they always deliver less than they promise: the "something" that enters Emily's bedroom is only someone she knows; the "spectacle in the portal chamber" was only the body of a stranger; the "black veil" itself discloses not a murdered woman but a wax simulacrum. Austen is not parodying Radcliffe, she is imitating her when the mysterious silver-locked chest at Northanger Abbey turns out to contain only the extra bedlinen and the difficult-to-open Japan cabinet contains only the washing bill. Nor is Catherine's humiliation and rage at herself Austen's invention: Emily feels the same way when she finds her imagination inventing more terror than circumstances legitimately provide. What distinguishes Austen's Catherine is that rage and humiliation are allowed to turn into self-reproach, which generates self-examination, which finally generates self-forgiveness and growth.

One of the distinguishing marks of both Austen's and Eliot's novels especially is this valorous attempt to use remorse. As we will see, the echo of "Mother Gothic" in these novels is the presence even in ordinary life of more remorse than it seems can be put to use in self-examination and growth, more dread than can be justified and carried off by the channels of maturation. We can feel this in the extreme precariousness of George Eliot's resolutions, in the unnecessarily awful ironies of James's, the continuing Frankensteinian yearnings of Lawrence's. And we can see it in the characteristically gentle dread, the faint ghost of narrow escape that breathes upon the Austen hero or heroine at their destinations' end—as Frederick Wentworth phrases it, they are all happier than they deserve. What a subtle hint at a supernatural or providential machine![13] Later novelists, weaving richer, thicker plots and characterizations and fortified by readings in protopsychotherapy, can afford to flirt more openly with the Gothic machine, the apparent supernatural presence. But it is the habit of the heretic to tinker, not to expunge. Like her contemporary, Mary Shelley, Austen is trying to be an atheist, or at least an agnostic. Thus the extra charge of dread is simply left unexplained, without a machine.

Setting is significant in both *Northanger Abbey* and *The Mysteries of Udolpho*, and it works similarly: Catherine, like Emily, moves from the childhood familiar setting, to an intermediate series of exotic settings in which she is ignorant, exhilarated, and bewildered, to a final lonely crisis-setting in which the apparently frightening and the truly frightening alternate to bring terror and anxiety to its height. To be sure, since setting is to be one of the Gothic conventions apparently most parodied, Austen seems to give it shorter shrift here than almost anywhere else. "Home" does not receive the eloquent rendering that gives Mansfield Park or Hartfield and Donwell Abbey or Pemberley or Kellynch Hall or even Barton Cottage an urgent signifi-

---

[13] In his provocative *The Improvement of the Estate* (Baltimore: Johns Hopkins Univ. Press, 1971), Alastair Duckworth argues for the presence of a tensely sustained almost "theological" Christian substructure to Austen's novels: "Jane Austen's fiction is intermediate . . . situated between two texts: 'Therefore that ye shall rise, the Lord sends down,' and 'Gott ist tot' " (pp. 24-25).

cation almost equal to the Radcliffean sublime. Our only vivid picture of Fullerton Parsonage—and it is vivid enough —is of Catherine "rolling down the green slope at the back of the house" (V, 14), which is more an anticipation of Emily Brontë than an echo of Emily de St. Aubert. But the middle ground of Bath and environ, where unfamiliar anxieties begin, is that same significant isolating Gothic labyrinth, subtly more frightening because it is filled with that ghostly intimidating crowd of "no aquaintance."

Austen begins the Bath chapters with a satiric reference to "the difficulties and dangers of a six weeks' residence in Bath" (V, 18), but when Catherine and Mrs. Allen first enter the assembly rooms, they are nearly "torn asunder" by the "common effort of a struggling assembly" (V, 21). The crowd absorbs them, carries them along, and only by "unwearied diligence . . . . a continued exertion of strength and ingenuity" can they achieve both a comfortable separation from the crowd and a vantage point for the dance. If the upper rooms are hateful to the stranger, they become even more charged, more labyrinthine, when it is a question of keeping oneself in view for the possible invitation of Henry Tilney while hiding from the hideous gallantries of John Thorpe. (Fortunately the crowd is democratic in its ruthless exercise of power, and it rescues Catherine: Thorpe is "borne off by the resistless pressure of a long string of passing ladies" [V, 76]). And if the Pump Room parade is lonely with no acquaintance, it is horrible when Catherine is staked out by the side of the friendly scheming Isabella Thorpe in the very seat that commands the eyes of all comers and goers. Catherine doesn't know that she is being used as signal and cover for the brother of the man she herself cares for, but she senses it. And that most unsettling of the anxieties of common social life, the sense of being used by the heartless or ignorant in pursuit of some unseen end, makes her miserable.

This terror of being used, this sense of being coaxed down a dark path by an invisible hand, is pure Gothic, and is at the heart of Austen's plots. This exercise of power by the knowing over the ignorant is the dynamic of all the charming young man/naive young woman relationships from Willoughby-Marianne on, and it reaches near perfect equilibrium in *Emma*, where the knowing Emma, organizing the wheels of her own plots, is grasped and gently moved onto a larger wheel by the sublimely opportunistic Frank Churchill. Only in *Persuasion*—a "breakthrough" novel in several senses—does this mechanism, applied by the only marginally interesting Walter Elliot to the intelligent Anne Elliot, fail to work. Only in *Persuasion* does Austen abandon the "student" heroine and the mentor lover-villain that was, as we shall see, the primary Mystery of Udolpho, transposed to the key of "common life."

A past-oriented device (the present being turned on the wheel of past sin or secret, the wheelmaster a superior intelligence turning on its own helpless wheel), this Gothic mechanism, transposed in Jane Austen from the language of sin and salvation to the language of character and behavior, is an essential motif in the novels of the "Great Tradition." Austen passes it on almost without change to James, who, avoiding in correct modern fashion all mention of sin or salvation, homes back like a doomed man to the pure Gothic of the haunted house of fiction, where he is back in the shadow of Grandmother Radcliffe but without her orthodox serenity. The more interesting grandchildren, I hope to suggest, are George Eliot and D. H. Lawrence, who add to this past-oriented mechanism, this haunting, a future-oriented mechanism, a straining out of haunting into prophecy (revelations) that gives these novelists their true identity as heretics.

The great Gothic place, the ultimate haunted house, what Eino Raillo calls "the secret chamber where the hidden presence dwells," is the ruined church—for the enlightened English mind, the abbey—the crisis setting in *Northanger Abbey* and one of the supreme crisis settings in *Emma* too. It is worth pausing for a moment over the special resonance that the monastery and convent seem to have in the English heart. Solid and enduring theatres of tyranny in the Mediteranean Gothic settings of English fiction, they were in fact "dissolved" in the great sixteenth-century movement against the old theological and pontifical machinery. Dissolved but not entirely wiped away; the gentry of England are now, in the nineteenth century, living blasphemously in them, along with all their displaced hosts. English mythos likes to conceive that the ghosts of monks and nuns in those expropriated abbeys are wailing over their own sins and weaknesses, but the most sensitive imaginations know better. To anticipate for a moment, there is a significant exploration of this phenomenon in Chapter 35 of Eliot's *Daniel Deronda*. Greeting Gwendolen Harleth Grandcourt at Diplow Abbey, Sir Hugo Mallinger recalls: "There used to be rows of Benedictines sitting where we are sitting. Suppose we were suddenly to see the lights burning low and the ghosts of the old monks rising behind all our chairs!" His is a playful sally, and Gwendolen's is a "playful shudder" in response; "I should be rather frightened to go about this house all alone. I suppose the old generations must be angry with us because we have altered things so much." (In *Daniel Deronda* of course the enlightened mind is doubly haunted—by the great old ones of the Catholic past and the greater old ones of the Old Testament.)

Clearly the alterations in English life since Benedictines kept their silence in the refectory are not only physical, and a certain nervousness about the direction of improvement is discernible even in Austen's Northanger Abbey setting, the most deliberately parodic element in the book. Catherine comes to the Tilneys' home prepared to find a ruined church: crumbling walls, dirty leaded windowpanes, inconveniently small passageways connecting formidably huge chambers fit for congregations rather than families. She is balked at almost every turn of the imagination by the General's improvements: everything was in good repair, servants were polishing and scraping (and bowing), the anticipated echoing spaces were scaled down to comfortable size ("the fireplace, where she had expected the ample width and ponderous carving of former times, was contracted to a Rumford" [V, 162]), and the approach to the abbey, "along a smooth, level road of fine gravel, [was] without obstacle, alarm or solemnity of any kind" (V, 161). Abbeys, as Emma remarks of Donwell, were built originally without any attention to "prospect"; they looked inward. But the new proprietors do a great deal of looking outward and so want an expanse of stately oaks, a sweep of elegant meadow, in view.

Now, Catherine's initial efforts to supply obstacle, alarm, and solemnity right out of Mrs. Radcliffe in order to objectify her discomfort at the abbey are amusing. But her feeling is dead right. There is something ominous in the Northanger setting—a hollow at the inward prospect that draws out all the poisons of the imagination. It is no longer a ruined church, true, but its restoration is not simply in the direction of comfort and "domestic economy." The furniture is overbearing and lavish: "The elegance of the breakfast set forced itself on Catherine's notice" (V, 125). Under the General's direction she tours the crushingly extensive gardens, enters "the real drawing-room, used only with company of consequence," and the library, "an apartment, in its way, of equal magnificence" (V, 182), ascends the richly carved staircase, and treads obediently through still more magnificent bedchambers. Through it all the General discourses on cost, dimension, and, if he does say so himself, the entire good taste and superb management of the estate and the extreme good fortune of anybody paying it a visit, supplying, in light of Catherine's ignorant silence, "all minuteness of praise" (V, 182). The whole place is "fitted up in a style of luxury and expense which was almost lost on the unpracticed eye of Catherine" (V, 166).

But these signs of a new idolatry in the ruined church are not lost on the reader. Whereas a Shelley, a Dickens, will deal in direct Gothic language with the new temples of money and the priesthood of pride, call for a cleansing and a restoration of the true godhead, Promethean or Christian, Austen's practiced and teaching eye will rove ironically over all extravagance of form and language. She will utter no direct call; her sense of the malleability of character, of the accidental in circumstance and the useful in money will mute her rage, "regulate" her hatred, in D. W. Harding's famous phrase. She will register the false gods in this newest of Gothic settings, the moneyed mansion, the Maple Grove. But her silence on the universal questions, the possible solemnities of life, will be profound.

In fact, the church, the parsonage, the cleric are not absent from her novels: they make rather an odd echoing center there. The Church of England is a special and subtle kind of ruin. In *Pride and Prejudice*, in *Emma*, early prospects for the heroines focus on marriage to clerics who are little more than clowns. These are, as Jane Austen pictures them, men without real work, holders of "livings" without life, shells empty of mystery or even ethical significance, invitations to ridicule. In both *Sense and Sensibility* and *Mansfield Park*, written respectively before *Pride and Prejudice* and *Emma*, the two male protagonists struggle more seriously with self-identity as clerics than do men in any other Austen novel about any profession. And though Elinor Dashwood and Fanny Price (and the reader, too) admire Edward Ferrars and Edmund Bertram for their independent stand against the clever and worldly, we do not know on what ground they stand anymore than the men do. The Church is Edward's "preference," and for it he sacrifices the interest of his wealthy family for whom "it is not smart enough" (I, 102). But the "living" finally presented to him by the worthy Colonel Brandon is "a rectory . . . at 200 pounds per annum," and though "it is certainly capable of improvement" (I, 283), it is the income, the lands and produce, that are to have the attention of this clerical improver, not the conduct of the parish, let alone anything more abstract. The rectory survives in Jane Austen but the

Church is a nonentity, a spiritual ruin to match Catherine's most fervid image of Northanger Abbey. When Mary Crawford learns that Edmund Bertram actually chose—was not forced into—the clerical profession, she produces an argument that in general the world of the novels unmistakably supports: "A clergyman is nothing. . . . For what is to be done in the church? . . . One does not see much of this influence and importance in society, and how can it be acquired where they are so seldom seen themselves?" (III, 91-92).

Men cannot "distinguish themselves" in the Church, Mary remarks, and though she needs perhaps a bit more flourish than normal in a man's behavior in order to be able to distinguish him, the phrase is singularly apt in an Austen context. The Church exercises a fading charm on men, for it is itself dissolving. The clergy are "lost in the crowds" of urban England, Edmund acknowledges. And though having given up the cities he gamely asserts that rural England may still be small enough to respond positively to the churchman as a significant regulator of moral conduct, he is silenced by his own peroration: "It will, I believe, be everywhere found, that as the clergy are, or are not what they ought to be, so are the rest of the nation" (III, 93).

The Church in English Gothic fiction is solid and massive, casting vivid shadows over the nation, an entity so weighty that it continually twists characters out of their personal orbits. As a result, the dread that is being exposed and explored in this fiction is the fear of being crushed. By contrast, the Church in Austen, Eliot, and Lawrence's novels is dissolving, becoming transparent. The dread is of becoming invisible, of being unable to "distinguish" oneself, of casting no shadow, of existing without "consequence."[14] Blacked out or whited out, the dilemma of personality is

14 Kellynch Hall's verdict on the curate of Monkford is curt and final: "Mr. Wentworth was nobody, I remember; quite unconnected" (v, 23)—a verdict that effaced not only the curate but his brother Frederick Wentworth in the eyes of *Persuasion*'s elder Elliots.

the same—"Gothic," as I have tried to define that word in earlier chapters. On the other hand, the novels of the great tradition provide little in the way of Gothic catharsis—that satisfying ripening and disposing of villainy, that restoration of the Holy Order, that climax when the sin of the father overtakes and is expiated in the son. For here we are moving away from the age of the father toward the age of the son. The evil father, the great old one himself, is whiting out, still terrifying in his transparency, from Mr. Woodhouse to Mr. Brooke to Mr. Verver to Mr. Crich, still oddly dominant in his muteness or passivity, but peripheral nonetheless. At center stage now are the youths of late Romantic and Victorian fiction, handed the cup of pain, repeating from some treasured memory, "not my will but thine be done." Yet with the fathers fading out and the Church dissolving back into the land, neither the simple exchange of wills, nor even the battle of wills seems possible, only the long and difficult task of finding amid the continual moral dissolution both a will of one's own that is not simply beastlike and a secular "thou" to confirm and sustain it.

It is in this context that C. L. Pitt's jape that one may turn a romance into a novel by substituting a marriage for a murder becomes truly interesting. For marriage is the feared and wished-for catharsis of the serious English novel as death is of the Gothic: the great tradition novel reinforced, perhaps even helped establish, a secular mythos of marriage as the gateway to reality in the same manner as the Christian mythos established death as the gateway to the fullness of life. And of course one can't get through either gateway alone: a mate, or a murderer, is necessary.

The Genteel Demon-Lover

Which brings us to the lovers in *Northanger Abbey*. Here in the ruined regilded Church, the evil father still seems to reign, exercising a constant "check upon his children's spirits" (V, 156). Even in his rented quarters in Bath, General Tilney's petulant violence of expression to his children and his mysterious "incessant attentions" to Catherine (V, 154) make tranquility in his presence impossible, and his normal behavior at Northanger Abbey, requiring strict punctuality at meals and thorough attendance on his own conversation at all times, is such that any seventeen-year-old would shrink from it—"in training for a heroine" or not. Now, this does not add up to a certainty that he murdered his wife; Catherine's arithmetic is faulty. But not too far faulty. When she knows the whole story, she considers that her vivid imaginings "had scarcely sinned against his character, or magnified his cruelty" (V, 247). The General is a Gothic villain, an egoist, a materialist, happiest when he can feel contempt over the comparative smallness of the Allen estate, which he thinks Catherine will inherit. The plot of the novel hinges on the General's mistaken notion that Catherine is an heiress; his heavy pleasantries are a courtship of her for his son. And if it seems a contradiction for him to scheme on behalf of an estate that it makes him happy to think is *less* considerable than his own —well, that would be a contradiction only for a reasonable villain, a Blifil, for instance. The Gothic antihero, as we have seen, is obliged to go on acquiring and devouring everything, of whatever size. When Tilney is misinformed by John Thorpe that Catherine's is a "necessitous" family bent on acquiring *his* substance, the "terrified" (V, 246) General retreats.

He fails to carry his son with him, however; the lovers stand firm, and the marriage is made. But really, Henry Tilney is a curious lover, even for a parody. The Theodores and Lorenzos, the Valancourts and Vivaldis are accustomed in Gothic tales to a rather passive, at best a rescuing role, and at first Henry seems to fit this model. Charming and experienced, handsome and good-humored, he has only to make kind and common conversation to the naive Catherine to be fallen in love with. And though, after acquaintance, we, like her parents, feel that "nothing, after all, could be more natural than Catherine's being beloved" (V, 249), the story of that love has a kind of shadowy undertone. This comes only partly from Austen's steady insistence that propinquity and naiveté were Catherine's great charms and that gratitude tinged with vanity was Henry's initial impulse. Austen has a thorough disrespect for the first moments of "love," as evidenced by her tart comment concerning her last pair of lovers, *Persuasion*'s Frederick Wentworth and Anne Elliot: "Half the sum of attraction, on either side, might have been enough, for he had nothing to do, and she had hardly anybody to love" (V, 26). These two pairs are the only Austen lovers who meet within the novel's time scheme and love each other immediately. The others have a long unromantic dose of propinquity—Elinor and Edward Ferrars, Emma and Mr. Knightley, Fanny and Edmund Bertram—except for Elizabeth and Darcy, who rather dislike one another on meeting.

No, Henry Tilney is not merely an unromantic lover, he is a threatening one. He is the first of a peculiarly Austenite series of lover-mentors. Like Knightley, whose Emma is sixteen years younger, like Edmund, whose Fanny had her mind "formed" by him as a child in his house, Henry has acquired so early and formidable a psychological advantage over his heroine that it would take a force of will positively saintly not to use this advantage.

This psychological advantage of the old over the young, the strong over the weak, again dates back to the Gothic. The temptation to use it patriarchally is the beginning of that drama of ego-manipulation which the Gothic antihero undergoes, though of course, to take up this irresistible mentorship and then drop it, as the case of Victor Frankenstein shows, is almost the worst sin of all. Austen's young men are not saints, but they are not fathers either and therefore do not possess the sanction for psychological shaping that a father's title affords. Henry and Edmund are still getting daily lessons on the terrors and frustrations that a man in that role both inflicts and suffers. But to forego that advantage entirely seems too much for a man; it may even be, as the case of Emma and Knightley suggests, immoral. A look at three similarly sinister sequences in *Northanger Abbey*, *Mansfield Park*, and *Emma*—sequences of the deliberate manipulation, almost terrorization of the lover-student by the lover-mentor—will show how Jane Austen has taken that inherited Montoni/Emily situation, the primary Mystery of Udolpho, and transformed it into the recognizable anxiety of common life.

One's memory of Catherine Morland's distress in *Northanger Abbey*—the expectation of the sublime and terrible thwarted, then reestablished, thwarted again and dilated again until the recognition that she has actually come to suspect her host of murder sends her rushing away in miserable tears—is that she did all that to herself—she and Mrs. Radcliffe. And certainly she is not blameless. But the real culprit is Henry Tilney, who embarked on a deliberate Gothic tease with Catherine as they approached Northanger Abbey in order once again to figure as the deflator, the reality tester, for the innocent and frightened girl. The amiability of his "My dear Miss Morland, what have you been judging from" (V, 199) rebuke does not disguise his glee in the enjoyment of the joke he has foisted on his father and on Catherine. If his joke turned real, his abbey legitimately "horrid," and his father into a true ogre, serve him right! And it did serve him well, for faced with a Montoni-father, Henry turned into a genuine Valancourt, found his real will to love and harbor Catherine, not just to tease and preen with her, and stood up a hero. But Austen hints at a very mixed motive in the lover: "As much in honor as in affection" is his proposal at the end, because he believes "that heart to be his own which he had been directed to gain" (V, 247).

"Directed to gain"? Was he in on the plot with his father? Not exactly. He is no energetic schemer himself, but he likes plots and is not averse to puffing off his own understanding at the expense of others. We, and even Catherine, can take sarcastic measure of John Thorpe's juvenile "Let us walk about and quiz people" (V, 59), but what are we to make of Tilney's "Only go and call on Mrs. Allen! . . . What a picture of intellectual poverty!" (V, 79). We should make of it what Mr. Knightley makes of Emma's similar remark to Miss Bates,[15] but Henry's lover has no such penetration, and prattles on. She and Henry's too-partial sister feel the sting of that careless self-regarding tongue a few days later, however, when Henry lets a misunderstanding between the two young women on the nature of the "something shocking" about to "come out in London" develop momentum so that he can score amused points by putting things right—and them in their places. Catherine's mind is on the latest promised thriller from the Minerva Press, "more horrible than anything I have met with yet . . . murder and everything of the kind" (V, 112), while Eleanor Tilney, whose study includes history as well as novels, worries that a political riot may be at hand. Henry's laughter has a jeering edge to it:

> And you, Miss Morland—my stupid sister has mistaken all your clearest expressions. You talked of expected hor-

---

15 Marvin Mudrick and D. W. Harding, the black knights of Austen criticism, argue, from the presence of extraordinarily cruel statements like this all through the novels, that no "gentle Jane" but rather a Swiftian spinster wrote *Northanger Abbey* and *Emma*. Mudrick finds Henry's "eagerness to turn everything to ironic profit" an example of Austen's own "compulsion . . . to look only for incongruities" in order to justify that irony with which she defends herself from commitment (see *Irony as Defense and Discovery* [Princeton, N.J.: Princeton Univ. Press, 1952] pp. 19 and 2, respectively). And of scenes like this, Harding notes that Austen's satire often "suddenly directs itself against the public" rather than against the specific object (see "Regulated Hatred: An Aspect of the Work of Jane Austen," *Scrutiny*, 1940; reprinted in *Jane Austen: Emma, a Casebook*, ed. David Lodge [London: Macmillan, 1968]). While it seems reasonably clear that in her mature work Austen purges her narrator's rather than her character's voice of sudden or obsessive irony, the case of Henry Tilney—her participation in or distance from him—is in some ways the most complicated of all, not least because *Northanger Abbey* is, arguably, both of her "juvenile" and of her "mature" periods of writing.

rors in London—and instead of instantly conceiving, as any rational creature would have done, that such words could only relate to a circulating library, she immediately pictured to herself a mob of three thousand men assembling in St. George's fields; the Bank attacked, the Tower threatened, the streets of London flowing with blood. (V, 113)

As many critics have noted, Austen's full intention is puzzling here: Eleanor looks "grave" at Henry's outburst, as Knightley does at Emma on Box Hill, as Fanny does when Edmund makes excuses for Mary Crawford's immorality. Henry Tilney himself fields Eleanor's silent rebuke lightly, and he agrees to make Catherine familiar with his "odd ways" of banter, which look so much, as his sister has hinted, like outright brutality. Sketching *Northanger Abbey* in the late 1790s, the years not only of the Terror across the channel but of the Combination Acts and the riots that the Terror both prohibited and provoked, can Austen really have thought these memories unavailable to "rational creatures"? Or can she be further undermining Henry's good opinion of his own rationality? Or can she be subtly linking these two "horrors," the public and the fictionalized private, as Lewis's *The Monk* does? Again there seems a question whether this, like the "not in the central part of England!" passage discussed earlier, or Tilney's rebuke, "Remember we are English, remember, we are Christians!" (V, 198), might not be a complex admission, rather than a rejection or parodying, of the Gothic.[16] In any case, the encounter

---

[16] Several critics, Lionel Trilling and A. Walton Litz among them, anticipate Duckworth's argument in *The Improvement of the Estate* that *Northanger Abbey* "subverts the falsities of such works as *The Mysteries of Udolpho*, but [that] it also retains enough of the extra-rational probing of the Gothic novel to put into question any easy acceptance of a rationally grounded existence" (pp. 84-85). Indeed, as is often the case, Mary Lascelles broke the ground for this argument in her important *Jane Austen and Her Art* (London: Clarendon Press. 1939). She suggests that Austen's "steady opposition to those burlesque

over the fictional "horrid" warns the reader about Henry Tilney as clearly as the play *Lovers' Vows* warns him about Henry Crawford or the little comradely charade with Emma about poor Jane Fairfax's piano forte warns him about Frank Churchill. All three men are without sufficient "weight" where the feelings, even the being, of other persons are concerned. They like games and shows, and they enjoy manipulating people and events.

But we may argue that while Henry is, peculiarly, the hero of his book, Crawford and Churchill are the villains of their little worlds, insofar as there are villains. We should not expect to find this Montoni-like quality of pursuit in the lovers of Jane Austen's more mature works. Or should we? Will there be anything in Edmund's behavior to Fanny or in Knightley's behavior to Emma to match the extraordinary, now one comes to look at it, cruelty of Henry's damning exposition of Catherine's imaginative follies, "his quick eye fixed on her's" at the end of volume three, chapter nine? *She* runs off in "tears of shame" at his sly reproach—"What have you been judging from? . . . Dearest Miss Morland, what ideas have you been admitting?" (V, 197-198). *He* has lightly forgotten (putting the best face we can on this lapse) that the ideas she was admitting were his. Driving her to visit the abbey, he had introduced the subject of her Gothic expectations, discoursing on all the dire distresses (cribbed out of *The Mysteries of Udolpho*) that would surely occur. At the beginning of the conversation, Catherine is exhilarated but she does not think she will be frightened at the abbey because it is her friends' home. Henry disabuses her of that notion, mostly for his own entertainment, until he "was too much amused by the interest he had raised, to be able to carry it further" and

writers who, like herself, attacked the contemporary novel for giving a false view of life" arises from her sense that cheap attacks on mystery, intensity, and romance in the name of a "distorting" and dull realism were really meant to "flatter the reader's own lack of moral strenuousness" (p. 70).

"was obliged to entreat her to use her own fancy" (V, 160). Thus insensibly directed, she reexperiences all of his fancies when she is alone in the abbey, concluding with one of her own about the General, which in fact has its own prophetic aspects and subsequently receives that unfair luxurious two-page dressing-down from her lover/teacher.

Fortunately Henry sees later how he has hurt Catherine and takes pains to show her more affection than ever; at this point his careless care turns into something more serious, strong enough to enable him to stand up to the General when he turns into the "heavy father." And fortunately, Catherine emerges from her misery with a modicum of independent judgment: "She need not fear to acknowledge some actual specks in the character of their father, who, though cleared from . . . grossly injurious suspicions, she did believe, upon serious consideration, to be not perfectly amiable" (V, 200). In fact the narrator is convinced that the General's "cruelty" rather strengthened their attachment than endangered it and sees them on the last page embarked upon "perfect happiness." To the inevitable undercut of that adjective, one need only add that Henry too is a clergyman—one whose "living" also does not, so far as we can see, include a church but only income-producing lands and a friendly curate—to feel again that their happiness will be a stroke of tremendous good fortune.

One would hesitate to call the gently manipulating Henry a Montoni, exactly, just a charming young man with a slight cast in the moral eye. Still less does the guileless Edmund Bertram seem to fit the description. By the time of *Mansfield Park* Henry Tilney has metamorphosed into the charming villain, Henry Crawford, and the General, Austen's devil-in-the-machine, has become the likeable Sir Thomas Bertram, whose most serious sin is in fact his failure to "form" his children's minds. Yet when Fanny Price refuses Henry Crawford, the Montoni fit comes over Sir Thomas with devastating effect: he browbeats the wretched Fanny ("You have proved yourself of a character the very reverse of what

I had supposed. . . . offensive and disgusting. . . . wilful and
perverse!" [III, 318]) until she too shrinks and bends, "crying . . . bitterly" (III, 319). He sends her away from Mansfield Park to visit her own badly regulated and unwhole-
some home in Portsmouth as a deliberate attempt to present
her with the horrible alternative to Crawford's offer, a
"medicinal project upon his niece's understanding" (III,
369) that would do perfect credit to Montoni.

And Edmund concurs. Her one friend, and as she is now
coming to realize, her beloved, Edmund is "entirely on his
father's side of the question" (III, 335). In love with Mary
Crawford and trying hard to ignore her moral faults, Edmund cannot very well enter into Fanny's reasons for disap-
proving the amoral Henry; he proves no friend but an
active enemy to her as Crawford, with the entire assistance
of all of Fanny's protectors, moves in: "As Edmund perceived . . . that it was to be a very thorough attack, that
looks and undertones were to be well tried, he sank as
quietly as possible into a corner, turned his back, and took
up a newspaper" (III, 341-342). "Grieved to the heart" at
Edmund's "arrangements," Fanny is well nigh flattened
when he too goes on the attack: "Let him succeed at last,
Fanny, let him succeed at last. You have proved yourself
upright . . . prove yourself grateful and tenderhearted and
then you will be the perfect model of a woman, which I
have always believed you born for" (III, 347). To Fanny's
Gothic "Never!" he can only sorrow, in best Montoni
fashion, "so very determined and positive! This is not like
yourself, your rational self," and regret that he and Crawford had not joined forces against Fanny sooner: "Between
us, I think we should have won you. My theoretical and
his practical knowledge together, could not have failed. He
should have worked upon my plans" (III, 348). The worst
of it, Austen affirms coolly, is that it probably would have
worked: had not Crawford overreached himself in the obsessed seduction of Maria Bertram, had Edmund married
Crawford's sister, Henry would have obtained in his favor

the greatest pressure of all, "the assistance of her conscience in subduing her first inclination" (III, 467) and a rechannelling of Fanny's affection for Edmund towards the man who was his brother-in-law.

In this sequence from *Mansfield Park*, we see Jane Austen using the Gothic pattern of *The Mysteries of Udolpho* with no parody. It is high seriousness, this "medicining" of the understanding, this battle of "looks and undertones," and though once again the alternative to marriage, Portsmouth, is unthinkable, the wrong marriage is shown to be hell. Hell in old Gothic was servitude to the devil; in new Gothic, as the Brontës and their female Gothic imitators down to Daphne du Maurier and Mary Stewart were to establish, hell is to find oneself attached to a charming young lover with a hideous moral blemish, perhaps expugnable, perhaps not. In *Mansfield Park*, Henry Crawford is a figure of genuine Gothic dimension, not the evil old man, now offstage and a figure of fun, but the willful, the obsessed, the rootless and therefore self-engrossed young man. At the very point of victory, just as his alienating trajectory was beginning to curve genuinely towards a shared life with Fanny, he wrecked his salvation because he "must . . . make Mrs. Rushworth Maria Bertram again in her treatment of himself" (III, 468). And this Frankensteinian project makes him a perpetual outcast from the reality of Mansfield Park. His portion is that "remorse" which the classic Gothic anti-hero eats to the end of his life—"vexation that must rise sometimes to self-reproach, and regret to wretchedness" (III, 468-469).

Here then are two women who have been brought to bitter tears by the actual heroes of the novel. But we may feel that Catherine and Fanny cry too easily anyway. We may be more attracted to an Emma Woodhouse, "handsome, clever and rich," no seventeen-year-old moldable cotton candy but a willful queen of the village, "nearly twenty-one years in the world" and above shedding tears for fathers or lovers. Yet Emma too is found at the turning point of her story weeping bitterly in self-reproach, going home in the carriage from Box Hill, "the tears running down her cheeks almost all the way home, without being at any trouble to check them, extraordinary as they were" (IV, 376). The author of this distress is Mr. Knightley, the unmistakable hero of the novel. As in the other two cases, the means is a severe tonguelashing, worse than any other scourge among the anxieties of common life, and the occasion is a foolish act, a lapse from rationality. "What have you been judging from?" Henry marvels of Catherine's suspicions; "So unlike yourself, your rational self!" mourns Edmund of Fanny's refusal to marry the well-thought-of Crawford: "How could you. . . . How could you," Knightley thunders at Emma after she gaily limits Miss Bates to saying only three dull things, "Emma, I had not thought it possible" (IV, 374). And while there is an extraordinary similarity in these sequences, the difference is of course material. Emma, we want to say, deserves to be made to cry; Knightley, we want to say, has no manipulation in mind but is acting in pure rectitude. Let us see.

We might allow a bit more Gothic into this sequence from *Emma* if we recall that it starts, properly, at another abbey, which is also the home of the hero. Donwell Abbey has no Northangerian mist or cobweb about it, even to the imagination; it is "sweet to the eye and the mind. English verdure, English culture, English comfort" (IV, 360), and to its shades at "almost Midsummer" come the whole significant cast of the novel to eat strawberries and plan the next day's excursion to Box Hill. The surface action looks simple enough: Mrs. Elton proses, Miss Bates chatters, Mr. Knightley talks to Harriet Smith about agriculture, Jane Fairfax betrays her usual unusual tension and weariness and excuses herself early, Frank Churchill is late as usual and speaks recklessly and charmingly of being "thwarted" in his desires, and Emma watches, disposes, and "presides," also as usual. She issues the invitation to Frank to join the expedition on the morrow, where the same activities ensue. Only this time

Jane's tension, Frank's recklessness, and Emma's presiding reach "a pitch almost unpleasant" (IV, 374), and Emma finds herself saying carelessly to Miss Bates what she and Frank have only privately joked about all summer. Knightley's reproach and Emma's wretched humiliation follow, and the next chapters—right down to the final pages where a series of incredibly lucky accidents and second chances allow all to turn out well—hold only additional humiliations for Emma.

It is Mrs. Radcliffe in reverse: when the veils are down, the situation is seen to be more, not less, horrid than one had thought. What makes this Donwell Abbey-Box Hill sequence as Gothic as anything in Jane Austen, far outweighing in dread the melodramatic material of seduction, illegitimacy, and adultery in her earlier novels, is exactly the sense conveyed, from the sudden disappearance of Jane Fairfax from Donwell to the appalled silence after Emma's remark on Box Hill, of the crust of polite behavior cracking over a real abyss, of an achieved self exposed as monstrous, and overthrown. Emma comes back from insulting the boring Miss Bates to redouble her concerned care for her boring father, "whose talents," the narrator has already commented with the alarming impartiality of the recording angel, "could not have recommended him at any time" (IV, 17). The association in Emma's mind is not accidental, and her terrified grasp at immediate expiation for the one cruelty by the other care is the measure of her explicit understanding that without care—even undeserved care—and the personal and social discipline that preserves care, all of it, the beauty, the position, especially the cleverness, pours itself out in brutality, so that "Emma Woodhouse, handsome, clever and rich," is hard put to distinguish herself from the commonest Gothic villain.

What George Levine refers to as "this harsher form of disenchantment" that Austen's heroes force upon the heroines amounts in the first stage not to a useful awakening to a more real life but rather to a profound self-loathing, a dislocation, almost a disintegration of personality. It is not too farfetched to think here of Ambrosio in the grip of his disabusing demon or of Robert Wringhim after his fell "enlightenment." If one has become a monster, one's necessary business may appear to be to continue disintegration, to die that death which is not a gateway to fuller life but an irreversible decreation.

That Emma can distinguish herself, a little, from the true monster of selfish egotism is owing to another significantly nineteenth-century Gothic element in the novel, perhaps the most interesting of all—the double, for Emma two doubles, Frank Churchill and Jane Fairfax. This is a subtle business of Austen's, for while in their overall story, Jane Fairfax and Frank Churchill are the shadow lovers to Emma and Knightley, Jane is Knightley's alter ego and Frank is Emma's—at first. Handsome, clever, determined to be rich, Frank has contracted a secret engagement with the upright Jane Fairfax, an act monumentally improper from both the moral and the pragmatic point of view, since the wealthy relatives on whom his pecuniary hopes depend will never accept the orphaned Jane. And the young Emma has similarly entrapped the upright Knightley, though not, of course, so consciously.

When Jane visits her Highbury relatives, Frank follows at last with a visit to his relatives there; loverlike, he wishes to be in Jane's company on whatever basis of charade, and loverlike, he enjoys punishing Jane's chastity by flirting with the eligible Emma. Jane's enthrallment is genuine and deep: "a smile of secret delight" (IV, 243) claims her countenance in spite of her pain when Frank first daringly chafes her with the name of the resort town where they met and fell in love.

Jane's enthrallment to Frank is also permanent, like Knightley's to Emma. Although on Box Hill both Jane and Knightley find strength to deliver the rebukes that may tame their respective enchanters, or even drive him/her away, the enchantment remains. And, more importantly, as I will stress later, what Emma learns after her "disenchantment" is not the superior claims of "reality"—that corrosive and inhuman, that abysmal environment—but rather the superior claims of romance, as she becomes, for the first time, genuinely the enchanted as well as the enchanter, as she learns bravely to enter "the happiest dream" of loving and being loved. In this her teacher, her dangerous Gothic foreshadowing double, has been Jane Fairfax.

In between disenchantment and reenchantment, Emma suffers. But it is Jane Fairfax's suffering at the hands of her enchanter that lends the Gothic undertone of erotic tension, of personality under siege, to the whole middle of the book, until Emma's suffering joins it and claims our attention. The mystery of Jane's suffering is hidden, like the body of the passionate nun-lover in *The Mysteries of Udolpho*, until the end, when the happy death of his obstructive aunt allows Frank to reveal their engagement. He, the ultimate lover-mentor, has been teaching Jane passion; she, accepting and resisting, persecuted by headaches, experiences passion as pain, as Gothic heroines do.

The Donwell Abbey-Box Hill sequence has been Frank and Jane's crisis as well as Emma and Knightley's; it was a ferocious quarrel with Jane over her refusal to walk alone with him from Donwell that caused Frank to attach himself to Emma for the following day's outing and to cruelly redouble his gallantries to her in front of Jane. This is torment past the point of bearing to her, as her "coldness" (that is, her all but shattered hold on her own integrity and identity) is to him. A sharp exchange takes place between them, right after Emma's hateful remark to Miss Bates, which, though spoken in the abstract and general, escalates the battle to the sundering point: "How many a man has committed himself on a short acquaintance, and rued it all the rest of his life!" Frank exclaims, and Jane retorts, "There is generally time to recover from it. . . . it can only be weak, irresolute characters . . . who will suffer an unfortunate acquaintance to be . . . an oppression for ever"

(IV, 372-373). While Emma goes home weeping from Knightley's rebuke, Jane, irresolution past, makes the decision rather to submit herself to the genteel slavery of the "governess trade" than to Frank's careless/careful pursuit, and Frank, hardening himself as well, goes back to his wealthy relatives to confidently wait for his enthralled lover to "make the first advances" (IV, 441).

There is a clear electricity, a kind of open mystery, to Frank's and Jane's behavior in the narrative; it is a Gothic subnovel within the larger novel. The story of Emma and Knightley, though of a similar shape, is buried deeper, in gentle hints. Only in retrospect, and then only by reference to the vivid picture of Frank and Jane, does it become clear how much more than the "little likeness" (IV, 478) she admits to exists between Emma and Frank, how much painful personal experience of loving a careless clever willful fatally attractive soul there is in Knightley's startlingly confessional "Jane! Jane! You will be a miserable creature" (IV, 426). Knightley has been in love with Emma for years against his propriety, against his judgment, against every self-protective instinct. She has known herself to be "first" with him all those years, felt it "her due" and "enjoyed it without reflection" (IV, 415). As the courtship between Frank and Jane has been carried on by way of painful charade and commonplaces with barbs underneath, so that between Emma and Knightley has been a series of reprimands and saucy arguments. Knightley's avuncular "interference" in the education of the spoiled heiress of Hartfield has been, he admits at the end, as much to keep in touch with the beloved object as to chastise and correct her. Indeed chastisers and manipulators should really be deterred by what happened to Knightley, who fell in love with the child he was trying to lecture into good behavior because "I could not think about you so much without doting on you, faults and all, and by dint of fancying so many errors, have been in love with you ever since you were thirteen at least" (IV, 462).

The novel's structure invites us to view Jane's sufferings as a key to Knightley's and Frank's careless dangerous flawed charm as a gloss on Emma's. And so it is proper to reexamine Knightley's rebuke to Emma on Box Hill in the light not only of Henry Tilney's and Edmund's similar chastisements of their lovers but of Jane's sharp rejoinder to Frank a few moments before, a disapprobation so strong as to suggest complete alienation to the listeners, Emma and Knightley among them, even when the exact circumstance is misunderstood. One can then detect in Knightley's outburst a special personal sting and a tinge of personal despair, a Jane-like nerving himself up to a resolved correction that may lead to a total sundering in his brief hesitation: "I will, —I will tell you truths while I can" (IV, 375). Likewise, knowing that Frank's faltering and quick recovery is a riposte in a love duel, we can see Emma's similar action— "blushed, was sorry, but tried to laugh it off" (IV, 374)—as almost a kind of flirtation, the kind she has always carried on with Knightley. Here Knightley's mentorlike punishing does not partake of the superiority of an Edmund Bertram or a Henry Tilney. But it is not a neutral rational moment either. Out of his dread—at his plight, at his risk—come the words that finally make dread a fully embodied part of Emma's world.

And yet, of course, Knightley suffers less than Jane, and Emma's charm is less dangerously edged than Frank's because Emma and Knightley have position, they are "placed" in their worlds, literally rooted, and therefore able to grow. Frank Churchill and Jane Fairfax are solitary figures in their worlds—the separated ones—Frank cut off from his father to the point where he doesn't bear his own name and lacking any profession except charm; Jane orphaned and adrift as only an unprotected woman can be in that society. Playing their dangerous game, they can depend only, as Frank writes with the hollow gaiety of the nauseated man, on "anything, everything," "time, chance, circumstance, slow effects, sudden bursts" (IV, 437) to bring relief. Surrounded by chattering people, they are yet alone with a poignancy that only increases when Jane's cry, "Oh! Miss Woodhouse, the comfort of being sometimes alone!" seems to "burst from an overcharged heart" (IV, 363). And at the end of the novel they seem alone together, isolated in the classic Gothic dimension they have inhabited in the novel: like Montoni and Emily, like Victor Frankenstein and the creature, they are a conundrun explored and fixed in a fantasy, not a marriage, an entrance into reality.[17]

Imagination and Terror

There is, finally, another crucial perspective that her Gothic inheritance can shed on Austen's *Emma*. A classic figure in Gothic is the overimaginative heroine, the young woman whose burning hypersensibility catches every tremor of dread in the ethos and imagines it into concrete horrid form. Life for these heroines seems a constant battle against the "superstition" (as Radcliffe's Emily calls it) that too easily gives vivid shape to the "causeless terrors" (as Austen's Catherine thinks them) that surround and/or arise from the soul. But of course, epistemologically "caused" or not, the terrors are there; and in classic Gothic, "superstitious" or not, one's most extravagant imaginings are always true, either "really" as in *The Monk* or "ironically" as in Radcliffe—and Austen—where the peripeteia of the expected being reached by an unexpected route always occurs. As Alastair Duckworth suggests, despite Austen's "ironic defense" of the rational, "wholly to affirm a life without terrors, wholly to reject the function of the imagination, was not part of her intention."[18] Austen's Catherine

[17] W. J. Harvey expands on this notion: "The invisible presence of the Jane Fairfax-Frank Churchill relationship . . . allows Jane Austen to accommodate the apparent randomness of existence to the precise elegance of her form. . . . The shadow novel-within-a-novel enables Jane Austen to embody that aspect of our intuition of reality summed up by Auden—'we are lived by powers we do not understand.' " See "The Plot of *Emma*," in *Emma, a Casebook*, p. 240.

[18] Duckworth, *The Improvement of the Estate*, p. 98.

and Emma are linked backward to Radcliffe's Emily and forward to Eliot's Gwendolen in this explicit grounding of the imagination in activities arising from terror. Emily sees corpses all around, and corpses there are—different ones than she had thought. Catherine sees murders all around, and so it proves, in its way. And if there is something to the notion that in the serious novel of the nineteenth century, marriage replaces Gothic murder, then we can see why Catherine's sister-heroine Emma sees marriage all around. If both young women are caught looking in the wrong direction when the actual "attempts" come, it is because the Gothic heroine is *always* looking in the wrong direction or else where would the plot be? The Gothic personality is endowed with superb spiritual percipience and faulty, although strong, sense connections—and that may almost be the definition of sensibility.

Both Catherine and Emma spend a great deal of time fashioning specific clumsy plots to carry, and to carry off, the unmistakable charges of intrigue, of outside manipulation and inner contradictions, of "plottiness" that make up the anxieties of common life. In this apparently irrational sensitivity, this willful clumsy activity of imagination, they are, Austen and her successors suggest, oddly rather better fitted to cope with life than the indolently rational or the self-congratulatingly cynical. In common life too, the fact that one is paranoid does not mean that there are no monsters in pursuit.

But here again, once the provocative similarity between the two story-making heroines has been noted, it is the difference that arrests the eye. The "fresh feelings of every sort" (V, 79) that the seventeen-year-old Catherine brings to charm the educated Henry are given in *Emma* to Harriet Smith: for the nearly twenty-one-year-old Miss Woodhouse —poignant reflection!—"it was rather too late in the day to set about being simple-minded" (IV, 142). Thus whereas Catherine is at least trying to keep a check on her imagination, knowing and guarding her own ignorance (invited to Northanger Abbey "she could not entirely subdue the hope of some traditional legends" [V, 141], but she tries, until her efforts are undone by Henry's teasing), Emma cannot remember the time she thought herself ignorant, and hence has no inner guards.

Catherine's chaperone, Mrs. Allen, gives advice like "Do just as you please, my dear" (V, 61), and "Young people do not like to be always thwarted" (V, 105), but this lack of outward check to her thoughts and plots is felt by Catherine to be a handicap: "I always hoped you would tell me, if you thought I was doing wrong" (V, 105). Emma, on the contrary, has been mistress of her father's house and on "equal footing" with her governess since adolescence, and her "doing just what she liked" and thinking "a little too well of herself" are delicately posed on the first page by the narrator as the "threatened alloy" to her charge's happiness. And while we are invited by the narrator of *Northanger Abbey* to trace Catherine's imaginative bent in the direction of castles, villains, and murder to the "training for a heroine" (V, 15) she received in books[19] and to her total unpreparedness for the actual dangers a young woman meets, Emma's imaginative and very melodramatic focus on marriage is a bit more complicated to unravel. The material of Catherine's elaborate fantasy about General Tilney points to her fears both about not being married (the ogre might prevent it) and about being married (the husband is secretly an ogre), and the fantasy is activated by the confounding hiddenness of intent she senses all around her in the common conduct of adult life, from Isabella's masking familiarity, to John Thorpe's witless

19 It is interesting to note that *all* of Austen's satiric emphasis in this famous description of the training of a sentimental heroine is on poetry: "All such works as heroines must read to supply their memories with those quotations which are so serviceable and so soothing in the vicissitudes of their eventful lives" turn out to be not Walpole and Radcliffe but Pope, Gray, Thomson, and Shakespeare. Novelists, as she says elsewhere in *Northanger Abbey*, ought to stick together.

fop-gallantry, to Henry's ironic tenderness, to the General's terrifying amiability. The material of Emma's fantasies points likewise to fears and fascinations about marriage and, more explicitly, about passion, but they seem activated much more by a sense of inner conflict, and the most extravagant, the most lurid fantasy of all, the one about Jane Fairfax and Dixon, stems from her picture of herself as ogre as well as victim.[20]

Emma, it must be remembered, has never really seen a working marriage; her mother died very early, and her sister's marriage to John Knightley took Isabella away to London. That marriage neatly removed both mediating personages from the Hartfield/Donwell Abbey "intercourse" (IV, 416), leaving Emma and George Knightley solitary queen and king of the two parishes. It is in the spirit of fantasy that Emma begins spinning her first elaborate tale about Harriet Smith, "the natural daughter of somebody" (IV, 22), who is to become Cinderella and marry the prince, Mr. Elton, under Emma's ruthless fairy godmothership. That eligible vicar has been in the neighborhood just long enough to constitute, like Miss Taylor and Mr. Weston, a figure out of pattern: it is time for him to be made a match. Whereas for Mr. Woodhouse, "matrimony, as the origin of change, was always disagreeable" (IV, 7), his daughter's willingness to engage in it on others' behalf is remarkable for both its clever transposition of her own distaste for marriage and its neutralization of all the eligible males in the district. And certainly this is a significant element in Emma's character: "Highbury . . . afforded her no

[20] Emma's fictions "are considerably less innocent than those of the passive Catherine," remarks A. Walton Litz in his *Jane Austen: A Study of Her Artistic Development* (New York: Oxford Univ. Press, 1965), p. 135, because they arise not from a wish to escape from but from a wish to dominate others. And also, one is tempted to add, because they are about marriage, rather than just murder. Since Mr. Dixon is already married, Emma's fiction about him and Jane Fairfax is less innocent still, not about marriage but about sex.

equals" (IV, 7)—and that seems a satisfactory situation for her.

Yet her marriage fantasies serve two other purposes in addition to uniting persons so that they can be fixed in place or discarded triumphantly like pairs matched in a card game ("When such success has blessed me . . . you cannot think I shall leave off!" cries Emma the gambler [IV, 12]). In the first place, putting the fantasies into action affords her a challenge ("so many people said that Mr. Weston would never marry again" [IV, 12]) and an occupation ("For Mrs. Weston there was nothing to be done, but Harriet, everything" [IV, 27]). Characteristically, her own work —her drawing, music, resolutions of every kind—remains unfinished. Thus "promoting" other peoples' business (which they may then complete by themselves) allows her to take credit, at least, for a finished product. In this sense Harriet's ignorance and pliability are irresistible to Emma —as Catherine's were to Henry Tilney. When Emma finds that Harriet has already sketched herself into a rough draft of the farmer Robert Martin's wife, it is inevitable that she should find it a greater work, a double work, to erase Harriet's own sketch and to begin a new one of her as Mr. Elton's wife. The embellishment of aristocratic birth—the casual invention of a "mind delighted with its own ideas" (IV, 24)—changes the sketch formidably, and the whole project backfires. The drawing that Emma exhibits to him confirms Prince Elton's own fantasy of marrying the queen herself, and Emma's disagreeable shock at this turn is only doubled when, identifying herself with the false sketch, Cinderella Harriet decides she ought logically to marry the king, Knightley.

In the second place, these marriage fantasies give Emma the chance to imagine—with safety—the state of love and marriage itself: fictions, as Frank Kermode has reminded us, are tools for finding out about life.[21] Underneath all her

[21] According to Kermode: "It is ourselves we are encountering whenever we invent fictions. . . . We have to distinguish between myths and

triumph at the Weston match as the book opens, Emma is coping with the rather alarming discovery that yes indeed a woman may desire to leave the perfect comforts of Hartfield for marriage, that a man may, despite a not very successful first match that common sense would think had been enough for him, wish and need to enter matrimony again. And while that marriage of the governess and the landowner was nothing like a Jane Eyre-Rochester match, of course, something about it was outside the smooth ordinary workings of class and sloth in Highbury, something about it spoke of an unusual force somewhere. That Emma thinks this force is herself only points the more directly to her curiosity about the force.

The fantasies she builds around the absent Frank Churchill clearly partake of this purpose: after all, "handsome stranger" fictions are the most useful of all for finding out about marriage and need.[22] The handsome stranger fiction is more dangerous than matchmaking because it is about oneself—but it is not too dangerous, since in the fiction it is always settled in advance that the handsome stranger, not oneself, will fall in love—not quite, well probably not, or only a little. Trapped into a *tête à tête* at the Westons' by the "overpowering Elton," Emma hears Frank's name mentioned and goes into a reverie:

---

fictions. Fictions can degenerate into myths whenever they are not consciously held to be fictive. . . . Fictions are for finding things out, and they change as the needs of sense-making change. Myths are the agents of stability, fictions the agents of change. Myths call for absolute, fictions for conditional assent." See *The Sense of an Ending* (New York: Oxford Univ. Press, 1966), p. 39. Marvin Mudrick also sees this motive in Emma's fictions: "Harriet begins to seem a kind of proxy for Emma, a means by which Emma . . . may discover what marriage is like" (*Irony As Defense and Discovery*, p. 203).

22 It is only fair to add that Mr. Knightley has a classic male handsome stranger fiction of his own: "I should like to see Emma in love, and in some doubt of a return; it would do her good" (IV, 41). It is by now not difficult for the perceptive reader to understand why Mr. Knightley would wish to have a flashy face and a hard heart to compare his own soft/strong one to.

> She had frequently thought . . . that if she were to marry,
> he was the very person to suit her. . . . He seemed . . .
> quite to belong to her. . . . she had a great curiosity to
> see him, a decided intention of finding him pleasant, of
> being liked by him to a certain degree, and a sort of
> pleasure in the idea of their being coupled in their
> friends' imaginations. (IV, 119)

This pleasure is important to Emma; it is one thing to
resolve, after the Harriet Smith/Elton disaster, to repress
imagination "all the rest of her life" (IV, 142) with regard
to other people, but the "coupling" of Frank and herself
is her own business and will go on. Being so well acquaint-
ed with him in her imagination, she is warm in his defense
when Mr. Knightley argues, in much the same way as she
had argued casually to Mrs. Weston when her imagination
was occupied with Harriet and Elton, that Frank ought to
have paid his duty to the Westons long ago. One of the
happier dividends of fictions is a readier, more flexible
sympathy with other minds and other situations than one's
own "real" one: "I can imagine," she ripostes to Knightley,
the evils and difficulties of Frank's dependency. On the other hand, Knightley's long independence and lesser fancy
makes him incapable of sympathy.

Self-seeking and mistakes aside, there is something to this.
In fact in most of their arguments Emma's imagination
gives her sufficient range to remain about even, despite
Knightley's formidable and unfair advantages in experience
and education. As for Frank Churchill, their separate
"ideas" of him have acquired such decided and opposite
form that Knightley's vexation and jealousy are almost as
full-fleshed and uncontrollable (the fiction degenerating,
in Kermode's phrase, almost into myth) as Emma's voluptuous pleasures. When Frank does appear, gratifying both
Knightley's and Emma's fancies by his immediate volley of
compliments to her, Emma wonders whether he also has
been fantasizing about "coupling" and "whether his com-

pliments were to be considered as marks of acquiescence or proofs of defiance" (IV, 192). And by the time they have shared their dislike for the "reserved" ways of Jane Fairfax and begun embroidering together a most improper and hurtful fiction about Jane and her friend's husband Dixon, Frank is thoroughly fixed in Emma's handsome stranger fiction:

> The distinguished honour which her imagination had given him; the honour, if not of being really in love with her, of being at least very near it, and saved only by her own indifference—(for still her resolution held of never marrying)—the honour, in short, of being marked out for her by all their joint acquaintances. (IV, 206)

By the time Frank is called away from Highbury, Emma is certain of his love and spends hours "forming a thousand amusing schemes for the progress and close of their attachment, fancying interesting dialogues, and inventing elegant letters" (IV, 264). She is, certainly, a little in love, finding it a thoroughly manageable exercise of the feelings carried on in the imagination and very useful too, she thinks: "They say everybody is in love once in their lives, and I shall have been let off easily" (IV, 265).

To do Emma justice, she senses that Frank's feelings are "changeable" and expects to let him off easily too. But it is interesting to note that, careful controller of her feelings that she is, Emma is surprised by the "sensations" (IV, 265) she feels reading his letters from Enscombe, and the reader must raise an eyebrow at the number of reflections that she experiences during his later visits: "It was a clear thing he was less in love than he had been" (IV, 316), or "That Frank Churchill thought less of her than he had done was indubitable" (IV, 326), or "Frank Churchill not too much in love . . . how very happy a summer must be before her" (IV, 332). It is as if she were scratching an itch, and only when she begins another "passive scheme" (IV, 335), the matching of Frank and Harriet, does the itch disappear, channelled off in the less dangerous fiction of somebody else's handsome stranger. And even then her attitude toward Frank's hectic attentions on Box Hill is a piquant mixture of real flutter and strange anticlimax: it seems that her first personal essay at love fiction inclined her to stronger stuff than Frank's hollow playfulness. She has, somehow or other, acquired a new susceptibility to and inclination for deeper passion, and yet, as she tells Knightley later in the confusion following the Churchill/Fairfax engagement, "I was somehow or other safe from" Frank all along (IV, 427).

She was safe from Frank Churchill, as Fanny Price was from Henry Crawford, not so much because of an innate coolness or power to resist but because a prior attraction existed. Fanny understands her attraction when Edmund falls in love with Mary Crawford; Emma feels hers subliminally when speculation begins about Knightley and Jane Fairfax. But her jealousy of Jane Fairfax, begun in past years while listening to the universal praises of that paragon, takes an odd turn when she hears the story of Jane's rescue from the waves at Weymouth by Dixon and her subsequent decision to come to Highbury instead of accompanying the Campbells and Dixons to Ireland. "An ingenious and animating suspicion" (IV, 160) enters Emma's imagination, which is confirmed when she actually sees Jane Fairfax, radiating sexual tension underneath her reserve.

While others see a disturbance in Jane's manner, only Emma identifies it correctly. However, the fiction she embarks upon to explore it is no marriage fiction but rather a passion story. If at the outset, Emma is jealously willing to think Jane "mischievous" in her passion, she now imagines a blameless, unlucky, deep attachment: Jane, despite her purity, is seen to be "sucking in the sad poison" (IV, 168) —a very accurate account of Weymouth and its consequences for Jane, if awry on the actual identity of the poisoner. When Frank Churchill appears, Jane's turmoil increases and in proportion so does Emma's fascination with her fiction of illicit passion. Frank manipulates and extends Emma's fiction about Dixon as part of his own cover, pretending to share Emma's disapprobation.

Or rather, not exactly pretending. So many of his teasings and ripostes to Jane even before the strawberry party have the quality of punishment that one can scarcely help, Emma-like, wondering whether Frank had tried to persuade "the most upright female mind in creation" to "stoop to" some more serious sexual adventure than a secret engagement and, having failed in his persuasion is now attempting to derive satisfaction from accusing her to Emma of coldness. "One cannot love a reserved person," he remarks to Emma, and he is justly rebuked by the intelligently imaginative answer: "Not till the reserve ceases towards one's self; and then the attraction may be the greater" (IV, 203). When Frank sends the gifted Jane a piano forte, Emma weaves that event into her fiction about Mr. Dixon's love for Jane, licensed by the steady increase of tension she observes in her, especially when Jane is in the presence of both Emma and Frank. So clearly smitten under her reserve is Jane that she awakes Emma's sympathy as well as her fascination, and she whispers to Frank in the midst of his teasing: "It is not fair. . . . Mine was a random guess. Do not distress her" (IV, 241). It is at this point that Emma begins to inhabit, as it were, both figures in her fiction; she is not only the provoker of passion, as in her earlier fiction, but also Jane, the experiencer—a profound and crucial turning for her. She has been the monster who chastises; now she uncomfortably sees the victim's distress, and she begins to understand and be fascinated by the force that causes the victim to risk, or even relish, the distress.

Frank ignores the appeal, looking, the narrator stresses, as if he had "very little mercy," and a short time later, as she sees that "smile of secret delight" survive all the hurtful provocation, Emma notes, with her own kind of delight, that "this amiable, upright, perfect Jane Fairfax was apparently cherishing very reprehensible feelings" (IV, 243). But reprehensible as she may think these feelings are, it is this love-adventure, this vicariously experienced passion, that prepares Emma's imagination for her own real adventure. When she learns almost simultaneously of the Churchill/Fairfax engagement and of Harriet's attachment to Mr. Knightley, the "suspicion" of her own attachment "touches" her mind, and her conclusion is that "Mr. Knightley must marry no one but herself" (IV, 407-408).

There follows one of the most poignant moments in the novel, when against the review of Knightley's "justice and clear-sighted goodwill" (IV, 416), Emma's imagination attempts and cannot achieve a vision, even a fiction, of Knightley's marrying *her*. This is the nadir of her humiliation; since "every other part of her mind was disgusting" (IV, 412) to her except her affection for Mr. Knightley, imagination can no longer operate even so far as to teach her, as it just tried to do by way of the Jane Fairfax fiction, that an upright person may indeed "fall" into love with a flawed one, that a clear-sighted person may nevertheless want no other than the one object of her, or his, irrational affection. The best fiction she can achieve is a "wish" that Knightley marry nobody and a rerun of the same stale fiction she has lived in for so long, the father and spinster at Hartfield one now frayed to pieces by the more exciting and dangerous experiments with the Churchill and Fairfax fictions and just shattered by the discovered fact of her affection for Knightley: "Nobody should separate her from her father. She would not marry, even if she were asked by Mr. Knightley" (IV, 416).

This failure of mind, consequent on a blow to the imagination delivered by Knightley, Gothic murderer to "murderee," as Lawrence will phrase it, is equivalent in Emma to the death of personality. "In *Don Quixote* disenchantment and death come very close together," Levine comments: "In *Emma* disenchantment and marriage come very close together. Both marriage and death are endings."[23] But in fact, although disenchantment leads symbolically to paralysis and death, explicitly to the flight *away* from marriage, *Emma* seeks another end: the return of enchantment in the enchanted Knightley and the resurrection of imagination in the enchantress Emma. But by the end of the novel she is inside, not outside, the fiction. When she *is* asked to join Knightley in marriage, the sterile fiction of father-daughter union disappears for good: she is herself "overpowered," as her imagination told her Jane Fairfax was. And yet she is happy in that dangerous and animating exposure to "power," as her imagination, overriding her reason and even her fear, told her Jane Fairfax was happy, "in spite of every little drawback from her scrupulous conscience" (IV, 420).

The point to be made from all of this is that Emma's imaginative fictions about passion and marriage, awry, sometimes gross, often apparently self-protecting as they were, have actually prepared and enabled her to say "just what she ought" (IV, 431) to Mr. Knightley. It is, in other words, dangerous to trust the imagination too far, just as it was dangerous for Catherine to allow Mrs. Radcliffe's imagination to overwhelm her own. But if one's "training for being a heroine" (and what else is life about?) is not to proceed wholly according to the Gothic shocks of a wildly adventurous life, not, on the other hand, to be limited entirely to the tiny trials of a sheltered or quotidian life, then the imagination, and its tutor, the book, must be relied on to supply in the theater of the mind the experiences that teach. "The expression of his eyes" does not, therefore, in a simple-minded way dispel "illusion" and confront Emma with "reality": rather it returns her from the bleak self-reproach and sterile withdrawal that occurs when one gives up on the imagination to the humanly natural condition of imaginative participation in the shaping fictions of men and women. And the most fertile and powerful of these is marriage. "The dread of being awakened from the happiest dream" (IV, 430) of Knightley's returned love is alleviated, as it always and only is in Jane Austen, by Emma's Johnsonian recognition that she does not "deserve" quite that happiness, that therefore the marriage *is* a sort of dream, a made thing, like a novel, but a harmonious and suitable made thing for all that, with good prognosis for its continuance, productivity, and grace. She accepts it on those terms, and we are fully embarked on one of the great themes of the English novel, where King Marriage, like King Death, exists as both a fate and a choice, wearing its eternal corona of dread but provoking in the encounter a sufficient measure of courage. And where the novel itself, with its peculiar dependence on and obsession with its hallmark plot of bringing about marriages and its haunted pursuit of morality through rooms of individual conscience just vacated by the providential father, is the model for life —quite self-consciously the fiction for finding life.

FOUR

GEORGE ELIOT: THE GARMENT
OF FEAR

IN Austen's novels the sublime fates of death and marriage function mostly offstage,. and the condition of common life is, in softer phrase, anxiety: only by taking the considerable risk of using that double-edged tool, the imagination, does one enter that intenser realm of reality paradoxically and crucially perceived as the "happiest dream," where dread waits, and also love. In George Eliot's more spacious worlds the sublime thrusts constantly at the common, breaking dynamically through those wadded layers of "stupidity" and chatter with which humans protect themselves from "the roar which lies on the other side of silence."[1] Where the Gothic mode is directly employed, as in the exquisite Frankensteinian monologue of "The Lifted Veil," it takes the form of participation in scenes of the future and the past, invasion of the unhappy narrator by the very rush and substance of other people's "stream of thought . . . like a preternaturally heightened sense of hearing, making audible to one a roar of sound where others find perfect stillness."[2] But this sense of hearing beyond the trivial chatter of the ordinary, beyond even the band of stillness, is also

[1] Quotations from *Middlemarch* (1872) are from the Riverside Edition (Boston: Houghton-Mifflin, 1956). This phrase occurs on p. 144. Subsequent references are to this edition and will be cited by page number in the text.

[2] Quotations from "The Lifted Veil" (1858) are taken from the Standard Edition of *The Works of George Eliot* (London: Blackwood and Sons, 189?). This phrase occurs on p. 301. Quotations from "Janet's Repentance" (1857), *Silas Marner* (1861), and *Felix Holt the Radical* (1866) are also taken from the Standard Edition. Subsequent references are to this edition and will be cited by page number in the text.

crucial to the quest of George Eliot's major protagonists,[3] as is the sense of frantic, half-resentful participation in and vulnerability to the general consciousness. At another level, of course, this painful keenness of hearing, this daring exposure to possession by other consciousnesses is the very formal condition of the novel. And that condition, explored to the edge of madness by Doris Lessing's novelist in *The Golden Notebook* and by her world-citizen, her "breakthrough person," Martha Quest, in *The Four Gated City*, is the painful grail of major characters in Eliot, Lawrence, and the current inheritor of the great tradition, characters "ardent" and "theoretic" for whom Gothic preternaturalism, no longer doubtfully and deliciously confined to the Alps and the north of England, must be sought in the center, in London, even in Middlemarch.

No one in whom George Eliot takes an interest is safe from the formidable claim of an intenser life upon the mind's eye and ear: always the claim is inseparable from dread: dread is the infallible sign. The soul cannot construct a cover, whether the soul is large or small, cunning or simple, or even nearly quiescent. If a Bulstrode builds his protective shell in the classic Gothic style of the hypocritical/schizophrenic saint out of the very materials of the fear of the Lord, or if a Rosamond constructs her egglike self-sufficiency out of the shallow certainties of "a waternixie's soul" (p. 475), their covers will alike be shattered by the one event, the one reproach, the one word, whatever it is, that they cannot stand. They will be exposed and made to feel where they really are: Bulstrode will find himself "unscreened" (*Middlemarch*, p. 533). Rosamond will

---

[3] Victorian writers and poets seem to have had a special sensitivity to the revelations of the ear; all over George Eliot's novels lovers recognize each other and disciples find each other through richness of voice, and Tennyson's and Arnold's poetry especially is filled with this kind of imagery. One thinks of the Lady of Shalott, shot through the ear by Lancelot's "Tirra-Lirra" and of the speaker of "The Forsaken Merman" and the Marguerite poems.

find herself "walking in an unknown world which had just broken in upon her" (p. 583). If, broken in upon, the soul immediately and blindly repels dread like an enemy, however, it will sit all its days "at this great spectacle of life and never . . . be fully possessed by the glory" it beholds (p. 206). To enter upon that possession, to join that feast, the soul must bring its dread along, its "garment of fear": like the man in the parable, it needs its wedding garment.

When Eliot's charming, personable, morally flexible Tito Melema puts on the elegant mail shirt in the chapter of *Romola* called "The Garment of Fear," he is acknowledging that he walks, like it or not, believe it though he scarcely can, in a world where honor and sin, salvation and damnation, actually exist, where his smooth exercise of constant self-interest has in fact been murder, and its wages are death, collectable by the devil who, as he knows, is going about the streets of Florence with a dagger meant for him. To know one walks in such a world, and to defy and challenge it to do its worst, is the part of the Gothic antihero. To know it, and yet to behave as though the surface world, this blurred material garden party of ill-assorted egos and cares, were the central reality to be negotiated with charm, is for George Eliot the modern sin against the Holy Ghost —what the visionary Mordecai of *Daniel Deronda* will call "the blasphemy of this time."[4] To know it, and to struggle to behave accordingly while the modern world whittles down and crowds one's perspective, to search for, or even to construct for oneself that "medium in which ardent deeds take shape" (*Middlemarch*, p. 612), within which dread yields its perfume of moral heroism, is the achievement of Eliot's adventurers into the future. They represent a false future who, like Tito, adapt too easily to immediate pragmatic surroundings, resist too sunnily old "supersti-

4 Quotations from *Daniel Deronda* (1876) are taken from the Penguin Edition (Harmondsworth, Middlesex: Penguin Books, Inc., 1967). Subsequent references are to this edition and will be cited by page number in the text. This phrase appears on p. 598.

175

tions" for "the hidden and the distant to grasp him in the shape of a dread."[5] They represent a true, though perhaps fragile possibility who, like Gwendolen Harleth, respond sensitively, even if confusedly or resentfully, to that grasp. In the first pages of her final, and in some ways most Gothic novel, George Eliot draws us with an awful snap from the worldly trivial gambling game into high drama and preternatural conflict, when, broken in upon by the challenge of each others' stare, the power of conscious beauty meeting the power of moral measurement, Gwendolen Harleth and Daniel Deronda begin wordlessly to respond to and resist each other. "Why was the wish to look again felt as coercion?" Daniel debates (p. 35). "Who is . . . the dark-haired young man . . . with the dreadful expression," Gwendolen asks the friends who see in Daniel only "a fine fellow" (p. 42). And Gwendolen's inner sin has been only to coolly consider marrying Grandcourt without love, without much attention, whereas Tito has acquiesced in his foster father's exile and slavery with selfish indifference—and profited from it.

But Tito has that fear of fear, that terror of pain, which in Eliot's world brings moral death. Securing his breast from his father's knife, his judgment, his claim, Tito stands archetypally in opposition to that figure who supports at the deepest level Eliot's moral order, that figure "with bowed head and crown of thorns" whose portrait Janet Dempster drew in *Scenes from Clerical Life*, whom, after her moral crisis, Dorothea Brooke sees under the wide skies being carried by its laboring mother, whose crucified image Romola says offers man "supreme fellowship with suffering" (p. 337)—the Suffering Son. This image is lost from the English landscape now, muses the narrator of *Adam Bede*. Travelling in Europe, he can almost believe himself

[5] Quotations from *Romola* (1863) are taken from the World's Classics Edition (London: Oxford Univ. Press, 1913). This phrase occurs on p. 107. Subsequent references are to this edition and will be cited by page number in the text.

in Loamshire until he comes upon the wayside cross that only the mature historian knows *belongs* among the "apple blossoms" and the "golden corn" if the landscape is to truly reflect God's natural scene—"no wonder [man] needs a suffering god."[6]

On the other hand, in *Daniel Deronda*, that testing glance from a stranger has fallen on rich moral soil, that "liability" of Gwendolen to "fits of spiritual dread" (p. 94) which will issue at the end in the remorse that is a definite power of the soul and keeps it from damnation. As her final crisis approaches, Gwendolen's soul becomes a battleground of the two powers that the Gothic tells us are at the bottom of each of us, the immediate ego-preservation that will murder if necessary and the apprehension of larger, less personal values that first makes itself known as dread: "Temptation and Dread met and stared like two pale phantoms, each seeing itself in the other—each obstructed by its own image" (p. 738). A "fuller self" prays for deliverance from this impasse, but the deliverance, that profound self-rescue that climaxes every Eliot plot, is a flight *toward* pain. As Dorothea's imagination shows her what peace, what moral grandeur, what rescue of self and others might be achieved "if she could clutch her own pain" (*Middlemarch*, p. 577), so Daniel Deronda's words articulate prophetically in Gwendolen's memory the agonizing first stage of self-rescue: "Turn your fear into a safeguard. Keep your

---

[6] *Adam Bede* (1858), the Everyman Edition (London: Dent, 1960), pp. 349-350. Subsequent references are to this edition and will be cited by page number in the text. Whatever Eliot's sympathy for the Feuerbachian "secularization" of religious imagery and ideals, Ruby Redinger argues in her recent biography that Marian Evans ran into emotional difficulties while translating Strauss's *Das Leben Jesu*, with its demythification of this important figure. Redinger quotes a letter from Sara Hennell to Cara Bray, written in February 1846, that reports Eliot's own comment that she is "Strauss-sick . . . [from] dissecting the beautiful story of the crucifixion, and only the sight of her Christ-image and picture made her endure it" (*George Eliot: The Emergent Self* [New York: Knopf, 1975], p. 144).

dread fixed on the idea of increasing your remorse" (p. 738).

Assessing Eliot's debt to her Gothic inheritance is a complex matter, if only because at one easy level it is so clear; and to the casual eye, especially one looking for Jamesian architectonics, it seems indeed a matter of "machines." She does not, like Austen, begin with parody of Gothic romance and then move decisively toward "common life," while the uncommon and intense, the dangerous and inexplicable, the Churchill-Fairfax angle of vision, buries its energies deeper inside the restraint of the dominant narrative.[7] Like Scott, Dickens, and Brontë, she takes the Gothic machines almost whole into her narrative worlds. There the transfiguration of community into crowd and then into rioting mob that instinctively, though unknowingly, punctures dilated ego takes place not only in the midnight streets of *Romola*'s Florence but in *Felix Holt*'s Loamshire and even in *Middlemarch*. There in the remarkable scene before the Reform election, Mr. Brooke is driven off the platform and out of the race by an eerie rag effigy of himself and a mocking "Punch-voiced echo of his words" (*Middlemarch*, p. 370) thrust up from the boisterous crowd. There too King Death is present in the ghostly flesh in brilliant set piece after set piece, where the dying see visions unmistakable in their authority, from lawyer Dempster's perception of his beaten wife's recent temptation and rescue—"Dead . . . is she dead? She did it then. She buried herself in the iron chest. . . . She isn't dead. . . . she's coming out of the iron closet" ("Janet's Repentance," p. 267)—and Raffles's acute impression that his benefactor Bulstrode, choking him with

---

[7] Barbara Hardy notes perceptively that "George Eliot moved from the ordinary man struggling with tragedy to the extraordinary man and woman struggling with ordinary life" (*The Novels of George Eliot* [London: The Athlone Press, 1959], p. 29). This is one way of accounting for the presence of "the marvelous" in her novels from the beginning to the end of Eliot's career, but it underestimates the extraordinary in the so-called ordinary life in *Daniel Deronda*, not only in Daniel's story but surely in Gwendolen's too.

178

deadly money and deadlier brandy, is in fact starving him to death, to Romola's brother's extraordinary foreshadowing of the whole doomed wasteland that the amoral humanist renaissance was to the ardent soul—"You came to a stony place where there was no water, and no trees or herbage; but instead of water I saw written parchment unrolling itself everywhere, and instead of trees and herbage I saw men of bronze and marble springing up and crowding round you" (pp. 166-167). There in George Eliot too is the apparatus, introduced by Scott and Dickens, of the interpolated legend or tale that the narrative symbolically upholds. The legend of the Virgin of St. Ogg's illuminates *The Mill on the Floss*, as the story of St. Theresa does *Middlemarch*. And the farmers of *Silas Marner* argue about the local ghost just before the shattered and haunted weaver himself appears among them, concluding, pacifically, that some have the right nose to smell a ghost and some poor souls "can't see ghos'ses, not if they stood as plain as a pikestaff before them" (p. 81).

There too the apparently casual rhetoric of supernatural reference irresistible both to the sophisticated narrator and the quotidian character accumulates into metaphoric patterns of great force: "The Dead Hand" is Eliot's chapter title for the hold Casaubon keeps on Dorothea both living and dead; and "Good God! It is horrible! He is no better than a mummy!" (p. 43) gasps Sir James Chettam before the Casaubon marriage. In a certain kind of rain, the ghost of a legendary criminal Dedlock walks the terrace at Dickens's Chesney Wold; at convenient trysting hours, the phantom nun glides past Brontë's Lucy Snowe; at a certain quantity of vibration, the panel drops in Gwendolen Harleth's drawing room showing a dead face and a fleeing figure. These preternatural shapes are immense and solid in the patterns of *Bleak House, Villette*, and *Daniel Deronda* and in the souls of the women whose inner lives these shapes seek to master and emblematize.

But the simple truth is that these preternatural shapes

and supernatural hints are not detachable from Eliot's novels. The characters, moments, messages that have struck many critics as "unassimilated romance" or fable[8] are at the center of Eliot's remarkably consistent if complex vision. Something surely must be wrong with the general critical invitation to ignore Romola and Daniel Deronda in their own books, to forget the higher flights of Dinah and Dorothea, to avert our eyes from the goddess-worshipping Philip Wakem and Will Ladislaw. We are left then only with psycho-social analysis and compassionate irony, and these useful qualities, not as uncritically celebrated now as they used to be, are only a part of Eliot's vision—a vision that at its center is unmistakably "yearning," "ardent," and, above all, "theoretic," key words in the novelist's vocabulary. The yearning is painful and often vague, the ardor dangerous, the attempt to act out a universalizing theory brings disbe-

---

[8] In essays studying that "turning" point in Eliot's work from *The Mill on the Floss* and "The Lifted Veil" to *Silas Marner* and *Romola*, George Levine and U. C. Knoepflmacher, for instance, descry an increasing attention to "fable" or "romance" or "the ideal" that required, for proper novelistic balance, a more profound "realism" than Eliot had had access to in her earlier provincial fiction. Knoepflmacher thinks that "*Romola* convinced the novelist of the impossibility of welding history with the fabrications of romance" (*George Eliot's Early Novels* [Berkeley and Los Angeles: Univ. of California Press, 1968], p. 9). But it seems unlikely that Eliot was ever convinced of that; rather she modified, to some extent, that sense of the inflexibility and unchangeability of character which (in Northrup Frye's definition) is a quality of romance. Levine notes that *Romola* is in fact "a genuinely experimental work" which, like *Daniel Deronda*, relies on "action external to character, yet somehow profoundly related to it" ("*Romola* as Moral Fable," in *Critical Essays on George Eliot*, ed. Barbara Hardy [London: Routledge and Kegan Paul, 1970], p. 81), and adds that an historical novel, after all, must hew to lines of action first and construct character within those parameters. Barbara Hardy disagrees with me vehemently here: "a split between realism and romance is inextricably bound up with her distrust of politics and ability to evade —not marvellously and timelessly transcend, please—that exploration of history which she keeps telling us is her subject and her form" ("Introduction," *Critical Essays on George Eliot*, p. xi).

lief and ridicule whether the theories are clerical, political, or just "Dorothea's notions," hence the compassionate irony and social analysis. And for George Eliot, it is not simply a matter of "society" inhibiting individual ardent theoretics. The formulations themselves are *inherently* dangerous: "There is no general doctrine which is not capable of eating out our morality if unchecked by the deepseated habit of direct fellow feeling with individual fellow men" (*Middlemarch*, p. 453)—hence Eliot's psychological realism, especially applied to those theorists of religion who might turn out to be hypocritical monks or schizophrenic saints in the Gothic mode.

To the high Victorians, wandering in that wilderness of parchment and iron statues, the yearning for a comprehensive theoretical conception of the world that would make for the spirit that "medium for ardent deeds" went both backwards and forwards, towards history and prophecy, historical Gothic and "future fantasy," toward the visible Father and the invisible "Holy Ghost," though what they knew most intimately in their own presents was the Suffering Son. Scott went back into history at the behest of a familial and instinctual inner drive, but George Eliot, after Carlyle and Ruskin and Darwin, wrote out of energies that were in addition racial and theoretical. For Austen the drift of Crawfords and Churchills downstream, without moral moorings, was a tragedy for two; for Eliot the defection of a Tito, the drift and then the committed anchoring of a Daniel Deronda, were world drama.

But for both Eliot and Austen, one transformed Gothic machine stands solidly in the way of the drift, offers an anchor to commitment—that "murder" which is marriage. "Marriage is so unlike everything else. There is something even awful in the nearness it brings," says Dorothea "brokenly" to Rosamond; marriage "drinks up all our power of giving or getting any blessedness" in a love outside that duty; it "murders our marriage—and then the marriage stays with us like a murder—and everything else is gone"

(*Middlemarch*, pp. 583-584). A second Gothic machine, which is used elliptically by Austen in the story of Henry Willoughby and Mary Crawford but which is everywhere powerful in Eliot, is the pursuing past, the living Dead Hand that must be grasped, though it burns like fire in its awful unalterability, or else the present and future will be false. "Good come out of it!" says Adam Bede "passionately" to the comforter who thinks he should "rise above" his misery over the deceit and the punishment of Hetty Sorrel: "That doesn't alter th' evil. . . . I hate that talk o' people, as if there was a way o' making amends for everything. They'd more need be brought to see as the wrong they do can never be altered" (p. 440). And a third Gothic machine, profoundly Eliot's own, is the Terrible Vision, which must, like murderous marriage and the destroying past, be grasped and steered by if one is to avoid the worst evil of the Wandering Drift, the enchanted Melmothian Draculan void of black repetition. "I am a man who am warned by visions," says Felix Holt to the light-minded Esther Lyon:

> Those old stories of visions and dreams guiding men have their truth; we are saved by making the future present to ourselves. . . . I want you to have such a vision of the future that you may never lose your best self. Some charm or other may be flung about you—some of your attar-of-rose fascinations—and nothing but a good, strong, terrible vision will save you. (II, 40-41)

For Eliot, vision proceeds from terror, and imagination is triggered, as it was in Austen, by dread. Elaborating the truth of "those old stories," making these Gothic machines god-filled again to the modern ironic eye, Eliot writes, as Leavis saw in *The Great Tradition*, like Cassandra in Herodotus's clothing: Cassandra's is really "the woman's lot" by which she anchors her exploration of her present.[9] In this essay I want to look at these machines in action in four of

[9] F. R. Leavis, *The Great Tradition* (New York: New York Univ. Press, 1969), p. 25.

Eliot's most interesting works: in the Gothic tale of "The Lifted Veil," in the historical Gothic *Romola*, in the social history *Middlemarch*, and in the prophetic, controversial *Daniel Deronda*.

"The Lifted Veil" and Romola

"The Lifted Veil" is a Frankenstein story; like Mary Shelley, George Eliot wrote one of her most self-revealing works in the voice of a brilliant and tormented man.[10] This Frankenstein, far from pursuing his unhallowed gift, shrinks from it. Yet the results are the same. Whereas Victor Frankenstein brings about the death of his brother by an egoistic penetration beyond the veil of life, Eliot's Latimer acquiesces in his brother's death by withholding the vision that has sought him from beyond the veil, the vision of his brother's fiancée, Bertha Grant, as *his* wife. If Victor cuts himself off from others because *his* private imperatives drown out their voices, Latimer cuts himself off because their streams of trivial thought, even their futures, invade his private mind, producing a "superadded consciousness" (p. 294) that makes them intolerable to him. Like Victor, Latimer "suffers" a great vision of his heart's desire, and although his vision is realized by inactivity rather than activity, the recoil of disgust when the vision takes flesh is similar. As Frankenstein's horror triggers the dream of embracing his mother's corpse that was at the heart of his unholy attempt, Latimer's watch at the deathbed of his father forms the basis for the "withdrawal of the veil" (p. 322) that had kept him believing that his dream-creature Bertha was beautiful and mysterious. Latimer sees himself through Bertha's "cutting gray eyes," as Frankenstein sees

10 U. C. Knoepflmacher works out other parallels to Frankenstein in *George Eliot's Early Novels*, pp. 140-142. Eliot used the masculine in her only other first-person narrative, *The Impressions of Theophrastus Such*, and Barbara Hardy, among others, has noted that her earlier omniscient narratives, before *Romola*, that is, contain "elaborate reminders of assumed masculinity" (*The Novels of George Eliot*, p. 155).

himself in the creature's "watery yellow" ones; "front to front" (p. 323) each pair recoils into that union of mutual hatred, that marriage-murder, which marks nineteenth-century Gothic. For both Frankenstein and Latimer, the quintessence of horror in the vision-turned-nightmare is the self-hatred that they finally embody: Bertha's silent sneer, "Fool, idiot, why don't you kill yourself then?" (p. 327), echoes Latimer's own thought, and Frankenstein's, too. But both men know the answer to that question: the marriage they have entered is some doomful arena where human desires and human will are irrelevant. "I was too completely swayed by the sense that I was in the grasp of unknown forces, to believe in my power of self-release," says Latimer (p. 325). "I was the slave, not the master, of an impulse which I detested yet could not disobey," says the creature in reference to his murder of Elizabeth, echoing Frankenstein's own feeling when he created the creature.

This is the very hallmark of the Gothic: where character steps entirely out of choice into destiny, past that twilight of choice-within-destiny wherein Eliot and all the great English novelists normally operate.[11] Self-abandoned, not self-rescued or released, Latimer makes inevitable Bertha's attempt to destroy him. And although that direct murder of a mate which haunts so many of Eliot's works is, as usual,

---

[11] Following up Barbara Hardy's contention in *The Novels of George Eliot* that Eliot is attempting to use the novel as a "tragic form" based upon Greek and Shakespearean models, Felicia Bonaparte (*Will and Destiny: Morality and Tragedy in George Eliot's Novels* [New York: New York Univ. Press, 1975]) argues provocatively that destiny has the best of it in the collision between the two forces that make up man's condition. In her reading of the novels, "there is . . . very little sanctuary for the will" (p. 160); indeed, "from the special angle of perception of any character who begins in the illusion of personal independence, Eliot's novels unfold like unrelenting lessons in the reality of circumstantial determination" (p. 84). Bonaparte's sections on "The Laws of Consequence in Irreversible Time" (pp. 22 ff.) and "Heredity as Potential and Inclination" (pp. 62 ff.) especially reinforce Gothic motifs in the novels.

just barely avoided, it is willed and announced in the most
splendidly Gothic scene of all. Latimer's friend Charles
Meunier, to whose compassion Latimer will no more trust
his story than Frankenstein will his to Clerval, pays the
couple a visit just as Bertha's maid Archer is dying, and
proposes—echo of *Frankenstein,* shadow of *Dracula*—to try
experimentally to bring the woman to life again with a
transfusion of his own blood. Archer dies—as we will see
many of George Eliot's characters die—with "a look of
hideous meaning in her eyes" (p. 336), while Bertha
watched "like a cruel immortal" (p. 337) to see that the
accusation is left undelivered. When the silent death is
complete and Bertha is gone, the reanimation takes place.
"Haggard" and "eager," the "dead woman" delivers her
message of hate and vengeance, causing Latimer to exclaim
in horror: "Great God! Is this what it is to live again—to
wake up with our unstilled thirst upon us, with our un-
uttered curses rising to our lips, with our muscles ready to
act out their half-committed sins?" (p. 339). Here the romantic faith in death of Frankenstein's creature—"or if I
think, I will surely not think thus"—gives way to the nightmare embodied in Melmoth and Dracula, to the belief that
immortality may hold only the ripening, the eternal repetition of the state of love or hatred we had already achieved
in life. This is, of course, again the orthodox sublime, the
Dantean Gothic, and it reflects the "foresight" Latimer has
already had of his own death and reanimation: the suffoca-
tion of angina pectoris, the absence of his mistreated servants at his call for help, and then the darkness—but not extinction—"darkness, but I am passing on and on through
the darkness; my thought stays in the darkness, but always
with a sense of moving onward" (p. 278). By his moral
cowardice, his shrinking from pain, Latimer has indeed
made his "insight" and his "foresight" a curse, and he is
eternally bound to what he has made: "living continually
in my own solitary future" (p. 330), he scarcely knows death

from life. The veil—or is it a mirror?—becomes identical on both sides, a field of visions entirely "unanimate" of "strange cities . . . gigantic ruins . . . midnight skies with strange bright constellations" in which "something unknown and pitiless abides" (p. 329).

A warning about this hateful sterile will-less repetition in the presence of something blankly terrible was the profoundest part of Latimer's very first "foresight," a vision of modern Prague where the people seemed "ephemeral visitants" and the statues of kings and saints seemed the real owners and inhabitants, "who worship wearily in the stifling air of the churches, urged by no fear or hope, but compelled by their doom to be ever old and undying, to live on in the rigidity of habit" (p. 287). To become one of these Gothic great old ones is fearful, yet a more dreadful possibility emerges from Latimer's fleshly visit to Prague. There are even more direful greater old ones than the Christian saints: in the old Jewish synagogue, Latimer receives the "shuddering impression" that this building is "of a piece with my vision," for even those stony saints "needed the consolatory scorn with which they might point to a more shrivelled death-in-life than their own" (p. 309). Passing on and on through darkness, Latimer has seen himself as the wandering Jew, "a wanderer in foreign countries" with "horror for my familiar" (p. 340), and confirmed it, as he confirmed that his Prague vision was real, by finding that ultimate previously seen detail, "the patch of rainbow light on the pavement transmitted through a lamp in the shape of a star" (p. 309). In this oldest Western covenant—in the icon of the Jew and of the English dissenters who took the language of the Old Testament for their profoundest self-image—lies Eliot's characteristic stressful confirmation of the sublime. In Daniel Deronda's use of philosophical Zionism to redeem that covenant, to break from that repetitive death-in-life, to bring that wandering figure home, we see no eccentric aberration on George Eliot's part but the climax of a decades' long attempt to transform that dreadful icon into the world's hope.[12]

"The Lifted Veil" was written in 1859 as a kind of relaxation into the form closest to feeling, at a time when George Eliot's thought was blocked by the enormous responsibilities and dismays aroused by the great success of *Adam Bede* and the public discovery of Marian Evans as its author. She was also at work on *The Mill on the Floss,* and she saw "The Lifted Veil" as a "jeu de melancholie" bracketed by those two "companion picture[s] of provincial life" that required "time and labour." The following year, in Florence, Eliot began the long time and labor of *Romola* from which she was to emerge, she said later, feeling like "an old woman."[13] Savonarola was the figure who caught her imagination first, the hypocrite monk, whose "double consciousness" (p. 548), like Latimer's, gave promise of sublime inner drama, the displaced time and setting offering the medium for ardent deeds that could evoke grand actions.

Savonarola's is the figure that holds together the separate stories of Romola and Tito Melema, who might almost be, as their names suggest, shorthand anagrams on the personal level of the world-historical, the entirely Gothic, dilemma, that Savonarola lives. Eliot's letters, as she tried desperately to build a story from the figure and the setting that held her, suggest that *Romola,* or more precisely the climactic scene where Romola "drifts" away from her difficulties and is carried to the plague-stricken village that she saves by her nursing care, provided a second symbolic shape to the story. Maggie Tulliver's two water journeys, one away from her murderous "marriage" with her brother and a last one back

---

[12] U. C. Knoepflmacher notes that "like Daniel Deronda, who would witness a similar scene at Frankfurt, Latimer perceives only the withered remains of a once-vibrant faith; but unlike Deronda's, his conclusions seem correct" (*George Eliot's Early Novels,* p. 146). All of Latimer's nihilistic conclusions, of course, seem correct in this wonderfully realized "jeu de melancholie."

[13] Quoted in Redinger, *The Emergent Self,* p. 400.

to it, surely supplied this element. The story of Tito
Melema, perhaps fashioned from a story once told her of a
father who had killed his selfish son and refused a confessor
afterward, hoping to follow the victim to hell and continue
his revenge came shortly after, and probably, as Haight
suggests, provided that "backbone" which Lewes records
finally jolted Eliot into the actual writing.[14] Here we have
come a considerable distance from Walpole and Radcliffe,
where the beautiful young man is an afterthought or simply
shares the female victims' distresses at the hands of the
murdering fathers. As with Jane Austen, although the
fathers are to be feared, it is the brother-lovers who can
really crack the heartstrings in Eliot.

There are three powerful fathers in the novel: Romola's
father, Bardo dei Bardi, the blind scholar; Tito Melema's
foster father, the half-mad Baldassarre; and the priest
Savonarola, who is father, with complications, to both
young people—Romola will follow and save him, Tito will
betray him to his death. And, interestingly, a fourth figure
has some claim to that title, too. This man is the oldest in
the novel, that "resuscitated spirit" who died in 1492, "still
in his erect old age," who now stands, in Eliot's Proem, gazing on contemporary Florence from San Miniato hill. It
was this father Eliot sought to assemble and raise from the
dust and bones of the research libraries she labored in, and
if he is, as some critics charge, like Frankenstein's creature
too large and clumsy for comfort, at least his creator feels no
disgust with him:[15] as the historian grasps the Dead Hand

[14] Gordon S. Haight, *George Eliot: A Biography* (New York: Oxford
Univ. Press, 1968), p. 352.
[15] The argument about whether Eliot's Florentine section lives or-
ganically or merely galvanically continues still, and, like the similar
argument about the Jewish section of *Daniel Deronda*, has no final
arbiter but the individual reader. Undoubtedly one can feel about both
of these participations in foreign cultures a special effort of imagination that results in that "stylization, as distinct from style" which
Susan Sontag has proposed "reflects an ambivalence (affection contradicted by contempt, obsession contradicted by irony) toward the

of the past, both her pain and her pity are awakened. This spirit is "charged with memories of a keen and various life" when living had "zest" and the "passionate intensity" that are harder to find in the narrator's wider more dispersed world—and in that she envies him. But he is to be pitied in this—according to the narrator, not even his awakened fifteenth-century soul could bear the shock of the sheer amount of change active in the scene he sees from San Miniato. Looking on the broad geophysical outline of the city, confident of the enduring general outline of the human face and heart, the spirit decides to go down from the hill, but his child, the nineteenth-century historian, compassionately warns him: "Go not down, good Spirit! for the changes are great, and the speech of Florentines would sound a riddle in your ears" (p. 8).

What the old man cannot bear, the daughter must, and can—the sight of accelerated change, the betrayal of hopes, the agonizing cost of faith. In the first chapter, the nineteenth-century historian is down in the city right on the pavement, watching Tito Melema start from his sleep like "a suddenly-awakened dreamer" (p. 10). Twice more, in the grand structural harmonic of the novel, this opening scene will be repeated, with a reverse twist: the woman will meet the old man on the hill and be told by him to go down into the city against her inclination to that young sleeper who needs to be awakened. When Romola reaches "rising ground" (p. 342), in flight from the husband who has crassly sold her father's beloved books, Savonarola blocks her, offering—part rescue, part spell—participation in the vision, "rapture in the cup" (p. 376) that is carrying him

---

subject matter" (*Against Interpretation and Other Essays* [New York: Farrar, Straus, and Giroux, Inc., 1969], p. 28). Ruby Redinger interestingly suggests that in the "foreigners" of Florence, especially Tessa, who lives a purely sensual life and is not punished, and Piero di Cosimo, who lives an atheistic aesthetic life and is validated, Eliot is subconsciously pondering some important truths that she is unable to admit into strictly English life (*The Emergent Self*, p. 452).

back to the city and his ambiguous apotheosis. He reminds her that she must act upon the marriage bond as well as the filial bond that is prompting her outraged flight. And when she comes next to San Miniato, Tito's father tells her of her husband's worse than selfish crimes against both the filial and the marriage bonds, and commands, "exaltingly, tightening the pressure on her arm, as if the contact gave him power: 'You will help me?' " (p. 462).

Baldassarre holds Romola in one hand and his knife in the other here; he wants her to be the brains behind that knife, to help him destroy Tito. In this important scene, in a sense, all three of the novel's great old men confront Romola with the demand to carry out the murder that they know her marriage has, must have, become. For her own father and Baldassarre are conflated in the figure of the maimed and betrayed scholar: Bardo dies on the day Baldassarre enters Florence as a prisoner in the King of France's train, and Romola's last words to her father, as at death's door he makes another of those ceaseless demands to help him, to be the pen in front of his brain, are "I am quite ready, father!" (p. 251). And as this new father brandishes the sword in place of the pen, there is even an added fillip of irony lending weight to the "I am quite ready, father" that Baldassarre expects, for Romola had guilty remembrance of having hoped that Bardo's death would make her and Tito's marriage "more perfect" (p. 251), and she knows now that remaining silent in obedience to the marriage bond is, and has been, tantamount to involvement in the murders of all her fathers. Unerringly, though without specific information on Tito's web of political and personal conspiracies, she reads Baldassarre's revelations about Tito as a threat to her Medicean godfather Bernardo del Nero. What she does not realize is that the same web of conspiracies will finally entrap Savonarola too, the greatest of her fathers, whose symbolic presence with Baldassarre in the composite figure of the old man on the hill, offers the ultimate paternal sanction for the murder of Tito. Baldassarre first saw Romola during Savonarola's sermon in the Duomo when she sobbed out in submission to the priest's powerful preaching. Since then the note of fulmination has grown even stronger in Savonarola, and Baldassarre, feeding the fire of his own hatred at that fountain during the Lenten sermons, believes he can count on Savonarola's spiritual daughter: "You go to hear the preacher of vengeance; you will help justice. . . . The fire is God: it is justice: it will not die. You believe that—is it not true?" (p. 465).

Baldassarre's question, "the fire is God—is it not true?" connects to an important cluster of images that I will return to later. But now it is necessary to look at the process by which marriage in Eliot's novels, entered into under "a rainbow-tinted shower of comfits," becomes at its deepest level, a murder.

In "Janet's Repentance" (1857) and *Silas Marner* (1861), Eliot has already briefly portrayed the murder that lurks under marriage. Janet married Dempster and enjoyed early days of rose-giving happiness before mysteriously, inexplicably, the transformation of Dempster and then Janet into self-murderers by drink began.[16] In the murderous intimacy of marriage, Janet's very capacity to take punishment— "standing stupidly unmoved in her great beauty while the heavy arm is lifted to strike her" (p. 103)—provokes her husband's brutality. She has become "necessary to his tyranny" (p. 211), a need far more demanding than the need for love. At the same time tyranny has mastered him, so that as he beats his wife he also flogs his horse so obsessively that the whole of Milby knows he will be thrown and killed one day. Like his wife, he has long felt the marriage "rushing on to some unknown but certain horror" (p. 199); one important night when he is in that killing mood, Janet goes to him with a certain sick sweetness of completion in her mind, the result of that "self-despair" which is near suicide. When she is thrown out into the cold, only the consolatory

16 It is interesting that Eliot never returned to this theme of a strong woman finding her way out of the slavery of a truly dark vice.

sharing of Rev. Tryan's own crime and suffering stops her in that course. Nothing stops Dempster in the same course; even in his death throes he is still flogging the bedclothes, obstinately convinced in his hysteria that his wife, that is, his marriage, is his murderer.

Silas Marner's Godfrey Cass has married secretly, following a "low passion," and as a result is being blackmailed by his vicious brother; Godfrey is certain that marriage will murder him if the facts of his ill-fated liaison become known. His wife is an object of hatred to him, yet he feels that she "haunts" even his daylight life where the conventional happiness of a squire's life depends on his orthodox marriage to Miss Nancy Lammeter. While he courts that beauty, his wife walks through the snow to expose him as her husband and her child's father. She is no pitiful sentimental Hetty Sorrel but a vindictive votary of the "Demon Opium, to whom she was enslaved, body and soul" (p. 165); this is a "premeditated act of vengeance" (p. 164). As drink killed Dempster, that final draught of opium kills Molly, but in both cases it was the misery bent on company, on the destruction of the marriage partner, that really triggered the suicide. Since she dies before she can expose Godfrey, it remains for him to complete the marriage as murder, which he does symbolically in his initial terror that the unidentified woman in the snow "was *not* dead" and in his subsequent flash of joy and relief when he finds that she is. Certainly it takes "a cute man" to know what makes "the glue" in marriage, more acute even than the parish clerk Mr. Macey, who wondered, after the minister absent-mindedly asked the Lammeter bridegroom if he took "this woman to thy wedded husband," whether it was the intention, the words, or the register that "made the glue" (pp. 76-77).

Two things make the glue in the marriage of Romola dei Bardi and the handsome stranger, Tito Melema. Romola, who has only the soul-wearying demands of her embittered father for current bond but who remembers her brother's

kiss and his "masculine face, at once youthful and beautiful," before he abandoned them (p. 62), marries Tito as
Maggie Tulliver would have married Tom, to achieve that
brother-sister-father trinity that seems paradisal: "I love
Tito—I wish to marry him, that we may both be your
children and never part" (p. 135). Tito, whose Gothic conflict with his foster father—"all maturity [is] a mere nidus
for youth. Baldassarre had done his work, had had his
draught of life: Tito said it was *his* turn now" (p. 121)—
has allowed him to abandon hope of rescuing the old man,
was raised in a motherless house. So far as his love is not
mere mindless pleasure or self-interest—Eliot allows that he
is not simply "a cockscomb" in this marriage as he is in the
toy marriage with the peasant Tessa—his love is "subjection
to" Romola's maternity, "that living awe . . . which is perhaps something like the worship paid of old to a great
nature goddess" (p. 100). He was "subdued by a delicious
influence as strong and inevitable as . . . musical vibrations"
(p. 124). Tito's nature is all commonness but for this one
spot of uncommonness. But that positive contact with sublime awe is less efficacious, Eliot makes clear, than the
dread that "should sit as the guardian of the soul, forcing
it into wisdom," that dread "which has been erroneously
decried as if it were nothing higher than a man's animal
care for his own skin," that dread of which, after a long
course of skeptical modern philosophy and petty self-interest, Tito's mind was "destitute" (p. 122).

In this state of simplicity, sister to brother, aspiring manhood to "noble womanhood," Tito and Romola marry
icons of each other and enter the complicated embrace of
actual alien flesh and spirit that marriage enforces. This is
George Eliot's first extensive treatment of marriage, and
murder is very close to the bone of it. That moral ascendancy in Romola which made Tito "deliciously" happy at
a distance becomes, in the "glue" of marriage, his burden,
his hated critic, finally the knife at his throat. And that
charming flexibility of mind and kindling physicality of

glance and touch which Romola loved in Tito's courtship becomes, in marriage, her anxiety, her dread, finally her "poison." From Tito's point of view, rendered brilliantly all along by Eliot, Romola's estrangement from him and his common-sense manipulations of Florentine politics is sadly the measure of her hysterical servitude to the willful hypocritical arrogance of the holier-than-possible Savonarola. Accordingly, Tito believes Romola to be a "modern simpleton who swallowed whole one of the old systems of philosophy, and took the indigestion it occasioned for the signs of a divine afflux or the voice of an inward monitor" (p. 491).

As it happens, Romola is no simpleton in this area. She has a horror of "superstition" and fantasies, of narrowness, of the visionary certainty that overwhelms fellow feeling, a horror rooted not only in her brother Dino's abandonment of herself and Bardo for the convent but also in that clear bent towards self-government and self-direction that struggles at the core of her nature with the yearning to give herself to some large unquestioned purpose. Her guard is up strongly against Savonarola; her maiden barriers are down before Tito precisely because he seems so unsuperstitious, so flexible, so clearly part of "the large music of reasonable speech, and the warm grasp of living hands" that her mind has always contrasted, rather schematically, to the "phantoms and disjointed whispers" (p. 336) that lead visionaries away from their fathers and sisters. At the end of her career, Eliot will finally produce in the young Daniel Deronda exactly the figure she denies herself in this early novel, a Dino whose voices lead him *to* his father and sister, a Tito whose resisting flexibility is drawn within the vision.

And yet, of course, the biblical injunction to leave family and "cleave" to the mate is remarkably similar to the one inviting the visionary to "come, follow me." To Eliot and Lawrence they are equally grand visions—perhaps the same vision. Certainly Savonarola's charge to Romola to look in her heart and see whether, despite loss of love and even honor, she can cease to be a wife, suggests the indelibility of his own vocation. Tito, who "leaves" easily but cleaves nowhere, finds the clinging of his father and then his wife a bitter thing, finally an animal terror. And Romola, who was "ready to submit, like all strong souls, when she felt no valid reason for resistance" (p. 210), finds her flesh and spirit revolting from the abstract vision, the marriage, to which she gave her first faith. It "flashes upon her mind" that her dilemma is the one Savonarola faces, too, "the problem of where the sacredness of obedience ended, and where the sacredness of rebellion began" (p. 483). With the sacredness of rebellion and Savonarola's crisis, we are on Gothic ground again: that marriage between God and the human church that the apostle likened, mystically, to the marriage of man and woman, has become a murder, "inevitably a life and death struggle," says the narrator, and it remains only to see who will kill whom first, Savonarola or God, Romola or Tito,[17] and whether (although the narrator says this is "less inevitable") Florence should "make itself the . . . executioner" (p. 587).

And so Florence does, in both cases. Tito's marriage to Romola has reached that intolerable stage where every time he walks into his home, he is blasted by his wife's bitterness that "you—you are safe" (p. 486) while better men are entrapped by the Florentine conspiracy. Indeed he has, in his subtle, shrugging, passive way, helped compass the death of Romola's godfather because he expects Romola and the two old men to cabal and betray him. Romola is the "unmanageable fact in his destiny" (p. 512), and if he were not, as Eliot beautifully dramatizes him, so habituated to intrigue as to be literally unable to do anything directly, he

17 Ruby Redinger contends that *The Mill on the Floss* ends as it does because Eliot, carrying to ultimate action her hostility toward her own brother and her guilt over that hostility, "decided that Tom could be drowned only if Maggie drowned also" (*The Emergent Self*, p. 61). In that sense *Romola* represents a sort of macabre advance upon the earlier novel, since Tito dies while Romola lives.

would surely have killed her. But the judicial murder of Bernardo del Nero accomplishes the desired end; Romola flees Florence, marriage, and duty a second time—"all bonds snapped"—abandoning Tito to the enemies from whom, in bitter duty, in painful instinct, she would have shielded him.

With Romola's departure, Florence becomes like M. G. Lewis's Madrid for a time, the City of Dreadful Night. The crowds that have been a powerful, jostling, occasionally irritating presence all through the novel, become a mob, as if, lacking this element of passionate upward striving, the community tears loose even from the exhilarating authority of Savonarola and the corroded intelligence of Tito Melema to put itself under the guidance of the lowest, most stupid element, the brutal Dolfo Spini. Spini heads that "Masque of the Furies," Riot, and Tito, who had affected to manipulate and betray both the Republican Savonarola and the Medicean Spini in a final plot to bring down both of these authorities, is caught by a mob of mixed parties that is bent on killing him not so much as a "Piagnone" or a "Medicean," those two incompatible identities, but more chillingly, more Gothically, simply as "a man to be reviled" (p. 562). His leap away from them into the river is a typical witty improvisation that leads only to more horror, for the "half motiveless execration" of mankind is permanently in his ears now, the "fancied" yells on shore confine him "panting and straining" to the river. There, "the current . . . having its way with him" (p. 563), he is carried helpless to the grass where Baldassarre waits like a great troll-father to hug him to death. The mad assassin, nearly dead himself, broods over the fair white body like a lover, "trembling" with "a fierce hope" that he may be allowed his share in the city's and the river's murder. Tito does awaken, but, like Latimer, doesn't know on which side of the veil he is, for "this chill gloom with the face of the hideous past hanging over him for ever" might, he understands, be the very marrow of the state of death (p. 654).

In Baldassarre's mutually death-dealing grasp, Eliot dramatizes more forcibly than anywhere else the strength and the inevitability of the Dead Hand's clutch. Tito's whole metaphysic has relied on man's capacity to strip himself of his past; he sells Baldassarre's ring not only for money but to escape "recognition, which was a claim from the past" (p. 148). As he leaves home on the fatal night, "the old life [with Romola] was cast off" (p. 561). But the past, as Eliot has shown in the Proem, as Romola has come to know in her efforts to mediate between her dead father's wish and her husband's will, is not to be so treated. Grasp it in fellowship, and it will hurt but promote growth; evade it, and it will become tremendous, and kill. On the other hand, as we saw in nineteenth-century Gothic, the pagan life energy that Tito represents is not that easily destroyed. Baldassarre has to clutch him literally all night, first kneeling, then sitting, then lying on the body of his son, sacrificing his own life in the process, until, like Dickens's Bradley and Rogue Riderhood, like Scott's legendary Burley and the pursuing Dutchman, they make one dead object, and "it was not possible to separate them" (p. 565).

Almost simultaneously with this exchange of deadly energies the torture of Savonarola reaches its peak, and he cries out, "I will confess." As the man who would have blotted out the past dies in the grip of the Dead Hand, the man who had claimed to have God-sanctioned visions of the future makes public recantation of prophetic powers. And it is really for this, as a false prophet and not as a political rebel or a personal immoralist, that the city deserts him and then becomes his executioner.

Here again Eliot's position is complex; the morally aware person may in fact no more evade the grip of the future than he may escape the tug of the past. In the first scornful flush of innocent confidence, Romola taxes the brother who left home, "what is this religion of yours, that places visions before natural duties?" (p. 162), and it is a warning always alive for Eliot. Fra Luca speaks his dream-warning about

Tito in a "low passionless tone," like a ventriloquist's dummy, and even when its essential truth is demonstrated, Romola does not regret her instinctive recoil from visions. Yet also present, also like her brother "taught and guided by visions," Savonarola speaks the same warning in "a strong rich voice," and Romola "vibrates" to the sound. Fra Luca's visions carried him apart from the world; and as the father lived more fully with the spirits of the past than with the realities of the present, the son lived in the coming world and knew his "fellow beings only as human souls related to the eternal unseen life" (p. 164). But Savonarola's visions are emphatically of this world, and they call him to act there. Fra Luca's vision told him "the meaning of the crucifix" and so did Savonarola's, but whereas the brother's action is confined to gazing at the crucifix, Savonarola wields it like a sword. In the deathbed scene, he suggests that the brother give a crucifix to his sister—" 'Fra Girolamo, give her. . . . the crucifix,' said the voice of Fra Girolamo" (p. 168)—and when Romola next sees Savonarola preaching in the Duomo, he is lifting the crucifix as the most sublime icon of his vision (p. 234).

Essentially, Savonarola's vision is the Augustinian Puritan one; he has argued for years that, all material appearances to the contrary, true vision shows that the Church is rotten and will soon collapse, that political and economic well-being are resting on the flimsiest supports of chicanery and self-interest and therefore war and tribulation are imminent, that sin and ignorance rule in the high places and therefore, it being God's orderly world and not some humanist fairyland, the "cup of your iniquity" will overflow and fall, that the sword of justice "is about to fall" and "the tyrants who have made themselves a throne out of the vices of the multitude . . . shall be hurled from their soft couches" (pp. 235-237). There are few ages in which this vision is not persuasive, and often enough, as Eliot allows Machiavelli to remark carelessly, circumstances lie at hand that, taken up and acted on by an aroused people, can accomplish the prophecy. And once in a while, the being gifted with the power to arouse is also at hand.

Like all the great Gothic antiheroes, Eliot's Savonarola is a man of powerfully mixed character who is at first the community's scourge and then its scapegoat, but, as in the Gothic, this central drama is linked to and dwarfed by a grand inner drama of aspiration, self-dilation, "double-consciousness," guilt, and remorse. Like Robert Wringhim, accustomed from his youth to being swayed by visions, the Frate soon grows accustomed to swaying others by his own force, a gift notoriously hard to handle. Burning with that consciousness of "Unseen Justice" and "Unseen Purity" (p. 218), which neither he nor Eliot ever abjure, Savonarola is drawn irresistibly into the manipulation and interpretation of particular events in that prophetic light. But the only candidate for bearer of God's drawn sword is the invading French king, and the suggested model for the new pure world is simply the Venetian republican general council; these forms cannot bear the mystical charge that Savonarola has given them. There is in Savonarola that "clear-sighted demand for the subjection of selfish wishes to the general good" and "that passionate sense of the infinite" that for Eliot are the very stuff of vision, but there is also that straining after particularities of prophecy, that viciousness of personal political denunciation, that blasphemous certitude about crowd-pleasing miracles that "vitiate" (p. 244), if they do not obliterate, the man's achievement.

Like Manfred's pride, Ambrosio's lust, Schedoni's ambition, Melmoth's contempt, and Frankenstein's "curiosity," these "dark spots" finally bring down the antihero. Inevitably for Eliot, like Tito's degeneration from occasional self-interest to the perfection of faithlessness, Savonarola's degeneration is a process, "a drama in which there were great inward modifications accompanying the outward changes" (p. 244). This drama of changes is narrated by the sympathetic historian, but it is also rendered through meetings with, and analogies to, Romola and Tito Melema, rendered in terms of the agonizing Victorian Gothic dilemma of will.

In his first Duomo sermon and in the first two meetings with Romola, Savonarola's best moments occur when he exemplifies "the state of yearning passivity" (p. 337) in which alone one may actually be touched by that supreme good which "is a river that flows from the foot of the Invisible Throne, and flows by the path of obedience" (p. 372). He communicates this state individually to Romola and publicly to Florence in the two great Duomo scenes, "In the Duomo" and "The Benediction," which encompass the monk's time of triumph before his trial. Romola retains this gift through all temptations; she keeps to this river even when, by grand paradox, acts of will, of "sacred rebellion" even against Savonarola himself, are necessary, even when, grand paradox again, the river carries her constantly *back* to Florence, so that "her place may not be empty" (p. 375). Like Maggie's Floss, and as we shall see, like the rivers of Lawrence's imagination, the "current" in Romola has two natures: it is both escape and return, both destiny and will. Feeling "orphaned," like Maggie felt, like Tito will feel when escaping from the mob (except that Tito likes the orphaned state), Romola casts herself will-lessly adrift in the currents of the Mediterranean. But like the river of her obedience, the river of her desire runs backward like Maggie's to the invisible good behind the familiar visible relationship. She goes back from the plague-stricken community where, in her courage and selflessness she is filling another's place, the priest's, to the plagued community where her own place waits. There she finds that Tito's river too has taken him home where his father, who once "refused his atonement" (p. 324), has at last, grotesque parody of the mystery, accepted it.

She also finds that Savonarola has abandoned the river, whose rhythm of will and passivity seems to be the measure of human possibility, for the fire, which is God's, and has met his doom before it. Earlier on, San Miniato Baldassarre had called the fire of vengeance that burned in his mind and in Savonarola's sermons God's holy fire. But God's holy fire is only to be approached with naked feet, and it is never to be penetrated. Eliot's dramatization in Chapters 64 and 65, the inward and then the outward drama of Savonarola before the fire, is masterly. For he is tricked into this impossible-to-win challenge to God not only by his enemies, by Tito and Dolfo Spini, who need to discredit him publicly before moving openly against him. He is also manipulated into undergoing the trial by his friends and by his own once metaphorical words. He has called God once too often to bear witness to His personal sponsorship of Savonarola and his prophecies. And to bonfire-loving Florence, the absence of God's lightning on the occasion of Fra Girolamo's challenge to Him to strike him dead if God does not approve his actions is no substitute for the presence of God's asbestos hand when the Frate walks into the fire to demonstrate the sanctity of his visions.

As "the Prophet in His Cell," Savonarola frets not only over the snare his enemies have prepared but also over the deeper abyss it has opened in his very vision: he knows that he must decline to call on God for a personal miracle as Christ rejected Satan's third temptation, but mixed with that theologically pure motive is a simple devastating human shrinking from an effort too great not only for the body but for even the prophetic imagination. When, praying in his private Gethsemane, Savonarola "imagined a human body entering the fire, his belief recoiled again. It was not an event that his imagination could simply see; he felt it with shuddering vibrations to the extremities of his sensitive fingers. The miracle could not be" (p. 541). Appalled at this inner recoil as much as at the malign confluence of outward circumstances, Savonarola "filled his mind with images" (p. 542) of the great works he will do.

He is now, desperately, the source of his own vision. In this expedient glow, with that "double consciousness" of inward failure and outward success, he activates, via the compromising letter he gives Tito, a political scheme to oust Pope Alexander and devises a way out of the trial by fire that can only be called a blasphemous trick. His last public use of the crucifix is craftily to provoke a disputation over whether a man may licitly carry that holy object into the fire with him, a disputation that delays the trial indefinitely.

These two moves together lose him his support and put him in the hands of his enemies: the confession he makes under torture that only repeats his earlier mental torture is the result of that intolerable remorse which the Gothic antihero would kill himself to avoid, but which Savonarola, like that lesser-failed prophetess Emma Woodhouse, sustains and grows with. The man who set Romola in absolute opposition by crying "the cause of my party *is* the cause of God's kingdom" (p. 508) laments at the end, "God has withdrawn from me the spirit of prophecy" (p. 592).

But there is a spirit of prophecy alive in the novel, and it belongs to the narrator. How could it be otherwise in a historical novel, that arch-form of a century whose philosophical first premise, from Hegel and Nietzsche to Darwin and Marx, was based on the fact that the full understanding of history was equivalent to phophecy. As Romola witnesses God's fire being gathered for the last time for the puzzling man who has been her prophet and has retracted his gift, and then retracted his retraction, she yearns for that "last decisive word" (p. 593) which will make it clear that Savonarola is a true martyr. The reader knows that no such word will be spoken by the priest because it has already been spoken by the prophet-narrator in grand peroration, first in her own voice:

> The idea of martyrdom had been to him a passion dividing the dream of the future with the triumph of beholding his work achieved. And now, in place of both,

had come a resignation which he called by no glorifying name. But therefore he may the more fitly be called a martyr by his fellow men to all time.

and then in Savonarola's voice:

He endured a double agony; not only the reviling, and the torture, and the death-throe, but the agony of sinking from the vision of glorious achievement into that deep shadow where he could only say, "I count as nothing: darkness encompasses me: yet the light I saw was the true light." (P. 591)

Thus Savonarola dies, as prophesied, and has his martyr's altar and his memorial day in the concluding epilogue. He dies blind, mute, and betrayed, like Romola's father; but unlike Bardo, whose visions were of the past, Savonarola is remembered, like Eliot, like Hegel and Feuerbach, because he was able to envision the true light in the future. The self-conscious, occasionally rather stiff and superior historian of *Scenes of Clerical Life, Adam Bede,* even *The Mill on the Floss* has found in *Romola* her loving, hurting grasp of the past, the past that prophesies not the present but the future, the past that is animated by "a good, strong, terrible vision" that is still to be seen and reached for, and spoken. Eliot's conscious and fearful responsibility in this respect is the same as Romola's in the epilogue, when she is confronted by the child of the pleasure-loving destroyed Tito with the ominous and central question: "Mamma Romola, what am I to be?"

Middlemarch *and* Daniel Deronda

This question rings all over Eliot's final works, with ellipses the only answers. Felix Holt will be . . . a radical? Will Ladislaw . . . a poet? Dorothea Brooke . . . a wife? Daniel Deronda . . . a George Washington? In *Middlemarch* those who think they know what they are to be—Bulstrode, Casaubon, Lydgate—are literally unmade. These stride confidently forward in response to a clear "vocation," like Romola's brother Dino, thinking, as Lydgate does of Fare-brother, that "a pitiable infirmity of will" (p. 139) ails the Fred Vincys, the Will Ladislaws, the Dorotheas, who drift in this less than epic age. But they are defeated, whereas the drifters survive.

It is important to remember that Bulstrode, Casaubon, and Lydgate also have, like Dorothea and Will, minds "altogether ardent, theoretic, and intellectually consequent" (p. 21). They too "yearned . . . after some lofty conception of the world which might frankly include the parish of Tipton and [their] own rule of conduct there" (p. 6). All five of these characters undergo that "ironic" deflation both of ardor and of theory that critics like to celebrate as modern realism and as evidence of the author's "control" of her own ardor and theory. But Casaubon and Lydgate are not merely deflated, they are really, despite Eliot's searching compassion, humanly reduced, as their "spots of commonness" eat deeper into their confident beings, and Bulstrode sustains that virtual decreation which is the mark of the Gothic, winding up physically as well as morally a shrunken ghost of his former self.

The Gothic substructure of *Middlemarch* is easy enough to find once one goes looking for it; from the entombment of Dorothea and the enchainment of Lydgate that mark the marriage-as-murder theme of the first third of the novel, to the theme of the clutching Dead Hands of Casaubon, Featherstone, and John Raffles in the middle of the novel, to the lightning that strikes balefully for Bulstrode and Lydgate, sublimely for Dorothea and Will at the end of the novel.[18] Of special note also is the recourse that even the

18 David Carroll has drawn attention as well to the "glimpse of vampires feeding off each other" we get in the relationship of Bulstrode and Raffles, one of the several Gothic patterns that "live a subterranean metaphoric life beneath the provincial surface of the novel." See "The Externality of Fact" in *This Particular Web*, ed. Ian Adam (Toronto: Univ. of Toronto Press, 1975), p. 84.

most phlegmatic or fair mind makes to the Gothic when it is hurt or enraged: the monsterific imagery surrounding Casaubon comes from the resentful Sir James Chettam, whose bride Casaubon has stolen, and from Will Ladislaw, who scarcely knows why his patron-uncle's marriage aggravates him so—"if he chose to grow grey crunching bones in a cavern, he had no business to be luring a girl into his companionship," Will grimly observes to himself (p. 264); and the strangling succubus imagery surrounding Rosamond comes from both the narrator and from Lydgate, who called her "his basil plant . . . which had flourished wonderfully on a murdered man's brains" (p. 610).[19]

Of special interest too in *Middlemarch* as we move from *Romola* to *Daniel Deronda* are the figures of Bulstrode, Will, Rosamond, and Dorothea. The latter is, of course, the major triumph of the novel, not so much, I believe, because in her Eliot achieved that "ironic distance" which was missing in the "idealized" Romola but because through Dorothea Eliot tenaciously, almost mystically, establishes and clings to that ambiguously dangerous and elevating concept of human and social fellowship that is expressed in perhaps the novel's primary image, the yoke. In the novel's opening scene, Dorothea declines the jewel-yoke around her neck, and Celia accepts it; in the Casaubon marriage, Dorothea bends her neck, fascinated, to "only the ideal and not the real yoke of marriage" (p. 353). But at the first crisis of her faith in Ladislaw, by heroic effort she "forced herself to think of [that scene] as bound up with another woman's life" (p. 577). Going to Rosamond to try and help her, she receives from her the news that restores her faith in her

19 We might think this an extravagant figure of marriage as murder for Lydgate to apply had not George Eliot previously told us at the bizarre story of Lydgate's first passion for a Parisian actress who murdered her play-husband, her real lover, onstage before Lydgate's very eyes. I want to return to this little-noticed episode in my discussion of *Daniel Deronda*'s Alcharisi, but for now it is worth observing that Lydgate's attraction to the succubus is of long standing.

own lover, and "the two women clasped each other as if they had been in a shipwreck" (p. 584). That same sense of yoking as calamity, as sublimity, accompanies the final yoking of Dorothea and Will; as lightning strikes outside, they seize each other's hands, and money, position, family, pride go overboard as they rescue each other from the worst fate in the world, yokelessness. In *Middlemarch* as nowhere else, this fundamental fact of Eliot's vision is dramatized; men and women properly draw the business of the world and seek the ideal future together, in harness with each other, strength calling on strength, will checking will. If the marriage of Daniel and Mirah in *Daniel Deronda* seems something of an afterthought, it is because by now that yoke has become an assumption underlying the useful life. Conversely, those whose wills grow too big for any harness, like Bulstrode, or whose wills are too small, their necks too smooth to hold the yoke, like Rosamond, slip out of human harness and become "good for nothing" (p. 129), monstrous, a horror to Eliot.

This is what Bulstrode and Rosamond and even for a time Will Ladislaw are about. *Middlemarch* has always seemed, with its Featherstone will and its Casaubon will as plot machines and with its curiously gypsy, laughing, Shelleyan Will for hero, a kind of devious allegory about will. Will Ladislaw, of course, orphaned, gifted, attractive, is thoroughly unyoked at the start. Dorothea's beautiful young man, like Romola's, is something of a pagan philosopher and skeptic, living off his foster father, like Tito, out of sympathy with old superstitions and duties and with the very concept of the yoke. Will's "the best piety is to enjoy" (p. 163) has much more to recommend it than Tito's animal pursuit of pleasure, certainly, as his resentment and final rejection of Casaubon's claims has none of the cold egoism of Tito's unyoking of himself from Baldassarre. But all the same, his "gypsy" life takes a decisive turn for the better when he comes to Middlemarch and, superior, irritated, fractious as he is, "harnessed himself" with Dorothea's uncle as a political journalist (p. 343). Eliot is amiably entertaining on the subject of Will's "choice" of a career in Dorothea's "neighborhood" and on the fanciful Platonism of his feeling for her. No more than Tito's awe at Romola's "womanhood" can Will's impetuous "you *are* a poem" (p. 166) be depended upon to anchor him solidly to love. But Will is fortunately gifted with dread too, a dread connected, as Daniel Deronda's will be, with the figure of his wronged mother, a dread that makes him fight to retain those qualities, laughter, ardor, argumentative candor, hopeful sympathy, that have earned him Dorothea's confidence: "He felt that in her mind he had found his highest estimate" (p. 566). Whereas Tito takes Romola's similar estimate of him for granted and uses it, Will knows that his ability to remain true to that estimate and so to confirm Dorothea's own confidence in the presence of virtue is the only way for either of them to keep that faith. Says Eliot, " 'If you are not good, none is good'—those little words may give a terrific meaning to responsibility, may hold a vitriolic intensity for remorse" (p. 565).

And so they do. When Will is discovered by Dorothea hand in hand with the lovely Mrs. Lydgate, the blasts of scorn, anger, and rage released in both of them are like nothing we've seen anywhere in the novel's world. It takes a genuine heroism for them to overcome that disaster of apparent betrayal and real destructive rage, and their reward is that marriage which is a yoke as well as a poem, not a murder, but "a beginning as well as an ending" (p. 607).

As for Bulstrode, he is, like Savonarola, neither hypocrite nor schizophrenic but a double consciousness, at once the elected "instrument" of a Divine Will that admirably parallels his own and that materially ambitious "Nick" who concealed his knowledge of a lost heiress so that he could wed her money and her widowed mother in a marriage that was an end to his Evangelical innocence as well as a beginning to his success. Like Savonarola, Bulstrode lives genuinely in the context of a fallen world overseen by a divine justice. His active conscience presents to him the accurate picture of the mixture of good and evil in each of his acts: he just strives very hard to underrate the evil in his questionable acts and to overrate the good in his admirable ones. Whereas Casaubon has stored up his unused emotional capacity in a spiritual bank and is disappointed to find that time and inflation have eaten it up, Banker Bulstrode knows better and thus keeps the capital of his good deeds out earning interest in the economy of philanthropy, but the problem is that the capital of his sins is out there earning interest too. At his gravest moral crisis, when his accomplice returns to threaten him with revelation, as Schedoni's does, as Bertha Latimer's does, as they always do in the Gothic, the wretched man cannot conceal from himself his wish to murder Raffles. But in the actual sequence of events that bring about the death, he can and must strive to keep his will clear of the overt acts. "A man may do wrong, and his will may rise clear out of it, though he can't get his life clear" (p. 510), says Eliot's homely theologian, Caleb Garth. But Bulstrode's will is not simply a man's will; it is dilated by the will of God, which surely cannot allow the destruction of the hospital-building Bulstrode by the drunken Raffles: "Imperious will stirred murderous impulses towards this brute life, over which will, by itself had no power" (p. 519).

In the context of Bulstrode's theology, we know what might have aided will to combat these impulses, but in his fear and rage Bulstrode has shut himself off from everyone else, closed off the channels of grace. After the murder is accomplished (it *was* murder, although Bulstrode raised no hand against Raffles), after the exposure that means exile and the breakdown of his double consciousness, grace comes to him, as it does briefly to Rosamond, through the only fellow human being that either had ever truly admitted to their hearts. A "great wave" of sorrow and identification rises in Bulstrode's stricken wife, passes to him through a hand on his shoulder, and allows him to break through his will, clenched against disaster, to cry.

Since Bulstrode's fellowship with Harriet is permanent, yoked in full marriage, he is probably saved from further exercise of "murderous impulses." But Rosamond's swan neck is too smooth to hold the yoke of Dorothea's fellowship for long and never really did take the yoke of marriage to Lydgate. "Hurried" by Dorothea's passionate, broken, paradoxical defense of marriage and of love into her one experience of dread, "oppressed" momentarily by a kind of "blood-guiltiness," she tells Dorothea that Will is faithful to her and then reaches again for the only morality she can really conceive of, "he cannot reproach me any more" (p. 584). This is her position with Lydgate too, as it was Bulstrode's before his deity. But of course the reproach comes nevertheless; Bulstrode's conscience arraigns him, as Lydgate's conscience arraigns Rosamond before his early death, for that flourishing on a murdered man's brains that in the Gothic world is the inevitable outcome of resisting the yoke.

These two figures, Bulstrode and Rosamond, are also crucial to Eliot's final most complicated novel. Having "rescued" Bulstrode from the worst consequences of his murder by activating grace through marriage and having discovered in her characterization of Rosamond her own ambiguous antipathy to and anxiety for the classic English murdering beauty, Eliot sets out to rescue her in *Daniel Deronda*. This time in the single character of Gwendolen Harleth, the demon behind all those murderous impulses will be fully explored. The necessary death will again occur. But this time there will be no marriage as rescue. Daniel, embarked on his own adventure towards fellowship-marriage, cannot be Harriet Vincy to Gwendolen's guilty Bulstrode, far less Will to Gwendolen's guilty Dorothea (Dorothea's "Oh, I did love him" recognizes some inevitable disloyalty during her marriage to Casaubon as Gwendolen's "I did, I did kill him in my thoughts" does of her own marriage). Instead, he will attempt to be to Gwendolen what Dorothea would have been to Rosamond had Rosamond allowed it: Eliot's model (not ideal) human being who, if he is not always unselfish or perfect, still has that sustaining dread of pure egotism, the "shame at the acceptance of events as if they were his only" (*Daniel Deronda*, p. 690), that gives men a hold on fellowship and an ontological ground for morality.

If *Middlemarch* owes its grand structural harmonic to Eliot's dramatization of "the stealthy convergence of human lots" (p. 70), one of the great technical achievements of *Daniel Deronda* is to show the stealthy divergence of human lots. Like *Romola* and *Middlemarch, Daniel Deronda* contains two stories, one dominated by the intuition that human life, even communal human life, must somehow be and form "a medium for ardent deeds," the other by the intuition that individuals and especially communities dream only squirellike dreams—freedom from pain, the pleasures of secured routine, and control of proximate territory. These stories, Romola's and Tito's, Dorothea's and Rosamond's, Daniel's and Gwendolen's, diverge at the root, merge only because that moral "rescue," one person of another, that characterizes George Eliot's plots, is the single certain ardent deed one can do in Eliot's world, although others—reform of the Renaissance Church, of the Victorian Parliament and the rural poor, reform of the ideas of progress and of nationalism—must be tried.

But *Romola* and *Middlemarch begin* in this ardent world, with the prophetic voice of the narrator calling for time travel and the vistas of the saints—the legendary Pope Angelico, the mystic St. Theresa—and then shifting comfortably back and forth between the two stories to accomplish, after a time, the convergence, the attempted rescue, the final divergence. The brilliant opening scene of *Daniel Deronda*, boldly artificial and dramatic after a headnote explicitly affirming "the make-believe of a beginning," establishes the convergence of Daniel and Gwendolen immediately, with great power. Two strikingly handsome persons are "arrested" out of the "serried crowds of human beings" in a gambling hall by each other's glance. He feels "coercion," she, "concussion." He "felt the moment become dramatic," and she, with "that nature which we call art,"[20] accepts the drama and makes it pure Gothic: "Deronda's gaze seemed to have acted as an evil eye"—where she was winning she is now losing, but "since she was not winning strikingly, the next best thing was to lose strikingly" (pp. 38-39). Though they speak no words to each other, "the young man with the dreadful expression" and the woman with the "Lamia beauty," they become "problematic" to each other immediately. To his theoretic mind, she is the problem of whether "in a dynamic glance, good or evil genius" predominates (p. 35); to her practical egoist's mind, he is the problem whether in a "measuring" glance, she ranks high or low.

The impact, and the romantic promise, of this convergence resounds over the rest of the novel, where it is, nevertheless, the narrative's business to restore separateness to both Daniel and Gwendolen, to show that their central dramatic moments have already occurred, that their minds are already engaged with the "terrible visions" around which their best (or worst) selfs will form. It is in confirmation of the vision on the painted panel in the drawing room at Offendene—the vision of a figure fleeing a

20 Rosamond too has that subtle gift, or is it a curse, of the beautiful English girl, the capacity to "act her own character" (p. 87) so well that she doesn't know she's acting it. Eliot's strongest and most anxious comment on this quality comes in her exploration of the actress Alcharisi: "The speech was in fact a piece of what may be called sincere acting: this woman's nature was one in which all feeling—and all the more when it was tragic as well as real—immediately became matter of conscious representation: experience immediately passed into drama, and she acted her own emotions" (p. 691). A complicated pride and guilt over this ruthless turning of experience into representation is, of course, close to the bone of Eliot's difficulties with her own nature, as the Redinger biography makes clear.

dead face—that Gwendolen has broken off her hypnotized near-engagement to Mallinger Grandcourt and escaped to the Continent. And it is in confirmation of the vision "burnt into his life" (p. 202) at age thirteen, of himself as the perhaps illegitimate child of a priest and a half-criminal, half-victim suffering mother that Daniel is arrested in debate and intimate scrutiny when he see the reckless Gwendolen. That "deepest interest in the fates of women" (p. 231) as avatars of his missing mother causes Daniel to "redeem" Gwendolen's pawned necklace there, as he will later rescue Mirah from her "drowning shroud" and Gwendolen herself from her demons—anything pawned, weighed down, trapped, might be his mother. Likewise, anything offering "enraged resistance" to fate, preferring to "lose strikingly" (p. 39) in a gamble, might be and, as we discover, is and has been his mother. And Gwendolen, willfully killing offending canaries and kissing herself cozily in mirrors, still suffers "fits of spiritual dread" (p. 94) connected with a real perception of the immensities of existence and with a mortal fear that she "can't love people" (p. 115) and that they will find out that flaw. His measuring aloofness, her defiant entrapment, raise deep personal response, but it is important to note that in the dramatic opening convergence they are merely ideas to each other, near mythic figures.[21] She is to Daniel immediately the subject of an "inward debate" that will find its crisis, though not, I think, its resolution, in his meeting with his mother. As for Gwendolen, "eager about something" (p. 42) and under all of her confidence uncertain, like Emma, of her powers, a friend suggests, jokingly, how Daniel will figure as her supreme moral test: "Perhaps this Mr. Deronda's acquaintance will do instead of the Matterhorn" (p. 43).

[21] In the gambling scene, adventurer against observer, Gwendolen is to Daniel as will is to destiny, in Felicia Bonaparte's terms, as autonomy is to value, and, despite the appearance of community in her stance and distance in his, we find from their inner monologues that she is to solitude as he is to society.

Gwendolen's story, in which Daniel will be a primary
model for the acquisition of her own balanced self-measure,
is a complex amalgam of Dorothea's and Rosamond's in
outline. She lives in the bosom of her all-female family like
"a princess in exile" (p. 52), taking the universe as "background" (p. 55) for that elegant conscious self-display of
pretty "spirit" as well as of pretty arms by which the women
of her world contrive to hide from themselves their essential
object-ness in their society. But Gwendolen's self-display is
less innocent than Rosamond's, and therefore, less powerful: her girlhood has been one long struggle with the astonishing intuition tht she is *not* free, not powerful, not
important—this despite, or rather, subtly, *because of* the
fact that she is the most striking, most deferred to, most
admired young woman of her circle. Like Dorothea, Gwendolen has no wish to be the ordinary brilliantly married
belle of her society; she too wants to "lead," to achieve real
things, not to go on "muddling away my life as other people
do, being and doing nothing remarkable" (p. 58). She too
is "ardent," but she is not, unfortunately for her, "theoretic"; she has had all of Rosamond's spoiling attention and
none of Dorothea's complex acquaintance with religious
theories of the uses of humility and duty and discipline in
the fight to become "remarkable." She has no theory of life
at all, right or wrong, within which to assemble and test
her often very fine intuitions about character and events,
only "a self control by which she guarded herself" from that
"penitential humiliation" that she somehow knows threatens her on every side and the "calculation" by which she
convinces herself she is really in charge of her life (p. 54). In
Eliot's words, "she would at once have marked herself off
from any sort of theoretical or practically reforming women
by satirizing them" (p. 83).

With these as her only forms for thinking about herself
and with satire as her major mode of perceiving other people, it is inevitable that the "life of passion" as well as the
life of achievement should, as Eliot phrases it, "begin nega-

tively in her" (p. 114). Men, as Gwendolen says, cruelly witty, are "too ridiculous" (p. 110) when they love; women too, as her cousin Anna is when her love for her brother Rex overflows. It is all so out of control, unguarded, "volunteered," and not calculated. Rex's declaration of love to herself, linked with his humiliation in the hunt and his resulting broken bones, evokes cold laughter and "a passionate aversion" (p. 114) in her. Avoiding love is one of the ways, the least vague way she has, in fact, of "not doing as other women do" (p. 101).[22] On the other hand, the only woman in her neighborhood who "does" anything, the authoress Mrs. Arrowpoint, is also the subject of Gwendolen's cruel wit, those light and bright and sparkling barbs by which she holds off the critical and managing world and preserves, just, her phantom independence. Mrs. Arrowpoint, who has made her biography of Tasso into a sentimental romance (p. 76), is almost ridiculous enough to confirm Gwendolen's policy of guarding herself against the risk of attempting any actual achievement in much the same way as Rex's virtual "illness" of love confirms her "fierceness of maidenhood" (p. 102).

[22] In *The Mill on the Floss* (1860), Eliot explores the complicated trap that love may be for a woman. The narrator notes that Maggie felt the "world outside books" to be one where "people behaved the best to those they did not pretend to love, and that did not belong to them. And if life had no love in it, what else was there for Maggie?" (p. 208). On the other hand, Maggie's experiences with Tom and her father and even Philip have taught her to think "there can never come much happiness to me from loving: I have always had so much pain mingled with it." She wishes she could "make myself a world outside it, as men do" (p. 361), but Philip remonstrates that such a separation would be not only a cowardly "escape from pain" but also a mutilation of one's nature, as, he might have added, it is for men. One of the achievements of *The Mill on the Floss* is to show the mutilation and pain of men as well as of women, inside as well as outside of love, but clearly Maggie's "susceptibility" is graver than Steven's or Tom's, or even finally, Philip's. Quotations are taken from the Riverside Edition (Boston: Houghton-Mifflin Co., 1961).

But even before she meets Daniel Deronda, two further encounters teach her the limits of satire. The musician Klesmer, ridiculous blend of arrogance, silliness, and genius that he is, lives by and criticizes by that "sense of the universal," of "deep, mysterious passion" and "conflict" that Gwendolen herself intuits in the negative as spiritual dread (p. 79). She knows as well as Klesmer that this quality is missing in the little song she sings him, the little tableaux she enacts in the drawing room and archery field—missing because she cannot risk living in its presence. She must quiver at his criticisms, whatever public defense of satire she erects, because they reflect her own deepest fears, and, on a more subtle level, because his vision, that terrifying "width of horizon opened" in their conversations, validates that spiritual dread which, half-mad as it seems to her, is really the only remarkable individuating power she has.

When in the family financial catastrophe the choices of ordinary female slavery narrow around her and she goes to Klesmer for encouragement about an acting career, he must foreclose that option with the truth. It takes living in the presence of the sublime and the universal, in the state of vocation, to achieve an artist's rank, and even a successful mediocrity requires surrender to the external slavery of patronage and the internal bondage of discipline. He must say it, and she must believe it, but as he leaves, "her burning eyes . . . would have suited a woman enduring a wrong which she might not resent, but would probably revenge" (p. 308).

Her rage is not at Klesmer but at the general dynamic of "girl's lives" (p. 101), at the empty charade of her royally independent girlhood, falsebottomed as "the packed up shows of a departing fair" (p. 306). The woman who thought she could will herself not to do as other women do has now only one last choice left: to give way silently or to lose strikingly. "I dread giving way" (p. 309), Gwendolen tells her mother, and when Mallinger Grandcourt appears soon after to renew his offer of marriage, she chooses to lose her freedom strikingly in a gamble that she can manage her enslaver.

Grandcourt, however, is a man impervious to satire, as he is to everything else. Like Rosamond's, his neck is too smooth for the yoke of marriage, and his mate's barbs slide off his water-nixie scales. Like Rosamond, he also opposes his mate not with will but with void: this consummate product of the English breeding of the gentleman has reached near total will-lessness, despite a certain hypnotic power of assumption, not assertion, that everyone, including himself, mistakes for will.[23] Grandcourt cannot "take the trouble" to cast off his mistress when he marries nor to kick his own dogs when they irritate him, or even, finally, to save his own life. Away from the sustaining element of servants, money, and class, he sinks like a stone into the waters of the Adriatic at the end of the novel without, one feels, even lifting his arms to swim. His courtship of the splendid Gwendolen is a triumph of void; it takes place in a terrifying series of "pauses" between the trivialities of conversation, pauses "during which Gwendolen imagined . . . interpreted . . . recalled . . . thought . . . speculated . . . reflected" (pp. 146-148), in a word, courted herself.

"Impassive," "unperturbed," "languid," "adorably quiet and free from absurdities" (p. 73), Grandcourt attracts Gwendolen by his smooth blankness—and not only because she feels able to manage it. At some fatal level, he represents that perfect freedom from dreads and pertubations, that perfect security from humiliations and the touch of other people, that she wants for herself, the quintessence of dead "ladyhood" because he is the ultimate gentleman. She recognizes "that a sort of lotos-eaters stupor had begun

[23] Felicia Bonaparte's proposal that "Eliot's darkest study of the implications of the nature of will [shows that will] craves not only power of mastery, but opposition," I want to argue, does not fit Grandcourt as much as it fits Alcharisi (*Will and Destiny*, p. 100).

in him and was taking possession of her" (p. 172), but for all her energy and wit, in her fear she is attracted to that stupor, partly, surely, as that revenge upon the phantasm of freedom of choice that had humiliated her with Klesmer. When Grandcourt comes to propose a second time, Gwendolen puts her conscience to sleep on the matter of Grandcourt's mistress and her children. And although from one point of view the narrator describes the resulting engagement as a battle of wills—"His strongest need was to be completely master of this creature. . . . And she—ah, piteous equality in the need to dominate!" (p. 346)—the truth is, it is a battle of voids. At "the turning of the ways," Grandcourt finds the perfect will-less way to propose—"Do you command me to go"—leaving Gwendolen the perfect negation as affirmation, "No" (pp. 347-348).

This is a yoke constructed in hell, a marriage which is murderous from the start, and its icon, as in *Middlemarch*, is a necklace. When Gwendolen receives the diamonds from her husband's vengeful mistress on her wedding day, she falls back in her chair, terrified but "helpless," and "truly," says the narrator, like some fell sister of the Brothers Grimm, "here were poisoned gems, and the poison had entered into this poor young creature" (p. 407). Grandcourt's entrance provokes "hysterical violence" from Gwendolen, but that is the last time her screams reach the air. Fighting Grandcourt the only way she can, turning herself to stone, Gwendolen means "to wear the yoke so as not to be pitied" (pp. 479-480). "Magnificent in her pale green velvet and poisoned diamonds" (p. 617), she presides over the months of her marriage like that similarly poisoned Tennysonian queen for whom she is surely named, the vessel of private damnation and public catastrophe. Like Guinevere, like Rosamond, she yearns for the rescuing Lancelot whose feeling for her will restore her confident self-value after it has been destroyed, unaccountably, by the marriage that she thought would be its foundation.

That opening meeting between Gwendolen and Daniel Deronda, binding and mythic, without words, like that of Guinevere and Lancelot, made his face and his judgment part of her innermost life. Like Lancelot's loyalty, Daniel's uprightness lodges in his queen's heart and struggles there against the demons of rage and self-pity. And as the crisis comes, Daniel's validation of Gwendolen's dread of wrong-doing stands savingly between her irresistible will to Grandcourt's annihilation (Bulstrode's "murderous impulses") and the deed. At the end, Gwendolen plunges into the water beside the sinking Grandcourt in a complex moral gesture: at once a "leaping away from myself" (the self that withheld aid and said "die" in its heart), a leap into a new and dangerous element of action (the lotos-eater returning to the sea-quest), and an effort at human rescue, "I would have saved him then" (p. 761). She has fled her crime, turned away from the dead face, according to the terrible vision she has carried with her from the painted panel in the drawing room at Offendene.

Like Lancelot, like Lydgate, Daniel has a story of his own, apart from the poisoned queen with whom he is linked. Unlike Lancelot and Lydgate, however, he finds the strength to pursue it, though it means walking away from a soul still just barely afloat in the perilous waters of self-recognition and remorse. But Gwendolen, alone and frightened as she is at the end of the novel, has two advantages over the drowned Grandcourt: she knows she may die and can therefore fight—"take the trouble"—to live; and someone has thrown her a rope. Daniel's rescue, spare, taut, never more than hand to hand, soon to be only mind to mind, is a rope, not a protecting, or choking, necklace. In their long, carefully managed parting scene at the end of Chapter 69 (analogous to Dorothea and Will's final scene in *Middlemarch*), no lightning strikes, only, in sequence, these wrenching human recognitions: "I have purposes that will take me to the East." . . . "I am a forsaken woman!" . . . "I am cruel!" . . . "I will try—try to live."

But along with her grief and solitude, Gwendolen acquires something crucial in that parting: like Dorothea she sees for the first time that she is not alone in the painful scenes of her life, and this recognition is the birth of rectitude—that terrible and sublime virtue. Rectitude in *Middlemarch* required Dorothea to overcome her hysterical flight from Rosamond and to go back in fellowship. An alarmingly "modern" rectitude in *Daniel Deronda* requires Gwendolen to resist her hysterical clutch at Daniel and to part in fellowship. And although "the burthen of that difficult rectitude towards him was a weight her frame tottered under" (p. 879) at the start, it is in George Eliot's world finally not a burden but the only possible support.

If Gwendolen no longer has Daniel as a necklace, she does have, through his agency, her father's necklace of turquoises, pawned by her at the beginning as Tito pawned Baldassarre's ring and Baldassarre his mother's Florentine *brevi*, or charm, in that reflex throwing off of the Dead Hand that is always utterly wrong in George Eliot. Returning it to her, Daniel is from the start the agent of that force which governs his own story, the force that decrees that the Dead Hand must be grasped as the key to the future. As Gwendolen's terrible but shaping vision is of the marriage that is murder, Daniel's is of the bludgeoning past that is prophecy. Orchestrating Daniel's discovery and self-discovery across the generations for all the world like Walpole's Alphonso the Good is Eliot's mysterious Daniel Charisi, born like Frankenstein before his time with the vision of the new man and with a ruthless desire to create the vision on his own, leaving out women. Poor Gwendolen thought right up to the bitter end that she was someone special, but "girls' lives" are seen to be ruthlessly pruned of heroic possibility by English society, and even George Eliot cannot lie to (or rather, fully imagine a truth for) Dorothea and Gwendolen about the lack of a medium for ardent deeds. In hideous compensation, boys' lives are doubly charged with heroic responsibility, especially in the culture Daniel finally connects himself with—any son may be the Messiah, the ultimate rescuer. Destiny, specialness, "chosenness," breathes hot behind him.

There are many ways to account for Eliot's choice of Judaism as the channel for the most positive terrible vision, the prophetic sublime, in this novel. For one thing, the open evasion of women in the Jewish vision of Messiah allows Eliot to show and question that evasion more clearly in Alcharisi's rebel mother than she could in Romola's rebel madonna. In addition, of course, as a medium for ardent deeds, the Old Testament outweighs the New, with its complicated morality and its ambiguous triumph, as the rhetoric of most Christian "reformations" testifies. The philosophic idealism at the root of both Judaic theology and German Romanticism to which Eliot responded so powerfully makes another link. And so, unmistakably, does nationalism. Deeply implicated in those great flawed avatars of universal brotherhood, "Christendom" and the Pax Britannica, Eliot is yet fascinated by the possibilities latent in half-developed nations and races, fascinated both mystically, so to speak, and politically. The long debate carried on in the workingmen's club at *The Hand and Banner* in the novel's "Revelations" book focuses on nationalism as the particular in the general argument about the necessity and direction of social change. And although the discussants on the whole seem to lean toward the easy position that "progress" is inevitable, that the direction of social change is benevolent, and that history is "setting against" nationalism and separatism, Eliot is clearly on the side of those who want to make room for history as surprise, for "explosions" of half-buried cultures and peoples, above all, for "resistance" to history itself if it grows too mechanical for visionaries to have a place in it.[24]

[24] Graham Martin argues that "the choice of Zionism has the effect of removing the ideal aspirations associated with Deronda from any effective engagement with the English scene" and therefore the book contains "the assumption that English life has become unhis-

In 1876 Zionism was politically the very picture of history
as surprise, mystically the ur-Western form of history as
prophecy, irresistible to a mind seeking, like Nietzsche's, to
resolve this paradox—that history must somehow be living
and lawful, yet not mechanically predictable, leaving room,
as Savonarola would say, both for sacred obedience and
sacred resistance. Finding this space in history is Daniel's
mission, and he accomplishes it through an agonizing grasp
of two Dead Hands, his grandfather's and his mother's.

Daniel makes contact with his past first through the
sister-self Mirah and then through the Gothic brother-figure
of Mordecai, the Jewish philosopher, whom he meets, as
Hogg's Robert meets his devil alter ego Gil-Martin, during
a casual walk from the familiar to the unfamiliar part of
the city, after a wandering that has been in fact a preparation. A solitary child with a bookish and sensitive disposition, Daniel has been raised by Sir Hugo Mallinger to be
the essential English gentleman-master in circumstances
that make that role to his mind as ambiguous and charade-

<hr>

torical" in the Marxist sense, no longer the theater of development
("Daniel Deronda and Political Change" in *Critical Essays on George
Eliot*, p. 149). This seems indeed to have been Eliot's fear, but if
Zionism demonstrated anything in 1876, it demonstrated that a nation may lie dormant for a time, out of history, and then regenerate
itself. Even England might do that if it has one woman, like Gwendolen, determined at all costs to live amidst the deadness surrounding
her. Again it must be emphasized that in this novel Zionism is *not*, in
any simplistic sense, merely the universal symbol for brotherhood and
human amalgamation; it is a grand *separating* of a nation amalgamated
and lost in other nations, a focusing of one race's energies as an icon
of that focusing which ought to take place in each nation and race.
His grandfather's friend Joseph Kalonymos reports to Daniel at the
end of the book that Daniel Charisi "used to insist . . . that the
strength and wealth of mankind depended on the balance of separateness and communication" (p. 791), a balance, as we shall see, at the
heart of Lawrence's vision too. One also notices in this connection
that Ladislaw and Daniel (as well as Latimer, the disappointed visionary) are connected with the figure of Shelley, for whom also, in the
end, England became a dead field of action.

like as Gwendolen's Lady-Queenship finally appears to her.
Showing that "blend of child's ignorance with surprising
knowledge which is oftener seen in bright girls," aware
from that "burning" initiating moment at age thirteen that
he has been born, like bright girls, "under disadvantages
which required them to be a sort of heroes if they were to
work themselves up to an equal standing with their legally
born brothers" (p. 205), Daniel resembles Maggie Tulliver,
or George Eliot, in his quest to give heroic, rather than
sentimental or destructive, form to that disadvantage. The
disadvantage that he thinks is bastardy and that turns out
to be Jewishness has powerful links with femininity. Daniel
blushes and has a perfect "delicacy of feeling" (p. 207); and
that "sense of an entailed disadvantage—the deformed foot
doubtfully hidden by the shoe . . . [which] easily turns a
self-centered, unloving nature into an Ishmaelite" (p. 215),
has instead "biased" Daniel's imagination to tender fellowship.[25]

But these are not alone what make the woman in him. An
affectionate nature has preserved him from the dangers of
Gothic Ishmaelitism, but his imperfect grip on a problematic self-image has skewed his ambition, raised in him a
kind of dreamy abstract tolerance, a "social neutrality"
(p. 220), "a many-sided sympathy, which threatened to
hinder any persistent course of action" (p. 412). An innate
susceptibility to the "losing causes of the world" (p. 413)

[25] "Daniel, like a later Ishmael, Leopold Bloom—is both solitary
and social, and the moment of discovery is both a joy and a shock,"
says Barbara Hardy (*The Novels of George Eliot*, p. 127). But Eliot
explicitly calls Daniel not the Ishmael his mother is, and the Ish-
maelitish Mordecai explicitly welcomes him as an Englishman, a
bridge for Ishmael back to Abraham. Daniel follows no visions unless
they are not merely social but familial. Bloom on the other hand sees
no bridge anywhere. It is interesting to compare Daniel's blend of joy
and shock as he contemplates his identity and plans his return with
Bloom's unrelieved alienation from the land of his fathers; Israel is to
him "the gray sunken cunt of the world," and its memory actually
darkens the sky above Dublin with the afflatus of Bloom's horror.

makes willful martyrdom for him, as for Maggie, the Scylla to the Charybdis of sympathetic neutrality. In a sense Daniel got both, when in a crucial episode he stopped studying for his Mathematics First at Cambridge in order to help his friend Meyrick win his. This rather childlike exercise of fellowship matches, in an oblique way, the older Daniel's habit of carrying a full cigar case for others' benefit although he doesn't smoke himself—he is afraid, the narrator says, of "turning himself into a sort of diagram" (p. 582) either of the English gentleman or of abstract goodness, of, one might almost say, the "good woman."

If in this profound sensitivity to the claims of others, this tense neutrality about the identity of the self, he is, as he thinks before he meets her, his mother's daughter, he responds all the more powerfully to Mordecai's invitation to be his brother, ultimately, as he discovers, his grandfather's heir. The mystic Mordecai, driven by the need to resurrect and focus the energies of his ancient race in that "halting place of enmities" (p. 595), Palestine, seems that very event "from outside" that Daniel desires to awaken and center his own "wandering energy" (p. 413). Since he has maintained his distance from the identities offered him—whig politician, English gentleman—because he sensed they were part of the charade concealing his actual self (in this recoil from the offered identity he is, as it turns out, really his mother's daughter), Daniel cannot resist for long Mordecai's astonishing certainty that he is the dream figure of his visions, the liberator, the translator, the "more executive self" (p. 530), the active embodiment of the return, the Shelleyan soul fled out of his soul. Just two evenings before the Jewish artist Klesmer listens, criticizes, then welcomes the rescued sister-self Mirah to her heritage—"Let us shake hands: you are a musician" (p. 541)—Mordecai welcomes Daniel to his—"I expected you to come down the river. . . . You shall take the inheritance" (pp. 550, 557). Mordecai tells the Englishman that he is a Jew, and more, that "visions are the creators and feeders of the world. I see,

I measure the world as it is, which the vision will create anew" (p. 555). Skepticism wars briefly in Daniel with his wish to respond to Mordecai's profound need and with his own wish to see the world heroically, and is then set to one side to provide the impetus—as it always must in George Eliot's theology—to check theory against feeling, lest any general theory "eat out our morality" (p. 453).

Mordecai's vision, "diagrammed" in passionate debate in *The Hand and Banner* section, has an importance for Daniel, and for George Eliot, beyond the political excitements of national regenerations, beyond even the defense of nationalism and the grand arc of wholeness followed by separation and hidden growth followed by return and larger wholeness that the Jewish odyssey symbolizes in Mordecai's eyes for the larger community of mankind. At the climax of the debate it becomes obvious that the Jews hold primary place in this vision, rather than the Italians or the Americans, because they are not only the chosen people but the choosing people. Here is Mordecai's peroration, with the full weight of George Eliot's passion behind it:

> I say that the strongest principle of growth lies in human choice. The sons of Judah have to choose that God may again choose them. The Messianic time is the time when Israel shall will the planting of the national ensign. . . . Shall man, whose soul is set in the royalty of discernment and resolve, deny his rank and say, I am an onlooker, ask no choice or purpose of me? That is the blasphemy of this time. (P. 598)

In "sacred rebellion" against this blasphemy, in full knowledge of their own and each other's distracting weaknesses, Daniel and Mordecai, like Savonarola and Romola, choose choice, action, Messianic time, kairos. Indeed their understanding is fuller than Savonarola and Romola's, for they know the epistemological fragility not only of human beings but of vision itself: "You would remind me that I may be under an illusion. . . . I face it," says Mordecai to

Daniel in the most existential moment of their meeting, "So it might be with my trust, *if you would make it an illusion. But you will not*" (p. 560).

As if in answer to that prediction, the narrative continues with dreamlike thoroughness to uphold the vision. All the wandering Jews accomplish return—Mordecai to his sister Mirah, Daniel to his grandfather Charisi, whose Messianic dream of Jewish rebirth and human community has lodged in Mordecai to act as a magnet for Daniel. Linked in concrete and symbolic marriage, the Cohen/Lapidoth and the Charisi/Deronda, Eastern and Western Jews, leave England at the end, enriched by it, for the symbolically larger field of Jerusalem, the center of the earth, to begin work on the concrete fabric of the vision.

That is, all but two of the wandering Jews return. For while the vision is tensely upheld by Daniel, Mirah, Mordecai, and essentially by Eliot herself, she has let it be shaken playfully by the brief return of a renegade Cohen/Lapidoth, Mordecai's father, and she cannot avoid its being severely challenged by a rebellious Charisi, by *the* Charisi, Daniel's mother.[26]

26 A less strenuous but still important resistance to the vision is provided by Daniel's friends the Meyricks, especially Hans and Mab. Hans's resisting of the incursion of the Jews upon his friend/mentor's life is sympathetically described, and he is the source of many a significant reproach and warning. My favorite, contained in the letter that Eliot puts, like a dash of cold water, just after the emotional meeting between Daniel and his mother, describes Mordecai's, or any man's, all-encompassing vision as "a worldsupporting elephant, more or less powerful and expensive to keep. My means," Hans continues, "will not allow me to keep a private elephant. I go into mystery instead . . . a sort of gas which is likely to be continually supplied by the decomposition of the elephants" (p. 703).

I owe to a friend's senior thesis (Kathleen Kiely, "George Eliot: Tradition and the Individual," Princeton, 1977) the recognition of Eliot's continual, often sarcastic attention to the fact that vision and culture are "expensive" in this Marxian way. Note for instance the observation in *The Mill on the Floss* that "good society, floated on gossamer wings of light irony, is of very expensive production; re-

Old Lapidoth is a comic enough Satan in this regenesis, playing the oily "curly" parasitic Jew in a self-conscious parody that has worked for forty years on three continents for him. He disappears at last in a virtual puff of smoke, like one of Melville's or Twain's Luciferian con men, with the expensive ring through which Daniel and Mordecai first pawned and then redeemed each other. He too represents the blasphemy of this age, the crafty onlooker with "a way of turning off everything . . . like a farce or a vaudeville, where you find no great meanings" (p. 257). But Alcharisi is altogether a more serious matter. Her challenge is not in the name of ridicule or parody but in the name of another great meaning that is in fact an integral part of the terrible vision itself. She was in her time and still remains the living embodiment of Mordecai's cry in *The Hand and Banner*, "Woe to the men who see no place for resistance in this generation!" (p. 585). Meeting her in Book Seven is for the reader, as it is for Daniel, like walking unexpectedly into a glass wall. She is not the mother he thought he had; she resists the vision he is making his own, and she raises in him and in us more powerfully than ever that question on which the novel began—what *is* the power of a dynamic glance, does good or evil genius predominate there?

Since that first meeting in the gambling hall, Daniel has come to know how bent and illusory Gwendolen's dynamism was: not for him the Gothic surrender to La Belle Dame Sans Merci. He understands too the quirky side of Mordecai's dynamic glance, but he has let it enter him and is committed to it. The piercing gaze of the Princess Halm-Eberstein, once the great singing actress Alcharisi, once Daniel Deronda's reluctant mother and Daniel Charisi's rebellious daughter, speaks, however, of another kind of genius than Mordecai's or even than Klesmer's. Deep-ranging, self-au-

---

quiring nothing less than a wide and arduous national life condensed in unfragrant deafening factories, cramping itself in mines, sweating at furnaces" (p. 254).

thorizing, "royal" as Mordecai's philosophy and Klesmer's music are, Alcharisi's acting has given her a personal power that makes the two other geniuses of the book seem human, almost homely in comparison. For Klesmer lives one grand artist's life, and Mordecai lives a sublime life enlarged by the whole consciousness of his race. But Alcharisi has lived, through her art, "a myriad of lives" (p. 688), accepting and mastering that exposure to multiple identities that was a horror to the Latimer of "The Lifted Veil." She is that figure profoundly upsetting to Eliot, and to Charlotte Brontë before her, the actress, that avatar of "performing heroism"[27] absolutely free to choose each night her face, her personality, her morality. Brontë's Lucy Snowe watched the actress Vashti in a kind of yearning terror, loving and fearing the energy, dreading and envying the amorality. Eliot's Lydgate watches his dream actress act out the murder of her lover onstage and witnesses the ultimate display of that demonic genius that Eliot will call "sincere acting" in Alcharisi: "at the moment when the heroine was to act the stabbing of her lover, and he was to fall gracefully, the wife veritably stabbed her husband, who fell as death willed" (*Middlemarch*, p. 112). In sorrow and desire, Lydgate follows Laure to another town acquitting her of anything but an accidental slip in the heat of the part. And so it was, in a horrible way, a willed murder of a husband grown wearisome and, dreadful portent for Lydgate, "too fond," yet not a coldblooded premeditated act but something suggested by the face and personality and morality she had casually put on that night: "I did not plan: it came to me in the play— *I meant to do it*" (p. 114).

27 In *Literary Women* (Garden City, New York: Doubleday, 1976), Ellen Moers describes "performing heroism" as a "compelling female fantasy" (p. 143) based at least partly on the unavailability of the experience in "real life," the experience that Mme. de Staël showed to Jane Austen's generation and George Sand to George Eliot's, the "myth of the famous woman talking, writing, performing to the applause of the world" (p. 176).

Far more than music or novel writing, acting is a display of that "exhibitionism" that her latest biographer, Ruby Redinger, says Marian Evans feared only slightly more than she desired; it licenses, not through the safe medium of books or instruments but through the instrument of one's very person, the display of all those conflicting passions and deeds that jostle together in what Stevenson's Jekyll understood to be "the polity of the self." And one of those deeds, Eliot unmistakably knows, is murder. At the peak of her career, we know from Sir Hugo Mallinger and from her own words, Alcharisi was almost pure amoral dynamism, like Stevenson's Edward Hyde. And we learn too that her genius not only leaves room for resistance, or enjoins it when necessary like Mordecai's and Klesmer's—her genius is virtually *made* of resistance, to everything but the entirely self-created. For bad as it is to be poor and obscure like Mordecai and Klesmer and to have to fight like them to get a hearing for one's genius, it is far worse, "unimaginable" to us, says Alcharisi, to "have a man's force of genius in you, and yet to suffer the slavery of being a girl" (p. 694).

In Gwendolen Harleth, the narrative has shown what it is to have no formal genius and yet to chafe against that slavery: the two women whom Daniel must abandon in his own great act of resistance are linked in the book called "The Mother and the Son" because the spirit of opposition has become demonic in both. Pursued by furies of hatred, Gwendolen ends the book with her near murder of Grandcourt. Yielding, momentarily, to the painful clutch of her father's Dead Hand, Alcharisi opens the book by allowing Daniel to come to her for his heritage, the documents of his grandfather's vision. "Shadows are rising around me. . . . I cannot go into the darkness without satisfying him" (pp. 691, 689), she groans, still in resistance, like the superb Gothic antihero she is. More than Savonarola, more even than Mordecai, George Eliot's female genius is the great Gothic separated one, terrible in her isolation—"I did not

228

want affection. . . . I wanted to live out the life that was in me and not to be hampered with other lives. . . . I did not want a child" (pp. 688-689)—yet crucially instructive, for "her errors lay along high pathways" (p. 695). More than Savonarola or Mordecai she gives us a sense of the true immensity and mystery of the moral universe. For where their visions of the profound and irresistible sweep of the human community towards brotherhood and justice make majesty in the midst of quotidian materiality, her counter-vision of the kingdom of the self lends the crucial dynamic to the mystery of the good and evil. The meeting of mother and son, says Eliot, is "something like a greeting between royalties" (p. 687): when Alcharisi is fully herself, "I have a right to resist" she says (p. 699), and yet in the presence of Daniel Charisi Deronda "some other right forces itself upon me like iron in an inexorable hand, and . . . is beginning to make ghosts in the daylight" (p. 699).

Alcharisi is there, like Manfred and Schedoni and Melmoth, like Frankenstein and Jekyll, to testify to that mysterious battle of royal rights. As with those other Gothic men of sorrows, "my nature gave me a charter" (p. 728), she affirms. And Daniel, like Frankenstein's child, and Manfred's and Melmoth's, must acknowledge what he sees plainly before him, "an expression of living force" (p. 729) finally uncontradictable.

And yet, in the transformations of Gothic themes wrought by novelists of the great traditions, as in classic Gothic itself, the figure self-chartered to live "a myriad of lives" in resistance to mortal seasons and the harvest of death must be, if not exactly contradicted, at least left behind. Daniel has his own charter, which makes him, in cruel paradox, adamant in opposition to her solipsism, as she must resist his mystic communion. He must be adamant in opposition to her amoral, almost inhuman power of spiritually distant "representation" of all emotions, as she must resist to the death that real emotion, love or hatred, that is "subjection"

(p. 730). In loving subjection to his vision. Daniel ends the novel putting hand to his work. And in the fierce but sterile freedom of her countervision his mother lets him go, in her exhaustion, in her Gothic rigidity and repetition, even in what Eliot calls her human "privation," still no less royal a figure than he.

FIVE

D. H. LAWRENCE: GHOSTS
IN THE DAYLIGHT

AUSTEN holds us to the fruits of our anxiety, George Eliot to the promise of our fear and dread. For the modernists, whose conquering travels over the globe and through the newly-mapped thickets of mind-science and time-science have killed off numerous poets and immeasurably toughened the rest, the conditions of vision are nothing so tame. "The horror! the horror!" cries Conrad's separated Kurtz when he reenters his old community at the end of his curve out and back through the Heart of Darkness, and Marlow, with the grim satisfaction of the artist, the stoic minimalism of the mariner, applauds: "Kurtz was a remarkable man. He had something to say. He said it." "I will show you fear in a handful of dust," says the first voice in T. S. Eliot's Wasteland, and shows and tells the horror with clarity and power. But then, almost immediately, "looking into the heart of light" after a surprise moment of connection and tenderness with the Hyacinth Girl—"I could not speak." And, as the world of the Wasteland "cracks and reforms and bursts in the violet air" of its apocalypse, that same voice records as one of the signs of the end that "bats with baby faces in the violet light/ Whistled and beat their wings/ And crawled head downward down a blackened wall," while Joyce's Stephen Dedalus, another classic modernist observer overwhelmed by the same image, briefly unlocks his clenched poetic will to write a fragment of a poem on a scrap by the sea: "He comes, pale vampire, through storm, his eyes, his bat sails bloodying the sea, mouth to her mouth's kiss."

The vampires are coming, Roused by the Western imperialist's invasion of ancient and barren lands, tempted by the fatness fed by the markets of the world, Dracula has come. And in the same year, 1897, the Martians of H. G. Wells's tricky fable, *The War of the Worlds*, turn their telescopes coldly upon England "as we view the infusoria under our microscopes" and invade her from their ancient and now barren land, seeking, like Dracula, that blood which is "the life." Under the special pressures of late Victorian anxieties about colonial counterattacks and fueled by the secret nightmare of Darwinism—reversion of man to beast, of science to magic, of future to past—the Gothic has mutated a companion form, as it had at the beginning of the century, one that calls not for the half-fascinating and creatively cathartic response of "terror" but for the almost wholly alienating response of "horror." The difference was never so clearly seen between the terror-Gothic of Mrs. Radcliffe and Maturin and the horror-Gothic of Beckford and Monk Lewis as it is between the fertile terrors of Dracula's deadly kiss and the screaming, finally numbing horrors of the Martians' meals, "injecting blood" by means of "a little pipette" directly from the veins of the still living animal, man, and bypassing all such messy transforming processes as digestion. The Martians had no entrails, and neither, says Conrad's station manager at the entrance to the Heart of Darkness, does he, fortunately. For men with entrails catch diseases and die of their exposure to their own crimes up the river. The mortally sick Kurtz, who went upriver on a journey of conversion, has become pure conversion, pure digestion: at their first meeting toward the end of the story, Marlow "saw him opening his mouth wide—it gave him a weirdly voracious aspect, as though he had wanted to swallow all the air, all the earth, all the men before him."

Both the victim and the image of the horror he has seen, Kurtz is an object of terror to Marlow. Both the victim and the image of the death who "claimed her, mouth to mouth's kiss," Stephen Dedalus's mother is an object of terror to her son. When in the darkening parlor of Kurtz's Intended,

Marlow adds to the darkness but postpones the final black-out by substituting a word of love for "the horror" as Kurtz's last word, when in the garishly gloomy parlor of the brothel Stephen smashes the lamp by which he is seeing fully at last his mother beastly dead and cries shortly after, "damn death, long live life," they are casting their lot with life, via the saving lie, the fiction of transcendence. But although Marlow and Stephen depend upon the saving lie, Conrad and Joyce do not—at least not entirely. For they are artists substantially (not, of course, perfectly) removed from their fictions, and their complicity is hidden, their desperation displaced. They are not *there*. They have, rhetorically speaking, only seen someone who saw the horror, the vampire, King Death.

But there is one great modernist artist who was there, and who saw, and whom we see seeing—frantic, unremoved, deeply complicit D. H. Lawrence.[1] Embedded in

[1] I am using Lawrence in this essay as the "modernist" artist who is closest to the subtle, yet comparatively unprotected, unironic return to Gothic energies I have been studying all along. Yet the question of his proper "placement" in literary history, or even the history of ideas, is a rather more difficult one than I have space to treat. I am using Leavis's argument that Lawrence connects back through Eliot and Austen to Richardson and the specifically English line of "serious" novelists. Julian Moynihan seems to agree that Lawrence's greatness arises partly from ambitions that go back to Richardson, but ends his book, *The Deed of Life* (Princeton, N.J.: Princeton Univ. Press, 1963), claiming that "if Lawrence is to be assigned with one particular tradition in the novel it must be the tradition of those nineteenth-century artists like Tolstoi, Melville, Dostoevsky, Proust . . . who offer themselves to us simultaneously as leaders and as scapegoats" (p. 225). Graham Hough (*The Dark Sun* [New York: Farrar, Straus, and Giroux, 1973]) throws up his hands at the question: "Just where does he belong? Not perhaps with the great European figures. . . . He is too idiosyncratic. . . . But he certainly does not belong either with his nearest English contemporaries, altogether more local, and restricted—Virginia Woolf and E. M. Forster—nor with his immediate seniors—Bennett, Galsworthy and Wells. . . . He breaks with the mainly sociological tradition of the English novel and does nothing whatever to advance the more rigorous aesthetic definition of the novel's outline that we asso-

the old-fashioned rhetoric, like Austen and Eliot a first-person commentator in his world and, like them, a complicit maker not only of a criticism of his world but of its fiction of transcendence, Lawrence feels, shows, and communicates the more dangerous emotions, seeks for the more dangerous responses. In Lawrence we find dramatized not just guilty terror but alienating horror at the mechanical twitching corpse of civilization and the vampire preying of person upon person, not just dread but bitter loathing of the dreary cycle of dominance and subjugation, of sensual rot and ghostly mental tumescence that the species of man has chosen for its fate and imparted like a blight to the life around him.[2]

---

ciate with Henry James" (p. 3). Although I hope to show some connections between the idiosyncratic Lawrence and Wells, Forster, and James, I maintain along with Leavis and Raymond Williams that the real clue to his place is in that "sociological" tradition of the English novel, sociological not in the scientific sense, a neutral study of "groups," but in the visionary, quasi-theological sense, an engaged and desperate study of organic bodies, communities.

[2] Critics and readers have from the start recognized this loathing in Lawrence, and they have recognized that it exists not safely tucked away in his characterizations but in the voice and sentiments of the author himself—a place where the great theoreticians of the art of the novel say contempt and loathing may *not* come. Flaubert and Joyce argue from aesthetic principles, Fielding and Meredith argue from moral principles, and Lawrence pays the price for this heresy in the outraged response of a reader like James Douglas, whose review of *The Rainbow* argued that "a book of this kind has no right to exist. It is a deliberate denial of the soul that leavens matter . . . [life] is not the thing that creeps and crawls in this novel" (22 October 1915, in *The Star*; reprinted in *D. H. Lawrence: The Critical Heritage*, ed. R. P. Draper [London: Routledge and Kegan Paul, 1970], p. 93). He also pays in the cooler assessments of critics whose tributes to Lawrence so often take the form of rescuing some fragment of truth and beauty from the admitted "failure" he is according to orthodox canons. Dorothy Van Ghent, for instance, admires the steadfast "otherness" Lawrence grants to the people, objects, and natural entities in his world and his depiction of the "creative relationship between people and between people and things so long as this 'otherness' is ac-

Gothic Overview

The automaton, the vampire, and the ghost are to Lawrence in his rage and fear and wisdom the very image of individual action and personal relationship. With these two values now reclaimed by the Gothic and made horrible, the whole human enterprise for Lawrence trembles at a massive crisis of confidence. That enterprise, small, hot, and "frictive," generates a vision of and a longing for its opposite, still, cool, and huge—a silvery state of "equanimity" for Joyce, of "star-balance" for Lawrence, a valley of white sand where the dry bones "sang, scattered and shining . . . under a tree in the cool of the day" for Eliot. Of course, only those who *have* personality, individuality, and emotion know what it means to want to escape from these things, Eliot adds in "Tradition and the Individual Talent." And Lawrence, having personality and emotion and the desire to escape, embodies this action throughout his works in a stunning series of tableaux that partake intimately of Gothic image and impulse and that offer, as T. S. Eliot's later work does, two routes for the escape—the stars and Sunday—whereas Joyce's work offers only one— the stars. (Both Lawrence's and Joyce's work are to some extent the battleground of one of this century's more significant art-inspired debates about life, the debate between Leavis and Eliot. Of this more in my conclusion.)

One such tableau occurs in *The Rainbow* in the chapter sorrowfully, not ironically, entitled "First Love." At the

knowledged," but she must first testify to the "disappointment and even perhaps shock" that "we" are bound to feel over Lawrence's "unrestrained emotionalism over glandular matters" and his " 'loose' and repetitious writing" (*The English Novel: Form and Function* [New York: Rhinehart and Co., 1953], p. 245). In a broadcast of April 1960 reprinted in the *Critical Heritage* (p. 344), E. M. Forster scolds, "The quaint quartet in *Women in Love*—have you ever met young men and women like that? And one of them is supposed to be on the Board of Education!" "Yet," he adds, rescuing, "do they not keep signalling to you, despite their arguments and adventures?"

end of the first vampire-meeting with Anton Skrebensky, where the man "sought for her mouth with his mouth . . . like putting his face into some awful death" and found himself forestalled by the victim-mouth, "seething like some corrosive salt around the last substance of his being, destroying him, destroying him in the kiss," Ursula Brangwen is "overcome with slow horror" at the demonism of the personal, the everlasting ignoble and finally futile struggle for the available quantum of human being, of "dark blood."[3] For after "she had broken him" by holding onto her own will, she had mated with his nothingness and become, of course, nothingness herself: "His heart was hollow. . . . but her soul was empty and finished" (p. 321). At this impasse Ursula looks away from the personal and the human to see, to long for, and to identify with "the delicate glint of oats dangling from the side of the stack, in the moonlight, something proud and royal, and quite impersonal." But almost immediately the meeting of star and life becomes hot and frictive again, the cool identification with oats in the moonlight becomes a stretching out of her arms to the "blind debonair presence of the night . . . a magnificent godly moon white and candid as a bridegroom" (p. 322), a hierogamous marriage, inhuman but certainly not impersonal. A Sunday morning follows, full of mysterious intensity and anticipation as Sunday so often is in Lawrence. But the grandeur and serenity of the myth embodied there, the untroubled quiddity of the god who holds up his end of mortality's rainbow not needing the validation of "the Ursula Brangwen who felt troubled about God," is spoiled for her by the comedy of the self-important Noah of the sermon. Ursula, irritated, flees in her imagination to the inhuman, once again, however, not quite achieving the impersonal:

[3] Quotations from *The Rainbow* (1915) are taken from the Viking Compass Edition (New York: Viking Press, Inc., 1961). This description occurs on p. 320. Subsequent references are to this edition and will be cited by page number in the text.

"Ursula wished she had been a nymph. She would have laughed through the window of the ark and flicked drops of the flood at Noah, before she drifted away to people who were less important in their Proprietor and their Flood. . . . Whatever God was, He was" (p. 324).

A similar action occurs in *Women in Love*, an action less sensuous, more verbal, as is the novel itself. Deeply ill at the core after a vampire battle of wills with his lover Hermione has nearly resulted in his murder, Rupert Birkin rows Ursula to an island in Willey Water where, surrounded by and lapsed into the stillness and coolness, they openly reveal to each other their discontents, "rousing each other to a fine passion of opposition." Birkin's hatred of the ordinary courses of life, his frustration at his own vampire insistency and his own ghostly mentality, explode in a whirl of metaphors: humanity is "dry-rotten . . . balls of bitter dust . . . a dead tree, covered with fine brilliant galls of people . . . a huge aggregate lie . . . a ghastly, heavy crop of Dead Sea fruit . . . myriad simulacra of people . . . one of the mistakes of creation . . . an anti-creation, like monkeys and baboons." And Ursula, whose resistance to Birkin's self-indulgent horrors—"too picturesque and final"— is one of the fine things in the book and the ultimate evidence, I believe, for Lawrence's good faith, speaks passionately for the richness and beauty of humanity when it loves. But even Ursula is shaken into acquiescence, even "exultation," when Birkin, in a voice of "pleasant sincerity," tempts her with the vision his loathing makes him desire: "You yourself, don't you find it a beautiful clean thought, a world empty of people, just uninterrupted grass, and a hare sitting up?" For a moment Ursula pauses over the vision, "a clean, lovely, humanless world. It was the *really* desirable." But she, one of the "daughters of men," sees it for a "phantasy," whatever its lure, while he, one of the "sons of God," wants it for his own, however fantastical.[4]

[4] Quotations from *Women in Love* (1920) are taken from the Viking

D. H. LAWRENCE: GHOSTS IN THE DAYLIGHT

In this opposition, the veil of consciousness "torn" momentarily, they reach not only humanlessness but impersonality, "like two impersonal forces, there in contact" (p. 124); and the foundation is established for Lawrence's version of the modernist quest—"a final me which is stark and impersonal and beyond responsibility. And it is there I would want to meet you—not in the emotional loving plane—but there beyond . . . [as] two utterly strange creatures [in] an equilibrium, a pure balance of two single beings:—as the stars balance each other" (pp. 137, 139).

Ursula's famous taunt at this point—"why drag in the stars?"— is her recognition that behind Birkin's "far-fetched" analogies and propositions, behind his Gothic (one must say) vision of a world of inhuman forces and deadly simulacra, is a theology.[5] But theology for her connects the stars not with Sunday but with the Sunday-school teacher, that pompous and stiff-necked absurdity who thinks he has a "relationship" with the Proprietor of the universe, who parlays what Lawrence elsewhere calls "this special kind of religious cheek . . . backed up by the Apocalypse"[6] into pure self-glorification. As Birkin struggles to articulate his "beyond," his "something else," his "we can go one

Compass Edition (New York: Viking Press, Inc., 1960). This incident occurs on pp. 118-119. Subsequent references are to this edition and will be cited by page number in the text.

[5] Graham Hough turned to his important book-length study of Lawrence, *The Dark Sun*, after exploring "the many attempts in the last hundred years to find satisfaction for the religious impulse outside Christianity," and only then did he gradually come to feel "that the only recent English writer besides Yeats to break into new spiritual territory outside the Christian boundaries was D. H. Lawrence" (p. vii). Hough's book, however, concludes with the argument that Lawrence in fact circled back to Christian boundaries in exactly the way a heretic does, his preoccupation with the modes of living and the terms of theological being he was leaving having become "so intense that he is able to orientate himself only by taking bearings on the Christian position he has abandoned" (p. 253).

[6] *Apocalypse* (1931; reprint ed., Harmondsworth, Middlesex: Penguin Books, 1976), p. 10.

better," he undergoes "this ridiculous, mean effacement into a Salvator Mundi and a Sunday-school teacher, a prig of the stiffest type" (p. 122). Birkin loathes this effacement too. And after the "Water Party" during which Diana Crich dragged her rescuing lover to their mutual death (can Lawrence have had Grandcourt and Gwendolen in mind here?) under a cold bright "impertinent" Saturday/Sunday moon like the one that shone on the unmanning of Anton Skrebensky, Birkin surrenders fully to a suddenly aggressive Ursula, fearing that in resisting her he "was becoming quite dead-alive, nothing but a word-bag" (p. 180). "Satisfied and shattered, fulfilled and destroyed," he settles into simple sensuous being, but "the other self" that "whimpered . . . not this, not this" (p. 179) still hovers, protecting the core of his desire for "another thing." Thus, as it was in *The Rainbow*, Ursula's Sunday morning is a discovery that passion's victory is nothingness, nullity, despair. For both the man and the woman, the least abstract, most sensuous, and only "other" thing than life in its modern contravened empty sense is death; in succeeding chapters first Ursula and then Birkin falls deeply ill, body counterpointing the soul's desire to see that world washed clean of humanity, "beyond our sullying," beyond even the power of science and progress to "nullify" the "great dark, illimitable kingdom of death" (p. 185).

This Saturday/Sunday movement from the world's dead-alive state to the kingdom of death strives for its completion in resurrection. But Lawrence's resurrections, his new creations, partake as they must of "phantasy" and, more disturbingly perhaps, of that fantasy which has already accomplished itself in the master myth of the Western world, the extreme forms of which, I have been arguing, are embedded in the Gothic. Partly for this reason, Lawrence bestows on each of his "resurrection" figures—from the Noah who returns from the waters to claim the rainbow's promise to the Quetzalcoatl who emerges from the lake to replace the saints in *The Plumed Serpent*'s village church—a woman, a nymph, an Ursula, a Kate, to flick the drops of the flood in his face and remind him that he is not, in fact, simply alone with the Proprietor of the universe. Only in the poetry and some of the prose essays does the full modernist epic-sweep and risk of Lawrence's resurrection theology come through. The Sunday-school teacher speaks in the desperate gaiety of "Books" (1924): "Now we've got the sulks, and are waiting for the flood to come and wash out our world and our civilization. All right, let it come. But somebody's got to be ready with Noah's Ark. We imagine, for example, that if there came a terrible crash and terrible bloodshed over Europe, then out of the crash and bloodshed a remnant of regenerated souls would inevitably arise. We are mistaken. . . . Catastrophe alone never helped man."[7] The cheeky chapel man speaks in the prophetic fire of "Resurrection": "The War was the Calvary of all real Christian men. . . . Christ has re-entered into the Father, and the pillar of flame shoots up, anew, from the nadir to the zenith. The world and the cosmos stagger to a new axle" (*Phoenix*, p. 738). In "New Heaven and New Earth," the poet speaks of the "maniacal horror" of self-absorption and self-consumption in the modern world, of the clean reducing "suffering of death," followed by a resurrection built on the discovery, finally, by touch in the tomb, that there is oneself and also the not-self, the not-nothing that is not the self:

> I, in the sour black tomb, trodden to absolute death
> I put out my hand in the night, one night, and my hand
> Touched that which was verily not me . . .
> Ha! I was a blaze leaping up!
>
> (Stanza 6)

And the critic, wrestler with ghosts, speaks everywhere, but

---

[7] Printed in *Phoenix: The Posthumous Papers of D. H. Lawrence*, ed. Edward McDonald (1936; reprint ed., New York: Viking Press, Inc., 1972), p. 733. Subsequent references are to this edition and hereafter will be cited in the text as *Phoenix*.

above all in *Studies in Classic American Literature,* where the evil resurrection and the good, the vampire/ghoul and the true spirit of place, the Holy Ghost, find powerful expression. "For it is true," he says in the essay on Poe, "that a spirit can persist in the afterdeath. Persist by its own volition. But usually the evil persistence of a thwarted will, returning for vengeance of life. Lemures, vampires."[8]

Vampire resurrections, "ghastly" visitations, occur for Lawrence when the personal will to love (or to hate) pushes one's being over its body's borders, even past the borders of the kingdom of death, towards the world, or another, in the striving to merge, unify, dominate, subsume otherness with oneself, or oneself with otherness. "This is the root of all evil in us," Lawrence judges; "We ought to pray to be resisted, and resisted to the bitter end" (*Studies,* p. 341). The ecstatic recognition of the new world occurs in the death of "craving," when, reaching out, one encounters and accepts "resistance," a presence—specifically, "the flank of my wife" ("New Heaven and New Earth," stanza 7). In that terrifying encounter with a full-bodied unknown— terror bringing the fruitfulness of dread rather than horror bringing the sterility of loathing—the crucial experience is not the discovery of the vulnerable self, nor even of the "unknown unknown." The crucial experience, the holy experience, is the recognition and admission of the space between, a live space, a breathing space, but an absolutely impersonal uninhabited space where resistance, balance, and above all "body" (in the curious ghostly Pentecostal sense that Lawrence means body) are made possible. For clearly for Lawrence, the body is the missing holy part of man, the ghostly presence always at hazard before the mind and the will. Between the wings of opposing desires, the body of the

8 Essays from D. H. Lawrence's *Studies in Classic American Literature,* reprinted in *D. H. Lawrence: Selected Literary Criticism,* ed. Anthony Beal (New York: Viking Press, Inc., 1966), p. 340. Subsequent references are to this edition and hereafter will be cited in the text as *Studies.*

bird Quetzalcoatl takes the shape of stability in *The Plumed Serpent*, between the trodden dead past that is memory and the vision of the new world that is desire rises the Holy Ghost, "It," the spirit of place in all of the places that fascinate Lawrence: the English midlands, Italy, Austria, and above all, America. The between—which for T. S. Eliot was an evilly haunted way station to the beyond, where the shadow falls between the idea and the reality, the motion and the act, the emotion and the response—the between is for Lawrence the great good place.[9] In that extended lyric to the between, *The Plumed Serpent*, "the dark middle," "the uncreated centre" that Kate Leslie sees over and over in the black eyes of the Indians is the space made for the morning star that rises "fearless between the sun and the night."[10] It is the space "between the flood and the great sky . . . between the vast universe of blood and the universe of breath" (p. 458) for the powerful heart that beats "between the bluish ribs" of the mountains (p. 119), for the new man "perfectly suspended between the world's two strenuous wings of energy" (p. 99), for the "poignant intermediate flashing its quiet between the energies of the cosmos" (p. 104).

Lawrence's heroines are equally "bored" with the beyond

[9] Leavis, the tradition's great defender of Lawrence and Lawrence's look upon life, argues that it was exactly Eliot's lack of faith in the possibility of new creations by, for, or between men ("I have heard the key turn in the door once and turn once only," he quotes from *The Wasteland*, as evidence of Eliot's solipsism) that accounts for his fear of the "between." Lawrence, on the other hand, looks mystically to every pause in time, every lapse in consciousness, every emptiness in space, not as a void nothing but as a fertile "uncreated," that is, not yet created, opportunity. "Uncreated" is thus, as Leavis sees, "a quasi-technical [I would add, theological] Lawrentian term" (*Thought, Words and Creativity: Art and Thought in Lawrence* [London: Chatto and Windus, 1976], pp. 29, 67).

[10] Quotations from *The Plumed Serpent* (1926) are taken from the Vintage Edition (New York: Vintage Books, 1959). This phrase occurs on p. 136. Subsequent references are to this edition and will be cited by page number in the text.

and the within, those two mythic dimensions that are the classic locus, respectively, of eighteenth- and nineteenth-century Gothic, respectively of the tyrannical Father and the suffering sibling self. Lawrence seeks a third mythic dimension, the "impersonal," "unhuman," "unknown" between, which is defined, naturally if paradoxically, by the presence of two deeply known persons or two deeply human ideas. His vision, an orthodoxy after all, charts the death of the age of the Father's reason (or "Law" as he calls it in "The Spinner and the Monks" chapter of *Twilight in Italy*), the dying of the age of the Son's suffering clenched will, and announces, explicitly through the Gothic figures of the automaton, the vampire, and the ghost or ghoul, the coming of the age of the Holy Ghost. George Eliot's dying aristocrat artist Alcharisi dreaded and fought the right that overruled her personal will to make her the impersonal link between her father and her son, the right that made "ghosts in the daylight" active interventions in life, not just passive visitations in the dream or the artwork. Lawrence would welcome that right, establish that ghost.

Lawrence was an artist deeply interested in the "Gothic" in several of its senses: architectural, literary, philosophic. The "timeless gloom" of Gothic churches fascinated him, their spirit of place, the placedness of the Spirit there, whether in his own Lincoln Cathedral or the Church of San Tommaso whose mystery is whimsically penetrated at last in the opening chapter of *Twilight in Italy*, or in the twin-pagoda-towered church of Sayula that in *The Plumed Serpent* escapes the fate of Mexico's churches to be made into schools and movie houses and army barracks and becomes instead, its high windows darkened, its soaring pillars painted like trees, its huge images burned and its new Trinity installed, the church of the returned old gods. All these churches are to Lawrence, in the more literary sense I have outlined earlier, the prime Gothic setting—the ruined house of power, its great idea still evident, still poignant, still capable of infusing terror and awe, but broken, the life ebbing and twitching in a way he will call over and over, in a word out of the Gothic vocabulary he will make peculiarly his own, "ghastly," the way of half-life. But, more than the sense of tyrannous enclosure, more even than the sense of greatness decayed, the Gothic church is, for this mystic philosopher of the between, the place of the arch.

For *The Rainbow*'s Will Brangwen, the sight of the cathedral arch is perfect fulfillment: Lawrence at the chrysalis stage of his affair with "the Church" is clearly figured in Will's passionate lyric to that shape:

> Here the stone leapt up from the plain of earth, leapt up in a manifold, clustered desire each time, up, away from the horizontal earth, through twilight and dusk and the whole range of desire, through the swerving, the declination, ah, to the ecstasy, the touch, to the meeting and the consummation, the meeting, the clasp, the close embrace, the neutrality, the perfect, swooning consummation, the timeless ecstasy. There his soul remained, at the apex of the arch, clinched in the timeless ecstasy, consummated.
>
> And there was no time nor life nor death, but only this, this timeless consummation, where the thrust from earth met the thrust from earth and the arch was locked on the keystone of ecstasy. This was all, this was everything. Till he came to himself in the world below. Then again he gathered himself together, in transit, every jet of him strained and leaped, leaped clear into the darkness above, to the fecundity and the unique mystery, to the touch, the clasp, the consummation, the climax of eternity, the apex of the arch. (P. 199)

But in Anna Brangwen the cathedral arch, "obsolete . . . confined . . . barren," awakes a "fear and joy" that she "mistrusts." She claims, like George Eliot's Alcharisi, "another right . . . the right to freedom above her, higher than the roof" (p. 200). Lawrence's nay-saying woman, mistrusting the roofed-in consummations and fulfillments of man, charts a larger freer movement for herself. But interestingly, that movement still has the shape of an arch, and the keystone of ecstasy is still at the apex of stillness, of suspension, at the place between:

> She wanted to get out of this fixed, leaping, forward-travelling movement, to rise from it as a bird rises with wet, limp feet from the sea, to lift herself as a bird lifts its breast and thrusts its body from the pulse and heave of a sea that bears it forward to an unwilling conclusion, tear herself away like a bird on wings, and in open space where there is clarity, rise up above the fixed surcharged motion, a separate speck that hangs suspended, moves this way and that, seeing and answering before it sinks again, having chosen or found the direction in which it shall be carried forward. (Pp. 200-201)[11]

At the place of the swerve, as in Trinitarian theology, as in Lucretian physics, arises the Holy Ghost, the creative spirit, holding the waters separate from the heavens, bridging the motion that is choice and the motion that is fate, giving both dimension and direction, as we shall see, to the separated union of lover and lover.

It is this idea that draws Lawrence to literary Gothic too, to the Hardy in whose novels "the condemnation shifts over at last from the dark villain to the white virgin," to the Dostoevsky whose Grand Inquisitor spoke from a "thinking mind in rebellion" of the dreadful need of man for "miracle, mystery, authority,"[12] above all to the fully Gothic Poe, whose "love stories" are "ghastly stories of the

11 Like many readers of this scene, Julian Moynihan takes the quarrel inside the cathedral to be one of roof against sky, closed system against open trajectory, an argument that Anna wins, forgetting that Anna's vision of a roofless movement still shapes into an arch, with the "carrying forward" occurring just before "it sinks again" (*The Deed of Life*, pp. 53 ff.).

12 Both the *Study of Thomas Hardy* and Lawrence's "Introduction" to *The Grand Inquisitor* are reprinted in *Phoenix*: these references are, respectively, to p. 437 and pp. 283-284.

human soul in its disruptive throes" (*Studies*, p. 330). In each of these writers Lawrence discerns a soul struggling with a truth it hates and wishes to call a weakness in man, a flaw in the universe. For Hardy it is the existence of that immense morality, "what we call the immorality of nature" (*Phoenix*, p. 419), whose axle is the purposes of life, not the purposes of man. For Dostoevsky it is that "the great mass of man *cannot* distinguish between money and life" (*Phoenix*, p. 286). For Poe it is that love is as destructive as hate, and that perfect love (or hate), seeking to possess utterly its object, results in "the dissolution of both souls, each losing itself in transgressing its own bounds" (*Studies*, p. 344). Of Hardy's dreadful discovery, Lawrence writes, "the morality of life, the greater morality, is eternally unalterable and invincible. It can be dodged for some time, but not opposed" (*Phoenix*, p. 420). Of Dostoevsky's, he writes, having reread *The Brothers Karamazov*, "At first it had been lurid romance . . . a display of cynical-satanical pose . . . showing off in blasphemy. Now . . . it is a deadly, devastating summing up, unanswerable, because borne out by the long experience of humanity" (*Phoenix*, p. 283). Of Poe's, he writes simply, "It is lurid and melodramatic, but it is true" (*Studies*, p. 344).

All these truths being both "ghastly" and true, Lawrence asks rather modestly, "Must we therefore go over to the devil?" (*Phoenix*, p. 286). It is the ultimate question for Gothic heroes and their creators. Up against the limitations of their humanity, Manfred and Melmoth, Frankenstein, Dracula, and the Monk Ambrosio go over to the devil. The consequences of crossing the boundary are pure Gothic, the orthodox sublime—that is, lurid and melodramatic and subject to rigorous *natural* (even if played out as supernatural) punishment. What Austen, Eliot, and above all, Lawrence, bring from the Gothic into their novels is this loyalty to what is true, however lurid and melodramatic, however visionary and impractical, however painful and "undeserved" in that ambiguous Austen sense, it may be.

What they attempt to mitigate for their characters is the orthodoxy of *punishment* for living within sight of the truths, dark or bright, of the sublime. Their heresy is a swerve away from the satisfied capitulation to the canons of punishing "realism," whether levelled by Shelley, Stoker, Stevenson et al. according to the self-destruction convention of classic Gothic, or by the spokesmen of communal morality, the Mrs. Eltons, the Mrs. Cadwalladers, and the Mr. Crichs, or by the modern realistic novelists. Lawrence hated the "resignation" that "seems like an acceptance" of Arnold Bennett,[13] the "hesitating between life and public opinion" (*Phoenix*, p. 440) in the Wessex novels, Hemingway's state of "*conscious*, accepted indifference to everything except freedom from work and the moment's interest."[14] And he wrote to a friend after reading *Under Western Eyes* that he "could not forgive Conrad for being so sad and for giving in."[15]

Refusing to give in, Lawrence offers instead a full-scale vision of the sublime, the first in English letters since Shelley and the first in English fiction since Radcliffe, Shelley, and Maturin. It is based, as he says, on the anti-Shelleyan insistence that the skylark (phoenix) is a bird, and man, man; and that both creatures derive their completion of being not from transcending their limits or changing their shapes but from filling (or flying) those shapes so intensely that they may feel the boundaries of their being by the resistance, the unpenetrated balance, between the self and the not-self.[16]

[13] Lawrence's remarks about Bennett occur in a letter to A. D. McLeod of 6 October 1912. See Harry T. Moore, ed., *The Collected Letters of D. H. Lawrence*, 2 vols. (London: William Heinemann Ltd., 1962), 1:150.

[14] Lawrence's review of Hemingway's *In Our Time* is reprinted in *Phoenix*; the remark occurs on p. 366.

[15] The comment on Conrad occurs in a letter to Edward Garnett of 30 October 1912. See *Collected Letters*, 1:152.

[16] In that astonishing and chaotic piece of criticism called *Study of Thomas Hardy*, whose principal theme is "the final aim of every living

D. H. LAWRENCE: GHOSTS IN THE DAYLIGHT

As a practitioner of the sublime, with excursions here and there (mostly botannical) into the beautiful, Lawrence is also deeply involved with the Gothic philosophically, as Burke and Ruskin defined this mode—concerned with the rugged, the jagged, the animated, the paradoxical and swiftly changing, the "obscure" in prose and in thought. Ardent and theoretic, like George Eliot's seekers, Lawrence too will risk the descent to the ridiculous inherent in the reach for the sublime theoretic: the combination may be, strictly speaking, impossible, like a plumed serpent, or at best temporary, like a star-balance before it degenerates into a star-satellite-balance. This philosophic ambition is especially evident in the three Gothic figures that form the special object of study in this essay: the ghastly (the ghoul as it expresses itself on the personal level), the vampiric-demonic (or marriage, when it attempts to elude the impersonal), and the spirit of place or placement (Lawrence's Holy Ghost).

---

thing, creature, or being is the full achievement of itself" (p. 403), Lawrence, not really digressing, challenges Shelley, that "transcendently male" poet, "Who would wish that the skylark were not a bird, but a spirit?" (p. 459). For Lawrence, Shelley was crippled by the absence of a quality apparently somehow female, that permits a soul to "belong to life"; the "pure male" on the other hand is "almost an abstraction." Lawrence has himself often been called a Shelley, interestingly, by critics who think it is his very abstractness that makes him not only an angel, in Lawrence's own terms ("But it were impious to wish to be like the angels"), but also ineffectual. In his April 1960 broadcast, Forster says that "Lawrence was a rougher, tougher propostion than Shelley . . . and though he did beat his wings against society in vain, he was ineffectual as a bird of prey rather than as an angel" (*Critical Heritage*, p. 344), and Louis Untermeyer argues that "it is the effort to find the self beyond selfhood that makes Lawrence seem another ineffectual angel beating his bruised wings; a darker Shelley of the senses. Sex storms about him. The lightning energizes, the rainbow arches to heal him. But he is not part of them" (review in *The New Republic*, 11 August 1920; reprinted in *Critical Heritage*, p. 135).

Flesh-Eaters: The Ghoul

Lawrence's first "work" was as a seventeen-year-old clerk in a factory in Nottingham that made, among other things, artificial limbs, surgical devices, and stockings. And though he had not the sort of imagination that could make direct Frankensteinian capital of the undoubtedly bizarre sights of that factory, the connection of work with automatism, the vision of a world of half-mechanical humans, pervades his writing. In *Sons and Lovers*, when Paul Morel sees the surgical limb on the notepaper of the man who hires him, he is deeply alarmed; he "dreaded" the business world and thought it "monstrous . . . that a business could be run on wooden legs."[17] Maturin had pictured the conventual world on which much classic Gothic was based as a place where old ritual had so eaten into the living mind that the voices and bodies of men and women took on the mechanical sound and movement of the bells and organs that guided their prayer. A few years later, Carlyle praised the same life in *Past and Present* for allowing a living and, in an almost Lawrentian sense, an impersonal dimension to communal life. In the chapter sarcastically entitled "Happy," he offered a wonderfully sarcastic automaton of the personal as *his* bogeyman: "Ever at a certain hour, with preternatural gnarring, growling and scratching, which attended as a running bass, there began, in a horrible, semi-articulate, unearthly voice, this song: 'Once I was hap-hap-happy, but now I'm *mees*-erable! Clack-clack-clack, gnar-r-r, whuz-z: Once I was hap-hap-happy, but now I'm *mees*-erable!'— Rest, rest, perturbed spirit!" But for Lawrence, Carlyle's solution is the oldest automatism of all: "Oh, my God, work is the great body of life, and sleep and amusement, like two wings, bent only to carry it along. Is this, then, all?

[17] Quotations from *Sons and Lovers* (1913) are taken from the Viking Compass Edition (New York: Viking Press, Inc., 1958). This phrase occurs on p. 92. Subsequent references are to this edition and will be cited by page numbers in the text.

And Carlyle gets up and says, It is all, and mankind goes on in grim, serious approval. . . . what a ghastly programme!" (*Phoenix,* p. 422).

For Lawrence, the work-is-life ethic is the very source of the ghastly, a haunting from the most primitive past whose sacralization in Western culture has made an unholy ghost of work, and above all, of the will that drives the machine of work. Not that there is really any escaping this ghost, this mechanical possessor of the body: even when he goes to work in the surgical factory, Paul Morel accepts a mechanical brace to hold his shoulders straight against the inevitable disintegrating slump of the copyist. This is exactly why, Lawrence argues, men must resist sacralization of work, because the boundary between work and life is already so fragile that some seepage, some possession of the organic by the automatic, is inevitable. The ghost of the machine, the body-eating ghoul of work habit and work worship, is already to some extent present in the flesh, and the true man, far from cleaving to this ghost, will cry, "Must I become one with the old, habitual movements?" Even when the answer is yes, self-preservation demands it, the true man will hold to his protest: "But why so much: why repeat so often the mechanical movement? Let me not have so much of this work to do, let me not be imprisoned in this proven, finite experience all my days" (*Phoenix,* p. 425).

Women, of course, are not haunted by work in this way; though Lawrence's lifetime saw the first major influx of women of all classes into the urban and professional work force, work is still, as Lawrence sees it, peripheral for them. For Paul Morel's fellow males at the factory, "the man was the work and the work was the man," but for the women "it was different. . . . The real woman never seemed to be there at the task, but as if left out, waiting" (p. 112). Mrs. Morel too is seen both at the start and at the end of the book, as Nellie March and Ursula Brangwen and Connie Chatterley will be found, working at jobs that, however

---

hard or tedious, do not eat into their souls because they are deeply waiting, because some instinct calls, more clearly to woman than to man, "What have *I* to do with it. . . . I wait, I wait, and what I wait for can never come" (p. 61). Meantime, as Clara Dawes tells Paul, "all women's work becomes sweated" (p. 261), as men take revenge on those who compete to be food for the sacred ghoul of work. And Paul responds with the classic image of man's concept of women's work: "You are waiting—like Penelope when she did her weaving" (p. 266).

Joyce, we see, is not the only modernist for whom the *Odyssey* looms large in the background. Lawrence's women are far less the Sleeping Beauty image that many critics see than Penelope unironized, competent, and active in her working but firmly and poignantly centered in her waiting.[18] When Paul and Clara Dawes ascend to the castle grounds above Nottingham and look down upon the working town, it is the woman who sees that "the trees are much more significant" and rejoices "cynically" that the town is "only a little sore upon the country yet." And it is the man, ghost-ridden but loyal, who replies: "The town's all right. . . . it's only temporary. This is the crude, clumsy make-shift we've practiced on, til we find out what the idea is. The town will come all right" (p. 271).

This loyalty to the idea of the town is what saves Paul Morel at the end of *Sons and Lovers* when, having broken

---

[18] Marvin Mudrick speaks from this perspective of the crisis at the end of *The Rainbow*: "The new woman is too strong, and the new man is too weak, the woman suddenly conscious of long-sleeping powers and the man suddenly confronted with a rival" ("The Originality of *The Rainbow*" in *Spectrum* (Winter 1959); reprinted in *D. H. Lawrence: Twentieth-Century Views*, ed. Mark Spilka [Englewood Cliffs, N.J.: Prentice-Hall, 1963] p. 47. And in his essay "*The Plumed Serpent*: Vision and Language" written for the same collection, Harry Moore finds "the Sleeping Beauty motif that underlies so much of Lawrence's work" in that novel too. But with Kate Leslie even more than with Ursula we can see the greater relevance of the Waiting Beauty image than the Sleeping Beauty one.

his mother's hold on him by euthanasian murder, having slipped "like a weasel" out of the hands of all humans who would relate to, and so possess him, Paul finds himself sickened by his failures, without a foothold in a vast dark universe. He sees two kinds of light: one, "a few grains" of stars "spinning round for terror, and holding each other in embrace," the other, the town, now almost pure idea, a "gold phosphorescence . . . the faintly humming, glowing town" (p. 420). To follow the first idea, the star-balance, would mean, at this stage of his life, surrendering to relationship, to the dreadful Poe-like love of his dead mother, an unthinkable haunting. "His fists shut, his mouth set fast," Paul chooses the other light, and the effort of will it takes to shed one ghost, the ghoul of woman-love, mother-love, becomes itself the new automatic driven limb, the ghoul of work, with whose exorcism Lawrence is most deeply concerned in his later novels.

Three figures carry the burden of this ghoul in *The Rainbow*—Ursula's Uncle Tom Brangwen, the man her uncle introduces to Ursula as her "first love," Anton Skrebensky, and the woman who is her second lover, her schoolmistress, the skeptic scientific intellectual Winifred Inger, who marries Tom Brangwen. Skrebensky is an early study of the doomed man of the West who, "fatally established" and completed in the man's world before his spirit can feel any mystery about life (p. 289), calls his "real home" the army and the world of work and politics and achieves at his best simply a magnificent "self" assertion connected with the working of one's will upon the finite rather than that "soul" possession (p. 301) that for Lawrence is connected with the chaste, reticent, graceful presentation, sometimes the submission, of the self and the will before the infinite. Skrebensky fascinates Ursula with his control over the events of the outside world, his certainty about the nation's "duty" with respect to the Arab-English conflict in Khartoum, above all by that *"perpetuum mobile"* (p. 292) that her sister Gudrun mocks in him and will later mock in

Gerald Crich as his "go," that continual rocking and "sharp starting" and "doing something" that is the sure and baneful sign of the automatism of the West. Winifred is an early study of the doomed "new woman" of the West, newly enfranchised to self-making work, clever and unsatisfied, given to the willful "humanization" of all thought and the demystification of all mystery, including love and man: "They don't come to one and love one, they come to an idea, and they say, 'You are my idea,' so they embrace themselves. As if I were any man's idea!" (p. 342). "Proud and free as a man," Winifred consolidates Ursula's love while in competition during a swimming race, much as Gerald will Birkin's in a wrestling match in *Women in Love*. And yet both of these loves are limited, doomed to end in hatred, exactly because they act out pride and freedom in the limited Western masculine sense, as a race between interlocked wills, as the strenuous making of self against self rather than the touching of soul to soul. In obedience to that imperative, Ursula hardens her female self against Skrebensky's "set and straining" will (p. 318), a "finite and sad" enterprise (p. 301). Nevertheless it "must go on, the passion of Ursula to know her own maximum self, limited and so defined against him" (p. 301). With Winifred the passion to know herself is not at first an opposition but a lover's submission; still it limits and defines Ursula to the schoolmistress, and "the inoculation" against mystery and the infinite and to the urban end-of-the-world skeptical materialism of the other woman "passed into her, through her love for her mistress" (p. 342).

Ursula ends by hating both of her definers, her inoculators; her own "self," limited concept though it is, is stronger than Skrebensky's or Winifred's, and her "soul," mere bud that it is, will drive her, as both her lovers know almost from the start, to "cast them off" (p. 343). But Ursula only comes to understand why and to make the connection of that personal rejection with the general process of corruption in the outside world around her when she and Winifred come to Wiggiston to visit the man who lies behind both Skrebensky and Winifred, her uncle, Tom Brangwen.

The chapter in which both the meeting with Winifred and the meeting of the two women with Tom Brangwen take place is called "Shame," a lament that explicitly links the "perversity" of the homosexual relationship between the women to the "barren cohesion," the "amorphous sterility," finally the "activity mechanical yet inchoate" (p. 345) of the great colliery town that Brangwen dominates. Although I will discuss Lawrence's response to homosexuality in the next section more specifically, for now it is necessary to note its linkage in this early novel with active, even self-enhancing, but ultimately, in the Lawrentian sense, sterile, *work*. Lawrence will make this even more clear in the opening pages of *The Fox*. Uncle Tom, the master of work in *The Rainbow*, and Winifred, the mistress of free inquiry whose life and loves emerge from her work in the school-room, are drawn to each other's "dark corruption" immediately. For though Winifred in her modernism protests the mechanism of work that leaves only "a meaningless lump" in man for his woman, "the bit the shop can't digest," her primitive feminism cruelly brings her, like Tom, to regard home and marriage as a "sideshow" to the life of intellect and progressive materialism symbolized, in both realistic and Gothic terms here, by "the pit." Men believe "they must alter themselves to fit the pits and the place, rather than alter the pits and the place to fit themselves," says this Mr. Colliery-master Brangwen, and although Uncle Tom and Winifred "cynically revile" this state of affairs, as Gudrun will mock the naming of people according to their work in *Women in Love*, it is clear to the repelled Ursula that secretly "You think like they do that living human beings must be taken and adapted to all kinds of horrors" (p. 346). It is not life that matters, but the pit, responds the realist Tom, accepting while pretending to deplore: "Every man his own little side-show, his home, but the pit owns every man"—or, as Winifred adds, "digests" every man, joining her future husband in what seems to Ursula to be a "ghoulish satisfaction in it" (p. 348).

The ghoul of work, of self-enhancing soul-destroying work, is digesting both Tom and Winifred, creating about them, Lawrence has Ursula feel, a "marshy" air, "the succulent moistness and turgidity, and the same brackish, nauseating effect of a marsh, where life and decaying are one," where the self clasps its devourer as its "mistress" (p. 350). What is especially interesting in a Gothic context in Lawrence's pervasive use of the ghoul is that a ghoul is, not to put too fine a point on it, a flesh-eating demon, not the blood-drinking one with which we are more familiar. This is surely because for Lawrence the *flesh* is the life, on the personal level. The part of the person that is not "ghastly," given over to the dead-alive twitching of the mechanical will, the automatic work, the pit-mistress, is the very flesh that is "hot" and "flamy" in Lawrentian imagery, whereas the ghoul is cool, moist, and marshy, carrying, to borrow an image of the ghoul from Joyce's *Ulysses*, the odor of wet ashes on its breath. The flesh, sacred to the personal in man, is the prey of the ghoul: the blood, which is somehow sacred in Lawrence to the impersonal, the universal in man (in *The Plumed Serpent*, Kate comes mystically to know and to dread the knowledge that "the blood is *one*"), the blood is the prey of the vampire—the demon who would make everything personal but who is clearly a nobler demon than the ghoul who would make everything nothing.

Tom and Winifred marry and are eaten more deeply by the ghoul that is work; even their reproduction is simply production, Lawrence laments, sex too harnessed to the process, the flesh merely "warm clay lifted through the recurrent action of day after day by the great machine" (p. 351). Ursula disengages from all this in loathing and rage; she would "smash" the colliery (p. 349). Yet like Paul Morel, she can only escape from the "darkness" that is her mother, the "tyranny" that is her father by fleeing to the world of work where she is "a separate social individual"

(p. 363). She will be a different kind of worker, she thinks: as a schoolmistress she will live according to the flesh, not the will, be "vivid and personal," work by love and not by power. Entering the humming, gleaming town on the tram with the other workers, she hears the automatic click of the ticket-taker's machine, and thinks "her ticket surely was different from the rest." But no, "her ticket was the same" (p. 368), and so, despite her, is her work, a question of mechanism and power over the classroom, which is a space "of hostility and disintegration, of wills working in antagonistic subordination" (p. 380), whose best expression is a mere nonantagonistic subordination of wills: "The headmaster and the teacher should have one will in authority, which should bring the will of the children into accord" (p. 382).

Ursula learns the lesson of will from the ghoul of work as she learned will in opposition to Skrebensky's will, learns to "obliterate" (p. 395) the students in negative impersonality as she obliterated her lover. She is finally, therefore, "broken in" to "the man's world" of pure will. When Skrebensky enters her life once more she "crushes . . . breaks . . . obliterates" him more finally than ever. She lets slip one cold tear, "glittering" with its "burden of moonlight," at what she has become, then abandons him. At college she hears from a female doctor of physics what she had heard first from Winifred Inger, that there is no more mystery about fleshly life than there is about emotional or religious life, that it is all probably "a complexity of physical and chemical activities. . . . We don't understand it as we understand electricity, even, but that doesn't warrant our saying it is something special" (p. 440). The scientist's name is Dr. Frankstone.[19]

[19] In the opening essay in *The Endurance of Frankenstein* (U. C. Knoepflmacher and George Levine, eds. [Berkeley: Univ. of California Press, 1979]), George Levine draws attention to the appearance, in this "rather amusing" and "surprisingly offhand way," of the Frankenstein myth in *The Rainbow*. Dr. Frankstone, Levine remarks, "articu-

This should validate forever the ghoul-world that is reality in *The Rainbow*. And yet the rainbow exists too, Lawrence affirms in the last pages. It is "arched in the blood" of men, and it can "quiver to life" in their spirit (p. 495). The hard shell of ghoul-eaten machine-ridden flesh can fall off and "new clean naked bodies would issue to a new germination," redeeming not only life but work as well, the old buildings and machines and factories "swept away" and a "new architecture" based on the arch replacing them. This hope will find expression in new shapes in new lands in Lawrence's later work (the zigzag shape characteristic of Indian weaving is a sign both of potency and of stability in *The Plumed Serpent*), but not in his next and greatest novel, *Women in Love*. There the full horror of the work-ghoul and the deep connection between work, will, and flesh-corruption holds so strong a sway that no redemption which includes work seems possible. Those who are doomed go down to corruption with the work-ghouls on their backs like the shiny shells of beetles. Those who survive do so by quitting work entirely.[20]

The preeminent figures in this scenario are the "glistening" "electric" Gerald Crich, adventurer, industrialist, "master," and Hermione Roddice, aesthete, intellectual,

---

lates the assumptions implicit in Victor's creation of the Monster—the transformation of spirit into mere matter" ("The Ambiguous Heritage of Frankenstein," pp. 26, 27).

[20] In his Modern Masters Series study *D. H. Lawrence* (New York: Viking Press, Inc., 1973), Frank Kermode remarks that while *Women in Love* opens "with two intelligent provincial girls talking, at about the same level of seriousness as the sisters at the beginning of *Middlemarch*, about marriage," the sisters walk almost immediately into the novel's true locus, "the solitary landscape, chthonic, post-mortem, a landscape of ghouls, hideous but with a strange inhuman vitality" (p. 66). Gudrun herself observes that "everything is a ghoulish replica of the real world, a replica, a ghoul, all soiled, everything sordid," but her artist's soul, already committed to work and to mentalism, stands apart from the sight in a kind of wierd excitement: "it's really marvellous—it's really wonderful, another world" (p. 5).

"mistress" of both Breadalby and (at first) of the Lawrentian protagonist, Rupert Birkin. Both are Cain figures,
alienated from life by that intense competitiveness (not
"opposition," which is good) of will that makes its practitioners either murderer or "murderee" (p. 27) in every
human relationship. Gerald has already "accidentally on
purpose" (p. 20) killed his brother; in an early chapter,
Hermione tries to murder her lover.

Gerald is a man who, in Lawrence's most pervasive
metaphor on this subject, lives from no "centre" but is
corruptly bound into a recognizable shape by outside
rather than inside forces: existential definition occurs not
from within, like a star exerting its field, but from without,
as a bubble or a shell randomly encloses emptiness. Life, as
Gerald describes it to Birkin, is a process of "finding out
things—and getting experiences—and making things go."
It "doesn't centre at all" but is "artificially held *together*
by the social mechanism" (p. 51). This artificial centre,
which is really a periphery, is will, "insane" and "fixed"
will, "demon-satisfaction" (p. 65) that absorbs all motion
into its own motion, the "ghastly wrestling" (p. 314) that
will not accept death itself as a master.

As Lawrence explores this ghoul-will, it manifests itself
for men in work, or doing, or going ("But where does his
go *go?*" Ursula's sister Gudrun mocks Gerald) and for
women in knowing. As man rapes the material world, subduing and reshaping it, women seek, mentally rather than
carnally, to know the world, to know above all the men
who connect them to the material world. Hermione is for
Birkin the last exquisite stage of the deathly knower, the
mind that knows even that "the mind is our death" and
yet continues its quest to "have things in your power" by
knowing (p. 34). This pure power relationship in mentality,
like the carnal one practiced by Gerald on the mines of
Beldover, the Arab mare, or Minette, finally brings on defeat by a more powerful mentality or carnality. At Breadalby, Birkin responds to Hermione's "dreadful tyranny

to know all he knew," loathing yet forced into the competition: "I know what centres" Hermione lives from, he reflects. And her knowledge of his contemptuous knowledge
breaks, collapses, swallows her: "She suffered the ghastliness
of dissolution, broken and gone in a horrible corruption.
. . . She strayed out, pallid and preyed upon like a ghost . . .
like one attacked by the tomb-influences which dog us. And
she was gone like a corpse, that has no connection" (pp. 81-
82).

These veritable ghosts in the daylight of modern life,
where "the substitution of the mechanical principle for the
organic" (p. 223) produces mere rotted mind and will-
eaten flesh "ticking" on in a motion, not an action, are a
crucial challenge to the still-living characters in Lawrence's
world because they are so numerous and because they are,
in their phosphorescent corruption, so desirable. Not only
do the ghouls outnumber the living, but they exist in all
shades and phases of corruption, so that the appetite for
competitive destruction finds better prey at each stage of
dissolution.

In *Women in Love*, this is beautifully rendered by Lawrence in the chain that links Thomas Crich, "The Industrial
Magnate," through Gerald, his son, to Gudrun Brangwen,
Gerald's lover, to Loerke, the industrial artist who is
Gudrun's final choice. The elder Crich is what Lawrence
describes as "the second generation" of "the idea" of industrial capitalism, an idea of work-as-life that is dangerous
enough in its first stage of pure greed and quite perverse
in its second "Victorian" stage of charitable dictatorship
and welfarism. Now, with the mastership of Gerald in the
third generation, it has become "a great and perfect machine," imbued with the rigidity of a philosophical principle (p. 220). The elder Crich, "the patriarch," inspired
like his tenants with "the last impulses of the last religious
passion left on earth, the passion for equality" (p. 217), is
trapped between his possessions and his love, between "two
half-truths" (p. 219). Like any man in the grip of the work-

259

ghoul, his shell is hardening against feeling, his will, holding off the tremendous contradictions from inside and out, is narrowing; he is fighting to die before this "armour" is breached, "as an insect when its shell is cracked" (p. 207).

On the other hand, like any man with a flame of passion, a religious impulse, he suffers deeply at some level from the narrowing process. His son Gerald possesses no such living impulse, but surrendered early to that "curiosity . . . to know," that "pure instrumentality" of the will by which a male and a worker "lays hold of the world" (pp. 214-215). In his early years of mastership, Gerald worked demonically to "reform" what had been all too visibly to *The Rainbow's* Ursula "the pit," purifying and mechanizing it, stripping away all the "sideshow" elements such as "widow's coal" and the butty system. Now as Gudrun enters his life and his father leaves it, the "pit" is clean, efficient, and perfectly joyless.

As the patriarch dies, however, Gerald experiences "more and more a sense of exposure"; without even the despised purpose of his father's charity to shield him, he must face the consequence of his idea, experience himself as pure instrumentality, "pure and exalted activity." And that is to experience oneself as no-thing, see one's face as "a composition mask" and one's eyes as "blue false bubbles that would burst in a moment and leave clear annihilation," feel one's mind as "a bubble floating in the darkness" (pp. 224-225). Gerald's will holds the bubble tensely around a "unit" of emptiness or corruption, but his similarity to his father makes him all but experience the older man's dissolution, and he requires toward the end of the book some powerful experience of another's will, another's dissolution, to compensate for his brush with death, "make good the equilibrium" between the dark fated outside world and the darkness within (p. 314).

"In this extremity" he turns not to Birkin, who would have him relax the will that is the only thing holding apart those two darknesses, but to Gudrun, who as he secretly realizes, shares in even greater measure the extreme wakefulness, "superconsciousness" (p. 339), of which his father has died, so to speak, possessed. Gerald's surrender to/possession of Gudrun after he leaves his father's graveside throws the pressure of maintaining the fortress of will most fully onto her; she sees herself, in one of Lawrence's most mysteriously arresting images, condemned forever to "pull and haul at the rope of glittering consciousness, pull it out phosphorescent from the endless depths of the unconsciousness, till she was weary, aching, exhausted, and fit to break, and yet she had not done" (p. 339). In this hellish competition, Gudrun is the stronger, as Gerald was stronger than Thomas Crich. Entering it for "balance," Gerald achieves the only kind of equilibrium possible in a mechanist's vision of The Good—the perfect stability of a pure frozen crystal of ice.

For the stronger but less "complete" Gudrun, who also recognized her "place," her desire, when she looked on the Alpine scenes of "Continental" and "settled down like a crystal in the navel of snow" (p. 391), a worse fate remains. The artist, more "conscious" than Gerald, less hypocritical than Hermione, more alienated simply by nature (and perhaps by her art) than anyone else in the novel's world, has known all along that in embracing Gerald she was embracing the machine. During their first kiss, she is carnally aware of the huge man/town/machine he controls; she responds viscerally to all that in "the vibrating inhuman tension of his arms and his body" (p. 323). Their first intercourse is tense with the constant notation of time and the ringing bells of the hours, and it ends in the precious "ache" and "nausea" of recognition: "I am like a workman's wife" (p. 341). By the end of the novel Gerald is for her not simply the workman but the work, not the clockman but the clock; in "Continental" he takes her once again during their battle of wills, the "passion" coming up in him "stroke after stroke, like the ringing of a bronze bell," his hands like "living metal, invincible and not to be turned aside" (p. 391). And the thought of entering life on Gerald's terms—"these men, with their eternal jobs!" (p. 455)—horrifies her. She sees herself trapped and helpless: "All life, all life resolved itself into this: tick-tack, tick-tack, tick-tack. . . .Gerald could not save her from it. He, his body, his motion, his life—it was the same twitching across the dial, a horrible mechanical twitching forward over the face of the hours" (p. 456).

Yet, of course, she has entered the relationship on these terms; even her opposition to Gerald has made her a machine like him, a "clock-face" mechanically ticking off her blows in response to his kisses. In utter weariness, in that turn of the century "boredom" that is worse than dread, Gudrun pictures her own face like a clock-dial, as Gerald had earlier imagined his mirrored face a mask over nothingness, and experiences that inward quailing and aging of the spirit that in classic Gothic turns the hair white. Here she only imagines it has turned white, "as it has so often, under the intolerable burden of her thoughts and sensations!" (p. 456). But it remained "brown as ever . . . a picture of health." Instead of settling down into pure, if stricken, dead whiteness, like Gerald, Gudrun will go on, ironizing even her terrors and loathing (p. 408), "laughing off" her clock-vision of the self (p. 456), brown, healthy, death-dealing and immortal, like Melmoth the Wanderer. Even before Gerald seeks death to end their competition of wills, Gudrun locks herself into this dreadful immortality by entering a relationship with the German worker-artist Loerke, who has gone the final distance into utter human detachment, utter mechanism. She sees him realistically as "pure, unconnected will" (p. 415), brutal and ratlike on a human scale, demonic on a national and racial scale—for he serves the god of work who protects one from the devil of hunger and weakness, and he serves that god not in repulsion but in delight: "the machinery and the acts of labour are extremely, maddeningly beautiful" (p. 414). Fascinated, doomed by her wish to *know* "every phase in her soul," even the corrupt ones, Gudrun hands herself over to "the troll," Loerke, "the creature, the final craftsman," ready to undergo "the last subtle activities of breaking down" that result from "an unbroken will reacting against her unbroken will" (p. 443). At the end of the novel Gudrun and Loerke go together into the land of "Willie zur macht" to "work for their living," will against will, craftsman against craftsman, beetle hardening against beetle, ghoul eating ghoul, each so many centimeters of dead flesh and tick-tacking motion. It is a doom worthy of Poe.[21]

Blood Sharers: Mystic Marriage

Rupert Birkin and Ursula Brangwen escape this doom because they understand and fight its fascinations, because in an uncharacteristically unfair slip of the plot both have been given sufficient income from somewhere to disengage completely from the ghoul of work without suffering the devil of hunger, and because they have each other, "flamily," in the flesh of mystic heterosexual marriage. One of the important things about Loerke, Lawrence's last-phase destroyer-troll, is that he is homosexual: the crucial thing about his and Gudrun's relationship is that while it will explore, we are given to understand, the destructively "frictional" depths of sensuality, it will not really be sexual.

Loerke's homosexuality is only briefly drawn in *Women in Love*: the large, fair, soft "love-companion" Leiter is pure object to Loerke, "a penniless dependent" who is "impotent with resentment" (p. 402), "kept in some sort of subjection, against which he was rebelling" (p. 412). Two

---

21 This "death in life" figure, as Julian Moynihan calls it, makes a final memorable appearance in Clifford Chatterley of *Lady Chatterley's Lover*, chained to, and in a ghastly way doubly energized by, his wheelchair. Moynihan sees Lawrence stating a hypothesis: "What will a man do with himself and with others when his physical attachment to experience has been violently and permanently severed?" and dramatizing an answer: "Such a man will create a 'simulacrum of reality'" to substitute for the missing parts ("The Deed of Life," *English Literary History*, March 1959; reprinted in *D. H. Lawrence: Twentieth-Century Views*, p. 78).

things are important about this picture of homosexuality: the subjection that characterizes it and the rebelliousness of the dependent. Of all the ghastly frictive flesh-possessions, the expropriative relationships Lawrence is concerned with, none is more hated by him than this one. For while the subjection of man to work-machine and of women to automatized man puts the will and "the pit" at the center of life and the flesh and the home at the periphery as a "sideshow," homosexuality for Lawrence is a deadly parody of marriage that makes any escape from "the pit," even a momentary respite in the sideshow, impossible. And yet— what Birkin wants with another man and Ursula says is impossible, what Nellie March has with Jill Banford until Henry says it is over, what Don Ramon and Cipriano have as an initiatory condition both for their great work and for their mystic heterosexual marriages, looks like homosexuality, surely. But it is not, says Lawrence, it is *blutbruderschaft*, sharing of the blood, an intersexual bond free of that subjection/possession modality that for Lawrence makes both homosexuality and most heterosexuality vampiric, yet one that connects persons by a blood relationship more demanding, because less willing, more "lapsing," than ordinary flesh relationships.

For Lawrence, to repeat, offers a systematic metaphysical anatomy, rather like his important predecessor George Meredith. Whereas Meredith's famous "triad" of blood, brain, and spirit makes brain the mediating force between the merely personal demands of the blood and the universal unities of spirit, Lawrence's Trinity of flesh, blood, and spirit (his Holy Ghost) makes blood brotherhood the next, the better phase after the purely fleshly, the independently personal, the bridge between the personal fleshly "self" and the attuned human "soul." It is the gateway to, the adolescence of, impersonality. When Ursula casts off her lover, her father, her child in the final pages of *The Rainbow*, retaining her "newness" and her independent personality but undergoing a kind of fleshly death in initiatory punishment, it is the pounding of her blood in unison with the sound of the horses on the hill, "a weight on her heart," that triggers the reentry into "the bottom of all change," a "dissolving" of the limbs that allows her—cruel and Gothic but necessary preemption—to substitute her own rebirth for the failed birth of Skrebensky's child. And the promise of newness for all people given in *The Rainbow*'s last paragraph is carried in the blood: "the rainbow was arched in their blood, and would quiver to life in their spirit." Whereas it is the flesh that separates itself (above all from the mother) to achieve selfhood, it is the blood that properly arches persons outside themselves towards a universality first perceived as an attraction to another of the same sex. The spirit, rising "between" those persons as a reminder that flesh must keep its singleness and blood its impersonality or the relationship becomes ghoulish or vampiric, completes the arc, provides the balance, makes the relationship star and star or wing and wing, rather than star and satellite, energy and object. The flesh is the locus of power, and the blood of sexuality, but the spirit is the place of marriage.

Thus the long idyll of the nineteenth-century's substitution of mystic marriage for Gothic murder reaches its' climax in Lawrence, for whom, as Rupert Birkin phrases it, "the old ideals are dead as nails—nothing there. It seems to me there remains only the perfect union with a woman—sort of ultimate marriage—and there isn't anything else" (p. 51). The strenuous grasp of marriage as both a "murder" of personality and an achievement of a greater impersonality, an ideality, becomes a desperate substitute theology—Pauline in thrust.[22] As man (or woman—giving

---

[22] Again I owe to a student the reminder that the story, as well as the theology, of Paul the Apostle resonates throughout Lawrence's work. In an unpublished paper on *Sons and Lovers*, "Our Father Who Art on Earth," David Schaeffer describes Paul Morel's "conversion" away from his mother towards his father, his father's work, and the "humming, glowing town" in terms of the story in Acts 9 of Saul's

Lawrence and Paul the benefit of the doubt, momentarily)
is to his/her body, so is partner to marriage partner, and so
is God to creation, arched within, "groaning in travail,"
quivering into life, with the unseen Holy Ghost presiding.
In *The Rainbow* we can see the travail of marriage, caught
in the bonds of flesh in two early Brangwen marriages.
Here briefly (and more dramatically in *Women in Love*
and *The Fox*), we can see the exploration of blood brotherhood, intrasexual bonding, as a possible new pathway to
living marriage. And in *Women in Love* and finally *The
Plumed Serpent* we can see Lawrence's desired end, an un-
devouring fertile impersonhood in a marriage whose shape
is a triangle, the most primitive of godheads.

The first marriage in *The Rainbow*, between Tom Brangwen and Lydia Lensky, has the unmistakable sanction of
the author; the Pentecostal wind "shook . . . boomed . . .
roared" at their meeting (pp. 39-41); and the condition of
their true mating, two years after their marriage, in a "confirmation" (p. 41) of it, is this, that they are to each other
the entrance into impersonality: "She was the doorway to
him, he to her," to a "further space, where movement was
so big, that it contained bonds and constraints and labours,
and still was complete liberty" (p. 91). Yet the marriage is
an early, imperfect form of its central idea (in much the
same way that the town that Paul Morel and Clara Dawes
saw was a predecessor of its idea), for it is formed between
a "Brangwen man," whose easy "lapse" inward into blood-
intimacy is without the "poetic" power of the men of
"thought and comprehension" (p. 5), and "a Polish lady"
who, like the "Brangwen women," has a streak of thought
and comprehension, a hunger for rebellion and "the out-

mystic encounter on the road to Damascus, a city where, the mystic
voice assured Saul (as it assures Lawrence's Paul), he will be "told
what to do." Lawrence's own "mission," apostolic, irascible, of wide
and pacific embrace yet tinged from the start with a dim violent impulse toward martyrdom, seems to parallel in many important ways
that of the apostle to the Gentiles.

side" in her. So foreign are they to each other, and so fundamentally placed in the woman is the newness, the freshness, the "leading shoot" of the species, that the star-balance is radically unstable from the first. Several years younger than the woman who is already the mother of a daughter, Tom Brangwen finds his stability and center in the marriage by taking "less than he wanted . . . to measure himself to her" (p. 78). Marriage is to him the center; no work exists to make it a sideshow; and yet his wife is less a mate than "all women" to him, the "powerful source of his life." It is marriage at its most primitive, heterosexuality in its first stage—mother and son. And to complete the primitive symmetry, the ur-triangle, the man who is subject to his wife turns to the daughter for "sympathy," and "soon they were like lovers, father and child" (p. 60).

The second marriage in *The Rainbow*, much more equal, and hence more "frictive," occurs between Tom and Lydia's daughter Anna and her cousin Will. But the degree of consanguinity present still makes this marriage a rudimentary one; Will, like Paul Morel, is engaged in a mother-love that Anna defeats at least partly by substitution. And Anna, who as a child had spent agonized years holding up "the broken end of the arch" (p. 92) of her mother's existence after the death of her father, finds in Will at least partly a release from the ambiguous intimacy of that triangle with her mother and stepfather. Once again an auspicious openness, however, hovers round the relationship's beginning: they share a kiss in a dark loft whose door "opens to the motions of wind and rain" and connects them to those "big, swooping oscillations" (p. 114). He is "the hole in the wall" to her (p. 109), and she, we see from the phoenix and then the creation of Eve that he carves, is the questing shape that "was issuing like a flame towards the hand of God, from the torn side of Adam" (p. 116). This is the marriage that Will, who is captured and yearning and unable to understand his sexuality, sees as "the solution now, fixed ahead" (p. 121), the marriage of which Tom Brangwen is "inspired" to say that "a married couple makes one Angel . . . when a man's soul and a woman's soul unite together—that makes an angel" (pp. 134-135).

But the angels in Will's carving stand "covering their faces with their wings," and he feels them "standing back" producing "darkness" when he goes to claim Anna at her farm (p. 116). Clearly this paradise is now lost or at least much more difficult to enter—made so by the sin whose name Will bears and that he can only lose by losing himself: "His will drummed persistently, darkly, it drowned everything else. . . . still he pursued her, in his kisses, and still she was not quite overcome" (p. 119). Losing himself, he pauses in exaltation during his honeymoon "at the supreme centre" of life, impersonal "at the centre of all the slow wheeling of space" (p. 141). But this door opens upon guilt and frustration.

After the honeymoon, unbolting the door, Will finds "the world there, after all" (p. 143), "the rind of the world: houses, factories, trains . . . work going on" (p. 146). The man is closer to this world than the woman, "hampered" and afraid, and feeling, with so many thousands of years of practice in him, that that attachment to the sideshow of marriage, however glorious, has something "criminal" about it (p. 146). He fights his fear, which is the same as his joy, with the weapon he has only too ready at hand, "his own tense black will" (p. 148). Between his male will to the world and her female one to her solitary self, their marriage is a "deep, fierce unnamed battle" (p. 165). Between his "blind" male attachment to the messages of his "blood" and her Brangwen female "worship of the human knowledge" (p. 168), they are a torment to each other on every field of engagement and desire except one, their desire for each other. Married love, that "third thing" created by two as a separate space in which souls can meet without selves destroying or possessing each other, issues in a living third thing, a child, and Will and Anna settle down, peaceful, "dazed out," and only half content to the old roles given by the old fixed solution, he to his work, she to her pregnancies. *They* are completed, but *it*—the human enterprise, the breakthrough—has not been accomplished in them because "there was no understanding, only acquiescence and submission" (p. 153). The will in both of them is present, but also "the blood is up" over and over in the chapter on their marriage. They are a half-success: the rainbow is arched in the blood. But there is insufficient understanding for the transition to the level of spirit. The marriage remains pure "blood," pure daze, pure passional sexual trance. The angels' faces are still covered.

In this context it is interesting that their daughter Ursula, the most vivid of Lawrence's "wayfaring" women, experiences her first really deep passion not with a man but with a woman, and an intellectual. Although intergender relationships can be the most vampiric of all, resulting almost always in the subjection and finally the death of one partner, still at one level, I believe the deepest, Lawrence's fascination with this kind of bonding reflects his desire that each gender know itself and its variations, its temptations and its extremities, better that it may finally engage. with understanding in that marriage which is more than personality, more than sexuality, which is "mystic."

When Ursula Brangwen meets Winifred Inger, it is true, she has already had, and "broken," Anton Skrebensky as a lover. She took him in confusion and anger and curiosity as the next step in "widening the circle" of her understanding of "the weekday world" after her discovery that "the Sunday world" of ecstatic vision in which her father has located his soul has no "reality" for her. In a sense it was a concretization of that visionary "passion of Jesus" in the Sunday world that drew her to Skrebensky: Lawrence puts the passion and the meeting with Skrebensky on the same page in the chapter called "First Love." Because she first experiences the weekday world through a man, she comes to call it the man's world; through her "breaking" of Skrebensky, she learns she has "secret riches," a reserve weapon for her attempt to conquer the man's world—"her femaleness." Her surrender to Winifred, who is in her modernity, independence, quickness of spirit, her fearlessness and unyielding mentality, both Ursula's enricher and her temptress, is immediate and full, physical and mental. No heterosexual friction of wills, no guard against the foreign "other" delays or chafes or narrows the bond, and from Winifred, and later a fellow teacher, Maggie, Ursula learns direct if ambiguous lessons about the positive side of that secret weapon of femaleness—that it cannot only destroy and manipulate man but, like man, it can both meet the world and directly manipulate it. She learns solitude, freedom, and pride, and the next step for her, as it was for Winifred, as it is for men, would have been subjection to that ultimate passion to lay hold of the world by will. "Inoculated" to work and will, the "new woman" has become a ghoul, and Ursula feels her lover turn from a presence clear, rushing, liquid, and blissful, like the swimming and bathing scenes that first united them physically, to a presence heavy and marshy: a "clogged sense of deadness began to gather upon her from the other woman's contact," "the fine rushing intensity" is gone, leaving "this heavy cleaving of moist clay, that cleaves because it has no life of its own" (p. 343). Wishing to cast her off, secretly but desperately complicit in the doom of this extreme form of her gender, Ursula brings Winifred and her Uncle Tom Brangwen together, two delighted feeders of the Moloch of materialism, two devotees of "the pit." Unwilling, unable to attempt the rescue of her gender-mate, Ursula escapes from her, stronger, unsatisfied, to mate with her fated lover in the later novel, Rupert Birkin.

It is a different story, interestingly, with the male mates of *Women in Love*, Birkin and Gerald Crich. There is blood between these men in several senses as we see in their first conversation in "Shortlands." For although Lawrence dramatizes by gesture and tone the fact of their "strange,

perilous intimacy . . . powerful but suppressed friendli-
ness" (p. 28) and although the powerful Crich mother
virtually bestows them on one another ("Gerald! He's the
most wanting of them all. . . . I should like him to have a
friend," she tells Birkin [p. 20]), the content of their
thought and conversation is bloody murder. Birkin responds flippantly to Mrs. Crich's invitation with a sotto
voce "Am I my brother's keeper?," introducing the biblical
theme that will color their whole relationship. Gerald, like
Cain, killed his brother, like Cain he is a city builder and
huntsman, a tiller of the fields of coal, proud of a great
work that, nevertheless, has no "respect" from the Lord and
is not acceptable to Him. And like Cain, Birkin sees, Gerald
knows the world only in terms of "striving," which makes,
as Hermione Roddice notes, "bad blood" (p. 23). Gerald
understands the spontaneous will in man to be wholly
committed to possession, and eventually, to murder, and
Birkin understands that Gerald's own spontaneity works
that way, alert to the threat that "every man has his knife
up his sleeve for you" (p. 28). Yet Birkin does have a kind
of knife-wish toward the other man, who represents so
beautiful and doomed a manhood, whose luckless striving,
destructive energy, and driven totemistic maleness it would
be so desirable to rescue, whose "bad blood" could be
turned good like water into wine by someone who wants to
believe, as Birkin wants to believe, in miracles:

> "You know how the old German knights used to swear a
> *Blutbruderschaft?*" "Make a little wound in their arms,
> and rub each others' blood into the cut?"
> "Yes, and swear to be true to each other, of one blood,
> all their lives. That is what we ought to do." (Pp. 198-
> 199)

It is a strange and frightening experience for these two
men to love each other as they do, for they love what is not
alien but extreme in each other's maleness. The love is
therefore radically unstable, always turning to contempt or

271

distrust—as Birkin once again encounters the completeness, the fixity, of Gerald's involvement with work and matter—or mistrust—as Gerald once again encounters the chameleon impalpability and fluidity of Birkin's commitment to vision and spirit. Undoubtedly, as Lawrence dramatizes the relationship, each man's contempt and mistrust could be made fruitful criticism for the other could he once get a firm hold on the surfaces of the other's maleness, each worn smooth by the thousands of years of shaping pressure applied by a cultural archetype that both men understand is doomed if it does not change. In "Gladiatorial" they seek that hold, Birkin on Gerald's matter-produced "force," Gerald on Birkin's spirit-generated "spell" (p. 262), and after a certain period of "mindlessness" consequent on the meeting of the flesh, they are called into harmony with each other, briefly, by the "great hammer-stroke resounding through the house" (p. 263) that is the heartbeat. In response to this laying down of mind and raising up of the blood, Birkin's own "spirit stood behind him," and it is here, on the interface between shared blood and single spirit, that the men achieve, momentarily, the blood-brotherly hold: "Gerald's hand closed warm and sudden over Birkin's. . . . [Birkin's] hand, in swift response, had closed in a strong warm clasp over the hand of the other" (p. 264).

What strikes Birkin most forcibly in the friendly aftermath is the difference between himself, touselled and careless, and Gerald, gleaming and richly clothed, the two men visibly "as far, perhaps, apart as man from woman, yet in another direction" (p. 266). Here is an individual's perfect placement, it seems, at the apex of a triangle whose lines of force encounter two other bodies with their single spirits behind them at the greatest possible distance consistent with contact.[23] For Lawrence is afraid of "love" in the old

[23] Here is another thematic that Lawrence seems to share with Joyce, with this important difference: Lawrence's wanderer desires distance with contact, whereas Joyce's Ulysses strays to the farthest distance "consistent with return."

"female" sense, Ursula's sense, Poe's sense, the love that merges, devours, leaves no singleness but encloses one being in the other, like the child in the mother. In the new sense that Lawrence is trying to articulate, love needs a mystic third to give dimension, to allow singleness, to prevent the collapse of two into one. And the most concrete, most sensible recourse seems to be to a third lover of one's own gender, to confirm that gender in its meeting with the other gender, and to allow for the exploration of the othernesses in one's own gender.

Clearly this is what Birkin seeks in Gerald, since he understands the implications of the relationship as it develops. Gerald finds that love "momentaneously" too, but his journey toward murder is too far advanced, he understands little and accepts less, frozen in matter's eternal mistrust of the spirit that awakens. When he makes his final trip into the Alpine waste, it is in search of sleep; it is to settle down into material at last, it is to experience in a perfectly tragically mechanical way the "tack" of victimization whose first "tick" so long ago was the murder of his brother. And Birkin, who is fighting his own mechanical "tick-tack" of male and then female dominance, grieves for the loss of his triangulation point: because Gerald closed the northern road with his death, there is now only "the old imperial road" going south toward the Italy that is love and sex and femininity. And the prognosis for the human species down that road is dim. Perhaps, Birkin "consoles" himself, it is "all up" with humanity, perhaps the whole enterprise will disappear into a cul-de-sac, leaving room for "the timeless creation mystery" to experiment with a "more lovely race" (p. 470).

It is Ursula, who at the end of *The Rainbow* was surrounded by images suggesting that she was, or could mother, the new race, who insists to Birkin on the last page of *Women in Love* that the way of triangulation, two loves, is "false, impossible." One scarcely knows how to read Lawrence here, for while the novel has demonstrated that if seeking to confirm one's own gender-self one touches the extreme archetypes of masculinity and femininity, Gudrun and Gerald, one may be swallowed up in their death and dragged down the river of dissolution, still the enterprise of heterosexuality and fertility that Birkin and Ursula represent seems blocked and "old hat" to Birkin and even to Lawrence. Birkin's attempted rescue of Gerald turns out to be as futile as Gerald's attempt to rescue "Di" at the water party; still, rescues are noble human gestures, and Birkin's attempt, untainted by the automatism of Gerald's, is touching and hopeful even in its futility. But no one, we remember, makes much of an attempt to rescue Gudrun. Is Lawrence's case, then, that woman indeed, unless she is "perverse," needs no one else but man and that in her need she closes off avenues of *his* more complex need? Does vampirism, the blood-lust that wants merging, not sharing, come from woman?

The Fox is instructive here. Written soon after *Women in Love*, it describes a kind of "water bond," a blood-sisterhood, between two women, that ends, as Gerald's and Birkin's did, with the death of the more extreme and modernist partner and the commitment of the survivor to heterosexual and mystic marriage. Yet the female survivor, Nellie March, feels the commitment an entrapment and a kind of anachronism, as the male survivor did in *Women in Love*. Her bond with Jill Banford, like Birkin's with Gerald, is partly an adolescent exploration of her individuality-in-gender. Like Gerald, Jill is abnormally aware of time, a manager, a talker; she is the "principal investor" in the farm that is to make the two young women independent. Whereas Gerald is the archetype of modern man's willful immersion in matter, Jill expresses modern woman's willful immersion in knowledge: he works himself to death, she reads herself into ill health and deals with the living world through the instrumentality of spectacles, as he does through his machines. Gerald's "totem" is the wolf, and he dies a wolf's death, self-exiled from warmth, frozen in the woods; hers is the bird, and she dies at the huntsman's hands: "He watched with intense bright eyes, as he would watch a wild goose he had shot. Was it winged or dead? Dead!"[24] Images of northern cold surround both: Gerald's element is cold water, cold iron, and Banford must sleep with a hot water bottle prepared by March. Like Gerald, Jill speaks to her gender-mate of self-development, self-defense, "self-respect," personal integrity, as against the dangerous self-loss and impersonality of heterosexual marriage. They both stand for that "old stable ego" that is a "dead letter" to Lawrence.[25] What makes Gerald tragic and Banford merely pathetic is that Gerald understands that the enterprise of "the self" has no more life in it, has become automatic, whereas Banford seems merely shrill in her attack on the male who enters to triangulate the intersexual bond.

A crucial difference, a continuous rent in Lawrence's often admirable feminism, then, is that there is no adulthood envisioned for the intrafemale relationship. Gerald dies classically because of his own contradictions, but Lawrence's Henry kills Banford with the "magic" of his falling tree, the power of his plexis entering, fairy-tale-like, into the world about him and accomplishing the "natural destiny" that makes woman fertile with man only. Birkin knows what his loss was, but Nellie March, sinking like "seaweed" into the impersonal currents of heterosexual desire, pulled "outside" herself toward sleep by "the deep, heavy, powerful stroke of his heart, terrible like something from beyond," like a "terrible signalling from outside" (p.

[24] Quotations from *The Fox* (1920) are taken from *The Portable D. H. Lawrence*, ed. Diana Trilling (New York: Viking Press, 1947); this one is on p. 298.

[25] "You mustn't look in my novel for the old stable *ego* of the character. There is another *ego*, according to whose action the individual is unrecognisable, and passes through, as it were, allotropic states which it needs a deeper sense than we've been used to exercise, to discover are states of the same single radically unchanged element." (Letter to Edward Garnett, 5 June 1914, *Collected Letters*, 1:282.)

280), knows only that she has "failed" in some obscure way to take enough "responsibility" for herself. What she wants is what Birkin wanted, star-balance, with something settled and anchoring and something else unfinished, drawing her forward, a poignant image, "to sit still, like a woman on the last milestone, and watch. . . . with him at her side" (p. 303). Whereas in *Women in Love* the woman tempts Birkin to love, to merge, to feel complete in a pair, the man so tempts the woman in *The Fox*. The tempter feels that that terrible hammer stroke of the blood that calls person to person impersonally comes from inside, begins and ends in love, begins in surrender and ends in "love will . . . lemurs . . . vampires." Those who understand better, however sweet the lapse together, know that while the stroke falls in the blood, the hammer is lifted outside, from beyond, from between, in the hand of the god, in the place of the spirit.

The Holy Ghost

No single aspect of plot, image, or mood says "Gothic" to us so clearly as the aspect of place. The castle, the tower, the graveyard, the prison, the rocky crag hung between wind and sea—all those settings scaled to purposes other than an individual normal man's—what could happen there other than what does, possession, preemption, decreation? Who could inhabit there other than the dilated, the separated, the monstrous? The unhuman, the god? Walpole's Manfred and Radcliffe's Schedoni work frantically to rebuild and keep solitary their houses; Frankenstein and Jekyll bar all entry to their laboratories; Dracula carries coffins of his earth across the sea. Unmistakably, power resides in place, from Scott's covenanter guarding his cave to Brontë's Heathcliff claiming his Cathy from Penistone Crags, to the scores of great houses that loom, wind-generating, behind the fascinated females on the covers of today's drugstore Gothic. Power, the Gothic says, resides in place, and as we can see from these examples, overwhelmingly, the kind of power that resides in place, in placement, seems to be male, and the power that challenges it, evades it, or that seeks place from a position of placelessness, is female. We can now see one of the reasons why the Gothic has been considered a "female" genre and one of the reasons why it appeals, both in its language and imagery and in its deepest forms of plot and placement, to Lawrence. For though the best works, as I have said, explore both the dilemma of placelessness of the female drifter/seeker/orphan and of the precariously placed, the enlarged or doubled male tyrant, the worse punishment (except in those black works like *Melmoth* that allow little success to any value) is for the male for pride of place. Indeed, quite often not only the proud man but the place itself is ruined: the walls of the Castle of Otranto, of the convent in *The Monk*, of the Inquisitorial prison in *Melmoth*, of Thornfield Hall and Wuthering Heights and Daphne DuMaurier's Manderley crumble, crash, go up in flames, as though power itself were being rebuked for locating itself too long in one place.[26]

Fascinated as he is on his "female" side by the power of place, by the location, the "there" of spirit, Lawrence is even more aware, in his maleness, of the shifting, the explosive departure and return, the "no longer there," the "coming again here" of power. This latter awareness gives his imagi-

[26] Discussing their differing responses to the classic Gothic place, the castle, Norman Holland and Leona Sherman agree that the castle-with-imprisoned-maiden symbol is perceived by male and female readers initially as a self with inner self imprisoned. Then the responses divide, Sherman citing her feeling of pain and pleasure at the prospect of that inner citadel's penetration, and Holland, interestingly, citing pure pain at that same prospect, with a feeling of pleasure connected to the "flinty hardness" of the outer self, the castle: "I want those stones to be inert, neither hurt nor hurting, whatever threats and penetrations go on between villain and victim. *They* cannot be penetrated, and if not they, then not I." See Holland and Sherman, "Gothic Possibilities," in *New Literary History* 8 (Winter 1977): 283. The certainty that one's outer shell will hold firm even if the inner citadel collapses is Gerald Crich's too. Classic Gothic demolishes both the certainty and the castle.

nation that racewide, specieswide, planetwide reach that makes him often sound not only apocalyptic and metareligious but actually fantastic, almost science fictive. His concepts of space, time, and the workings of "the great creative principle" have frequently a Wellsian largeness and bluntness; his visions, like Birkin's, have the glib extremism of the arrogantly scientific romancer that earthbound Ursula suspects; like Wells and a whole pantheon of philosopher-fantasists who took up science fiction at the turn of the century, Lawrence must "drag in the stars."

Yet there is a crucial difference, one that roots Lawrence in the true Gothic and separates him from the mainstream of science fiction as Wells and Verne and Olaf Stapledon defined it and C. S. Lewis later criticized it. For Lawrence, mankind derives its real and only power from placement, not displacement, from a living root, not a spectral freedom. Mankind's power is in its form and that form's home; its first place is its body, and behind that, the body of the planet, over both of which bodies the Holy Ghost, as another devotee of that aspect of God says, "broods with, ah bright wings." And when this form is fulfilled, or develops into a cul-de-sac, then the human enterprise will be over. Lawrence's imagination, rejecting both the insect adaptation of pure sensual instinct by which he thinks Egyptians and African cultures have survived their real form's time and the mechanical mentalism by which technology is adapting man's body and Western culture to "the pit," wants simply to rejoice and lay a wreath, if necessary, on the grave of old-style "mankind." Not for him the species-greed that Dracula-like, would make every place its own and every alien body its own. That adaptation won't work anyway. Dracula abandoned his own body, his mortal span, to live purely on the power of his place; when he leaves that place, he initiates his extinction.

As a place of power, body is a Lawrentian given. Its levels and sources of plexic power are explained at perhaps tedious length in essays like *Fantasia of the Unconscious* and in long monologues in the novels. Perhaps the simplest and clearest dramatic account we have of this, however, is in the short stories.[27] Here we see the power of body most often derived directly from light, from the sun; in "Sun," "The Woman Who Rode Away," and "The Lovely Lady," for instance, it is woman's body, mother's, that absorbs the sun and then generates power—maliciously in the latter story, self-fruitfully in the former, mystically and communally fruitful in the middle one. The strong implication in such stories (another rent in Lawrence's feminism) is that woman's body/sun power is properly a temporary possession, one that should emerge eventually in children, although to do Lawrence minimal justice he faithfully records the woman's restlessness with this destiny.

Juliet of "The Sun" recovers her health in the rays of that "other power" than her own, but she shies away from the peasant who fully expressed the Sun's "procreative power" in order to return to her husband, who is only half aware of the sun, to bear his child. Pauline, "The Lovely Lady," is carefully trying to absorb just enough sun to live "practically forever," refusing any of its excess to her sons, one of whom is dead, the other "sucked dry." The anonymous wife in "The Woman Who Rode Away" takes part in a mystic recapturing of the sun, which according to Indian lore was stolen from the dark man by the white man and then secretly (as we can see from "The Lovely Lady" and other stories) stolen again from the white man by the white woman. At the end, Juliet is caught in the white woman's "fatal continuity," condemned by her fear to bear only "mongrel" children from the half-monstrous white race. Pauline, who hears from the very walls of the house, though actually from her hidden and deprived niece (really from her own punishing conscience), the tale of her vampiric, sun-grabbing misdeed, finds the artificial bond between her

[27] All of the short stories discussed in the following pages can be found in *The Complete Short Stories of D. H. Lawrence*, 3 vols. (London: William Heinemann Ltd., 1955).

will and her body exposed, symbolically, by the electric light and dies of the understanding. The woman of the latter story, Lawrence would have us believe, participates with some elation, or at least understanding, in the sacrifice by which she "opens the gate" for the sun's release from the domination of the white race.

All of these haunted mothers share the discovery of placedness, stillness, as the gateway to power and the further discovery that the power of their bodies, new and precious and secret *to* them, is ultimately a secret *from* them too, larger, more "other" than they. Though they must come to the place of power—the beach, the rooftop, the cave—to become the bodily place of power, power itself moves from place to place, person to person, and as Lawrence argues at the end of "The Woman Who Rode Away," from race to race.

Getting to the place of power is a dominant action in Lawrence's stories. Juliet is sent by her doctor, Pauline climbs alone to her aerie, the woman is carried to her place "automatically" by her horse. In the poignant and terrible "Rocking-Horse Winner," the young boy, like Lawrence's women a seeker after place, has only a wooden horse on which to *"get there."* And he does get there, travelling through the "violent, hushed motion" of his body to the place inside, where he is a winner, "absolutely sure"—and thus in contact with all the others who are sure, at their body's center, the race horses who are winners even before the races. But the cost is too high for him, as it was for the women. The outside world gives no fertile invitations to seek full placement in the body; one reaches the place hampered, corrupted, or driven, and then, as with Gerald Crich, or Pauline, or the woman who rode away, "something breaks" in the soul—as with Paul, the "winner," something "falls, with a crash."

This crisis of placement in the modern displaced world, the fact that one cannot bear real fulfillment but must break up in death on the very threshold of completion, is nowhere more powerfully and simply dramatized than in Lawrence's finest story, "The Prussian Officer." Here it is not mother and son or wife and husband but two men who fight for the sun, to be fully body. Ironically, the men are part of an army practicing an attack on an imaginary enemy: in this genuinely absurd and life-draining atmosphere, the Captain and the Orderly emerge from the "neutrality" of their role relationship into a personal awareness whose terms Lawrence casts over and over as sun and shadow. The story opens on a landscape of "glare" interspersed with "shade," the Captain on horseback containing the sun, a "gleaming" figure, and the Orderly connected to and following that figure "like a shadow." The mute competition for the place of the sun from the place of the shadow contains several seesaw switches of place: closer awareness of the Orderly's more embodied "person" begins a slow transferral of being from the Captain. He grows "irritated," he "corrodes"; his own body "flames" into agonizing presence, but the other man's person is still stronger, more placed. He kicks and abuses that threatening body, trying to reduce it to shadow again, and the Orderly wavers toward "nullification," then "regains himself," and the Captain "began to grow vague, unreal." Horsed again, the Captain recaptures the "hot bright morning" in his own person, "a quick bright thing, in which was concentrated all the light of this morning," and the Orderly empties "like a shadow." More bodied than he has ever been, though with the help of the horse and at the expense of the Orderly, the Captain, in "an act of courage," makes contact with his body-brother, gives him a command, orders it "quick." The word itself, a Lawrentian code-word for vitality and embodiedness, gives the Orderly back his strength; he now sees the Captain as "less real than himself." It is then within his courage to join the Captain in the woods, where the light lies ambiguously "splashed," predicting violence, and the two, now equally bodied, meet "man to man." Since the source of the Orderly's body is "instinct" and the Captain is a figure of "will," it is the Orderly who moves first; the Captain dies in the sweet "pleasing" sensation of body meeting body, and the Orderly's own inner death follows. Having achieved a bodily oneness through the mutual rising of the blood, they suffer an equal diminution to shadow, like Frankenstein and the creature, men unable, after a thousand years of lessons bred in the bone, to sustain equal place, equal body, without competition, hatred, death. And so the light returns out of both into the world again: "It surprised him that the leaves were glittering in the sun, and the chips of wood reflecting white from the ground."

The final portions of "The Prussian Officer" show the Orderly, a shadow in the darkness of the woods, begin a long journey away from "the place of light," the source of human power, through the "open land"—"he had never been here before." The sun, "drilling down," will finally sever all the automatic bonds between will and flesh that are keeping his shadow-body alive: "the world" is simply a ghastly "shadow on the darkness." But between the sun and the dark, between the sky and the earth, stand the mountains, "blue and cool and tender. . . . They did not move." Still, clean, "between"—in this landscape the mountains are the ultimate body between energies, the abode of the inhuman and impersonal power, the place of the Holy Ghost: "and the mountains . . . seemed to have it, that which was lost in him."

Like Shelley and Wordsworth, the neo-Romantic Lawrence found impressive lessons in the very situation, the placement, of mountains—an inorganic and cool holding place for the opposite forces of sky and earth and, so located, a power in their own right. The Alps of *Women in Love* are like this and the Rockies of "The Princess," strangely consoling even to the self-destroyers who go there, drawn by the sense of a "secret Heart" and an "inhuman core." On the earth's body the mountains gather, speaking to Lawrence's eye not of rising but of sinking, "kneeling," heavy, "ponderous, involved," intricately "knotting," centering around them all vistas, "tilting away," the veritable plexus of the planet between the cold north of mind and will and the hot south of sensuality and submission.

In his early works, during and after his exile/escape, Lawrence writes of the ghosts and demons of the north— British automatons and wolfmen, Prussian ghouls and vampires. After *Women in Love*, the errant mysticism, the heretic narrative of the English soul turns south for its nourishment, as it did a century and a half before in classic Gothic. Taking "the imperial road South" at the beginning of *Twilight in Italy*, Lawrence passes through the mountains, bathing in "the radiant cold of changeless not-being . . . which waits to receive back again all that which has passed for the moment into being," and he discovers, of course, that man cannot really live a mountain life. "The eternal issue," that is, the "steaming up" of hot being towards cold not-being, is "too much revealed there."[28] His passage from north to south is marked by a change in the nature of the mountain crucifixes, the Bavarian ones expressing the worship of pain, the "triumph of death;" the negativity, that Lawrence finds in the north, and the more southern ones showing a "tendency . . . to become weak and sentimental" (p. 11). Only "very high up" does the traveller find a Christus "uncouth" and "significant of the true spirit, the desire to convey a religious truth, not a sensational experience" (p. 14). But this genuine god is broken, and Lawrence passes it in holy fear, wondering "who would come and take the broken thing away, and for what purpose" (p. 15). It is a question he will answer, fantastically, in *The Plumed Serpent*.

Lawrence's much loved, much criticized Italy, his south, is the other end of a world axis already "complete" and therefore "finished" in his estimation, an axis that his

---

[28] Quotations from D. H. Lawrence's *Twilight in Italy* (1921) are taken from *D. H. Lawrence and Italy* (New York: Viking Press, Inc., 1972). This one occurs on p. 6.

fundamentally Trinitarian imagination connects in the chapter entitled "The Lemon Gardens" with the movement from the southern "tiger" to the northern "Lamb" in iconography, from the "terrific eagle-like angel of the senses" to the "great reconstructed selfless power of the machine," from God as material "Me" to God as immaterial "Not-Me," from God the Father to Christ the Son, a movement from south to north along the axis of love, willed perfection of the self as lover of the not-self.

This axis is envisioned by Lawrence, the last of the Victorians in this as in so many other ways, as a railroad. At the end of "The Lemon Gardens," his southern padrone joins the young Italians and the driven Englishman on vacation in a general yearning for the northern direction: "He wanted to know the joy of man who has got the earth in his grip, bound it up with railways" (p. 53). In *Fantasia of the Unconscious*, the whole cultural enterprise since the Renaissance is captured in a superb railway image; Western man has been "laying down love like the permanent way of a great emotional transport system" whose great virtue is that it "goes" and whose great drawback is that it can only go in a straight line—forward "the English way" to "the New Jerusalem ahead" of progress and humanistic materialistic unity or backward "the German way" to "the New Jerusalem behind" of atavistic unity in power-worship. The Germans having "reversed their engines" and caused "one long collision all along the line," humanity is now, in the nineteen-twenties, seen "encamped in an appalling mess beside the railway-smash of love," while the English and the Germans continue their quarrel about who should control the engine for the next dreary run down the line.[29]

But although for the Lawrence of *Twilight in Italy*, "south" is still a viable journey, a joy even worth walking through the dullness of Switzerland to obtain, west is the

[29] D. H. Lawrence, *Fantasia of the Unconscious* (1922; reprint ed., New York: Viking Press, Inc., 1960), pp. 167-168. Subsequent references are to this edition and hereafter will be cited in the text as *Fantasia*.

true beckoning direction. In the final section of *Twilight in Italy*, it is a doomed Gerald-Crich-like countryman, not Lawrence, who makes "The Return Journey" north. And if, "when one walks, one must travel west or south" (p. 145) and south is simply, nostalgically, backwards on the already fixed line of culture, then one must set out west—not north as the padrone would, not fix immobile in disgust and resolution as "Il Duro" does, but set out west. At the end of the railroad passage quoted above, Lawrence himself blithely sets off away from feeding, breeding humanity encamped at the railway smash of love on the line running north and south: "Goodbye then! You may have laid your line from one end to the other of infinity. But there's still plenty of hinterland. I'll go" (*Fantasia*, p. 168).

Another exile from the north-south line in Italy is young John, who puzzles even Lawrence with his desire to leave Italy. He "could not say himself" why he was leaving land and family to go west, but his "soul," Lawrence says, is "in trajectory," rising as Ursula earlier hoped hers would, to seek a new direction: "His father was the continent behind him; his wife and child the foreshore of the past; but his face was set outwards, away from it all—whither, neither he nor anybody knew, but he called it America" (p. 119).

America, that soiled dove that Lawrence wanted to cast as Holy Ghost to his southern fatherlands and northern Christendoms, the place of cool meeting and relating, was finally to fail him in the fully concrete way England had, by banning his book. And from the beginning there was a great deal to anger him about the continent and its devil-ridden hero the U. S. of A.: a negativity about the parade of freedom and democracy, a shallowness about the parade of activity—like a cinematograph, he calls it in *St. Mawr*—a secret servility to the old in its parade of newness. One can easily imagine Nellie March of the early *Fox* recoiling from her Canada as later *St. Mawr*'s Lou recoils from her Texas and *The Plumed Serpent*'s Kate from her Mexico, its people groveling to their automobiles, its culture corrupted into a hunt for sensation—political as well as social and material.

Yet America, hung suggestively between east and west, north and south, between prehistory and the postmodern, is above all for Lawrence the place of surprises, its massive and disappointing extension of European "go" and Christian "love" a kind of mask. In the lyricism of *St. Mawr* and the mysticism of *The Plumed Serpent*, Lawrence works out his complex vision of the continent as the hinterland of hope, as morning star, as locus for the wild spirit of "something else" than kingship (law/self/God the Father) or sonship (givenness/love/Christ)—the Holy Ghost, in fact. But interestingly, this vision is founded upon insights derived from reading American authors—one Gothic imagination responding to others—and it is set down in Lawrence's first and in some ways most important American book, *Studies in Classic American Literature*. Separated from the Gothic wellsprings of his own heritage by three generations of transforming artists, Lawrence rediscovers them safely, as a critic, in the place where the Gothic went west—in the American tale.[30] Meditating on Hawthorne and Poe, Cooper and Melville, Lawrence clarifies the foundation from which he has been working all along in apothegm after brilliant apothegm from *Studies*:

> Never trust the artist. Trust the tale. (P. 297)
> Men are free when they are in a living homeland, not when they are straying and breaking away. (P. 301)
> Poe . . . is absolutely concerned with the disintegration-processes of his own psyche. . . . This makes him more a scientist than an artist. (P. 330)

[30] In his *D. H. Lawrence and the New World* (New York: Oxford Univ. Press, 1969), David Cavitch too finds Lawrence's imaginative reach for the American scene a matter of restoring magic to the landscape of his fictions, the mountain and desert vistas yielding the lost continent of his intenser visions, "an alien world that includes ghosts, satyrs, gnomish wizards, spellbound, nameless women, lost Indian tribes, sacred mountains and lakes" (p. 149).

Woman is the nemesis of doubting man—she can't help
it. (P. 356)
It is, perhaps the most colossal satire ever penned. The
Scarlet Letter. All begins with A. Adultress. Alpha.
Abel, Adam. A. America (P. 352)
Hot-blooded, sea-born Moby Dick. Hunted by mono-
maniacs of the idea. . . . The *Pequod* sinks with all
her souls, but their bodies rise again to man unnumer-
able tramp steamers, and ocean crossing liners. . . . Post
Mortem effects. Ghosts. A certain ghoulish consistency.
A certain terrible pottage of human parts. But what of
Walt Whitman? Was he a ghost, with all his physicality?
(Pp.391-392)

What fascinated Lawrence about American "art-speech"
was its "perfect duplicity," the longing for innocence hiding
its worship of guilt, its praise of white deflecting its hunger
for black and red, its rhetoric of creativity governing a
powerful national destructiveness. Above all, its mono-
maniacal love that loves death. In Whitman's "I" as in
Ligea's and Ahab's and Dimmesdale's, Lawrence finds the
greed to merge, absorb, retake all matter and energy (and
sin and guilt) for one's own, a greed licensed in the very
Constitution as the "pursuit of happiness." Happiness
Lawrence has diagnosed in *The Fox* as an object without
a referent other than death—and death, he repeats in the
essay on Whitman, though a fact and an end and even a
consolation if rightly viewed, is not properly a human goal:
"There is something else." Whatever the something else is,
it clearly comes in that "pause" of which Lawrence speaks
so often, not in that pursuit which has come to be America's
and the West's form of happiness. Pursuit is the core of the
American tale for Lawrence; not only Melville's captains
and Poe's lemur-vampires but Hawthorne's Puritans too
pursue their objects with that self-congratulating love that
he calls "dirty understanding. . . . the aeroplane *sensation*
of knowing, knowing, knowing" (*Studies*, p. 351). Even

Cooper's Natty Bumpo is an American in this: "What sort of a white man is he? Why, he is a man with a gun. He is a killer, a slayer. Self-effacing, self-forgetting, still, he is a killer. . . . He is the stoic American killer of the old great life" (*Studies*, p. 326). But he kills, Lawrence records Natty's explanation, only to live. Exactly. Perfect duplicity. Gothic.

In some ways Lawrence's essays on Cooper are the most interesting of all. Poe is a scientist and "true," Hawthorne had "magical allegorical insight," Melville was "the greatest seer and poet of the sea," Whitman "meant so much" to Lawrence as the first man of flesh-consciousness, the first soul out on "the open road." But Cooper he rather envies and resents: "This popular wish-fulfillment stuff makes it so hard for the real thing to come through, later" (*Studies*, p. 306). For Cooper, blue-eyed and duplicitous like the rest, had like Lawrence two vibrations to his wish, the disintegrative and the creative. Cooper "shot the bird of the spirit out of the high air" (*Studies*, p. 326) into dead materiality like the true American killer, but he also dreamed the dream of the "new thing" without mockery or desperation, for he wrote before the *Pequod* went down and left only the disintegrative love-merge vibration still operating.

And as Cooper pictured it, and as Lawrence was to recapitulate in *St. Mawr* and *The Plumed Serpent*, the "new thing" in America and the West has something to do with the land itself and its watchful first citizens. While the Indian and Mexican races struggle and finally merge in "the great white swamp" of the nineteenth and early twentieth centuries, their "unappeased ghosts" work up a frenzy of guilty destruction, "the great American grouch," in the unconscious white usurpers. But "a curious thing about the Spirit of Place is the fact that no place exerts its full influence upon a new-comer until the old inhabitant is dead or absorbed." Then, Lawrence argues, when the last Mohican, the last Indian dies, "then the white man will have to reckon with the full force of the demon of the continent

. . . the demon of America!" Then "we shall see real
changes" (*Studies*, p. 304). And that Holy Ghost will be no
blue-eyed white dove but the "dusky body" (p. 303) between the two wings of American energy, disintegrative and
creative, the black-eyed red man. His avatar in Cooper is
Chingachgook, "the great Serpent." His dramatic forerun-
ner in Lawrence's own work is St. Mawr, the vital red horse
who, overridden by white masters, becomes purely demonic
until he finds his wholeness with an Indian groom, and
finally on Arizona Indian land. His pure form, Lawrence's
own wish-fulfillment, is the Indian God Quetzalcoatl, the
Plumed Serpent of Lawrence's final American work.

St. Mawr contains several familiar Lawrentian figures,
the woman for whom everything in the familiar white
world is "turning ghastly," who seeks a place to pause and
be alone with her singularity, the animal icon of isolate
virility, and the men, Morgan Lewis and the Indian,
Phoenix, who share that energy and integrity, though it is
partly corrupted, "contravened," by the world. It also
contains one of the most remarkable evocations of the spirit
of place Lawrence ever raised—the American demon of the
Arizona mountain ranch that is the place of the soul. The
demon is half-breed, like the last Indian, Phoenix; it attracts and it "piths" at the same time; half "beating light"
and half pack rat, it energizes and it "eats away." In 1924,
Forster published *A Passage to India*, raising the demon
of the Eastern Indian for his Christian Englishwoman in
the Marabar Caves, an ancient "white worm" that swallows
all meaning as soon as it is uttered. That summer Lawrence
raised the demon of the Western Indian in the story-
within-the-story that ends *St. Mawr* for the "little New
England woman" who preceded St. Mawr and his mistress
to the "place":

At the same time, the invisible attack was being made
upon her while she revelled in the beauty of the luminous
world that wheeled around and below her, the grey,

ratlike spirit of the inner mountains was attacking her from behind. She could not keep her attention. And, curiously, she could not even keep her speech. When she was saying something, suddenly the next word would be gone out of her, as if a pack-rat had carried it off. And she sat blank, stuttering, staring in the empty cupboard of her mind, like Mother Hubbard, and seeing the cupboard bare.[31]

After these surprisingly similar visions of the unhuman speech-stealing spirit at the ancient heart of being comes, for both Forster and Lawrence, the vision of "the temple," in the former case a concluding section of the novel, in the latter case a separate novel, *The Plumed Serpent*, which describes the recapture of meaning through myth. Invulnerable in his irony, Forster's narrator offers the "coming" of the Hindu god in "Temple" as a truth for those inside the myth and as a possibility for the reader, who balances between the elegant dictum of Dr. Godbole—"absence is not the same as non-being"—and the elegy of "no, not yet . . . no, not there" on which the novel closes. Naked in his earnestness, his sarcasm, his irritation, and his need, Lawrence offers the coming of the Indian god in *The Plumed Serpent* as a fiction to be touched into truth by a living faith, Pentecostal, not perfectly intelligible.

It is a curious book, full of rage at the way life is lived by moderns, slyly "picking over the garbage of sensations" (p. 26) in the arena of politics as much as in the bullfight arena where the story begins. Love, ghastly merging love, has been abandoned and so has one-direction, railroad-straight progress—this "first half" of protagonist Kate Leslie's life is over. Hope too, "the bright smooth vellum of hope, with initial letters all gorgeous upon a field of gold," has been abandoned, and "the bright page" gives way to the dark (p. 52). It is her fortieth year, and the choice is clear before her—either go on to something new or, now poised

[31] *St. Mawr* (1925; reprint ed., New York: Vintage Books, 1953), p. 149.

290

at the apogee of the old way, fall to the "widdershins" spin of reversal that seems to have the whole universe in its grip, the "unwinding" toward disintegration and antilife, toward the centerless blackness of fatality that seems to live in the black eye of the Mexican Indian (p. 113).

Yet here too, Lawrence wants to argue, absence is not necessarily non-being. The vision of centerlessness becomes the sense of "the uncreated centre" (p. 83), and, of all things, at a "Tea-Party in Tlacolula," Kate meets the men striving to create that centre, call the god into being in the holy place that is their own bodies. By the end of the novel, the landowner/craftsman Ramon and the military leader Cipriano have become "golden Quetzalcoatl" and "red Huitzilopochtli," taken thrones in the emptied Catholic Church, and invited Kate to join them as the woman between, third and crucial point in the triune godhead from which a new world of fullness is to emerge, the mastery, that is, the meaningfulness, of life, passing from the white to the red race, from the unholy ghoul of Europe to the brooding Holy Ghost of America.

From one perspective this is all quite laughable and dangerous, and Kate Leslie, like Nellie March before her and Ursula Brangwen before her, and Radcliffe's heroines before any of them, fights to retain that skeptical perspective. For it is less skepticism than simply self-respect. Like Ursula, Kate loathes the corruption, the halfness, the vulgarity, finally the self-contradiction of the Salvator Mundi complex; like Nellie March, she struggles to keep awake, to keep above water, as the tide of myth, dreadful and obliterating and yet secretly, somehow, life-giving, rises over her head. In the final pages of *Women in Love* and *The Fox* the life-bearing, quarrelling heterosexual couples plan a move, south or west: because Birkin and Ursula, Henry and Nellie March lack a centering, balancing third figure, they must continue the quest. But the final chapter of *The Plumed Serpent* is titled "Here," suggesting a solution, a place to stop. The presence of a mystic third, the "hoverer between," the subtle, intense and yet distant Ramon, brings Kate, at least for the moment it takes to close the chapter in tenuous place, in slightly fractious pause, into position with Cipriano as the life-bearing quarreling man and woman. And this place, pause, rest is governed by a certainty that is a living presence, a preternatural not-self, a spark struck between, an impersonal abider that outweighs all one's hard-forged individuality. "Was it true? . . . Was it true? . . . Was it true?" Kate asks herself in dread about the God-world she is asked to enter (p. 426). And the answer Lawrence gives is the one the Gothic imagination always gives—not, finally, "it is true," but in lightning, on the Road to Damascus, "it is here."

CONCLUSION

A HIGH, VIBRATING PLACE

WHEN T. S. Eliot and F. R. Leavis met in debate over the
virtues and vices of Lawrence, they often focused on the
issue of tradition and the orthodoxy-heresy relationship
that is implied in the concept of tradition. Eliot sees no
tradition in Lawrence, no loyalty to guides and master-
works like Dante, Goethe, or Donne, and therefore he sees
an ignorance. He argues that without a "wise and large
capacity for orthodoxy" an artist like Lawrence can hardly
avoid "the solely centrifugal impulse of heresy." Leavis
replies that Lawrence's tradition, less one of masters than
of nonconformist and working-class ideals and attitudes,
gives him an orthodoxy clear enough to provide a background for development, strong enough to assert its presence in every departure from it. Eliot responds that heresy
is always merely centrifugal for him, ending in solipsism; he
can see nothing good in a mentality that could depart, for
instance, from the Trinitarian formula not by abjuring
it but by "huddling" the Father, the Son, and the Holy
Ghost "into a variety of costumes" while still using that
sacred terminology. On the other hand, Eliot concludes in
his review of J. M. Murry's biography of Lawrence, "perhaps if I had been brought up in the shadowy Protestant
underworld in which [Lawrence] moves, I might have had
more sympathy and understanding: I was brought up outside the Christian Fold, in Unitarianism."[1]

[1] Eliot attacks Lawrence in *After Strange Gods*, and Leavis replies in
D. H. Lawrence, Novelist; both men honed their arguments in reviews
and articles first. All quotations in the text are from Eliot's famous
review of J. Middleton Murry's controversial biography *Son of Woman*,
partly reprinted under the title of Eliot's *mot* for the relationship of

Eliot's religious and aesthetic journey from atheism to orthodoxy, like Joyce's journey the opposite way down that two-directional railroad track, did indeed unfit him, just a little, for understanding the hinterland of heresy that Lawrence and George Eliot and even Jane Austen found so fruitful. In their shadowy Protestant underworld, what matters is the space one can make in the old terms for new personal discoveries, new arrangements of concepts. What matters is the movement out from the either/or form of discourse to the both/and form, or the first/then form: God and man and the imagination, both one and many, both beautiful and terrible, first "real" and then true, first "here" and then everywhere. For Austen, urging novelists to stick together against the attacks of the orthodoxy of poets and critics ("We are an injured body" she says of her sect in *Northanger Abbey*) linked the nineteenth century with its Gothic heritage by affecting to draw away from transmundane terrors and visions and in fact restoring them to common life, where "imaginists" like Catherine Morland and Emma Woodhouse struggle to contact with reason that part of the mind, the imagination, that awakens to terror and converts terror to human vision. And George Eliot, licensed by the earthly seriousness lent by Austen to the debate about the imagination, swung still wider into studies of visionaries past, present, and future, hoping for an infusion of terrible vision not only in the individual mind, which can indeed scarcely bear it alone without corruption, but also in the community, nation, and race, where it can take more productive root. Lawrence, one of the greatest of apostles and heretics in both religion and aesthetics, explores most directly of all the development of

---

Lawrence and Murry, "The Victim and the Sacrificial Knife," in *D. H. Lawrence: The Critical Heritage*, ed. R. P. Draper (London: Routledge and Kegan Paul, 1970), p. 261. The general Leavis-Eliot debate is well summarized in editor Mark Spilka's introduction to *D. H. Lawrence: Twentieth-Century Views*.

human visionary intuition from Austenite concerns with imagination and order ("The Father"), to Eliot-like concerns with imagination and sympathy or love ("The Son"), to that modern yearning for a profundity beyond personal love that he calls the Holy Ghost. And the vehicle for that search, ultimately for the discovery of that profundity, he calls the novel, that "bright Book of life," the holy book of the Protestant underground that is to be, for reading man, the instrument by which he detects those "tremulations on the ether," those ghosts in the daylight, those mysterious anxieties of common life that are the special life, the preternatural intensities that are man's real birthright.

The Gothic above all seeks to remind those caught in its plots of larger powers, of finer tremulations located in places outside (or inside) the scope of everyday life, located in places apparently abandoned but secretly tenanted, places apparently blank but secretly full of signals. For Austen there are equivocal, not just parodic, powers at Northanger and Donwell Abbeys; for Eliot there are living tenants, honest ghosts, in the Florentine or Middlemarchian or continental past, in the Zionist future. For Lawrence the places on the earth's body that once harbored powers still do, and the zone of human mind where live the great animating myths, Indian, Christian, Persian, Achaean, is a real place, and accessible through the hinterlands.

Nowhere is this novelistic search for the place of power more clearly pursued than in the works of Doris Lessing, whose debt to Lawrence and George Eliot seems clear, whose debt to the Gothic as I've tried to define it lies in the serious use she has made of this century's special branch of the Gothic, science fiction. Lessing brings her heroine Martha Quest across thirty years and four novels for the moment she discovers, through the "instrumentality" of her lover and their mutual command of "the real high place of sex," that there is a still higher place, a "high vibrating place" above the personal, a "wavelength" of the best hopes and truths of the human race into which she can tune if she marshals her whole keen self as a path and a contribution to that wavelength.[2]

In *The Four-Gated City*, Martha makes a friend of the science-fiction writer Jimmy Walker, whose plots, conventional to his field, contain the potential for the most serious discussion of the nature and future of man, except that the visionary element in his science fiction is always being overridden by the "computer element." She meets and admires the "madwoman" Linda Coldridge, explores with her all those "Gothic" sciences—witchcraft, parapsychology, tarot —that contained the guides to that high vibrating place until they were vitiated by whimsy and unbelief or destroyed by jealous disciples of more conventional guides. All of the whispers from discredited sciences and trivialized arts are part, Martha finds, of the wavelength that unites the mental community of man. But that band of noise is guarded by dread: "Terror struck" every time Martha entered the band, where some claim or debt or challenge connected with the oneness of the human race waited to shriek at her (p. 40). Martha gives this dread a name: the self-hater. He is a person in the country of sounds, an aspect of self encountered in the zone of mind where realities larger than the ordinary single self wait, and he manifests this reality as hatred of the questing or imagining or risking self, as that dangerous mode of feeling which the Gothic warns us can be either the crucial condition for growth or the cause of permanent moral paralysis—remorse. Or worse: "Remorse?" Martha thinks, "No, it was more that her whole life was being turned inside out, so that she looked at it in reverse, and there was nothing anywhere in it that was good; it was all dark, all cruel, all callous, all 'bad.' Oh, she was bad, oh she was wicked, oh how very evil and bad and wicked she was" (pp. 535-536). This resembles Austen's Emma, turning on her own imagination in disgust.

[2] Doris Lessing, *The Four-Gated City* (New York: Bantam Books, 1970), p. 62.

But although Lessing's Martha will receive no help from a Mr. Knightley to continue her journey, neither will she stay frozen in proud Gothic remorse.

As the novel draws to a close, Martha retreats to a private space in the top of a house in London, a house "haunted" by other peoples' breakdowns, one ambiguously marked by its government purchasers for "demolition or redevelopment" (p. 527), thus reentering the zone of shrieking voices in her mind. The risk, of course, is breakdown, madness, but the goal is full immersion in, participation in, the organic human entity. Clutching her pain and her terror and her loathing, like Eliot's Dorothea and Gwendolen and Latimer, she goes on "charting the country of sound . . . accompanied by the self-hater" (p. 536), and as "time passed" and the self-hater is not defeated but sustained, survived, he becomes for Martha less a hater than a mocker, a familiar almost comforting, figure: "The self-hater had become, logically enough, the Devil, and commented or exclaimed or jeered or criticized her every move, thought, memory" (p. 544). And finally, jeering and criticizing, asking the questions that if sustained, lead closer to answers, the devil metamorphoses, mystically, into the tutor. On the last page of the novel proper, before the personal and social and racial apocalypse/resurrection hinted at in the appendix, Lessing's Martha, like Lawrence's Kate, wanders alone, half mad in her quest for place, and receives a kind of relief:

> She thought, with the dove's voices of her solitude: Where? But *where*? How? Who?
> No, but where, *where*. . . . Then silence and the birth of a repetition: *where*? Here.
> Here?
> Here, where else, you fool, you poor fool, where else has it been, ever. (P 591)

Where is "here?" As Manfred and Melmoth and Dracula confront their castles and Frankenstein and Jekyll their laboratories, as Emma draws near to Donwell Abbey and Daniel to his Jerusalem and Paul Morel to the humming, glowing town, we may speculate that "here" is no longer the God-made heaven or the natural Eden. The place of power, source and goal of preternatural gifts, is now the works of man. While eighteenth-century Gothic novels were creating in their gloomy caves and lurid landscapes a dark pastoral to accompany the artificial bright ones of the poets, while the nineteenth-century serious novels were creating, in their plague-cities and their prison-cities, an urban anti-pastoral, these linked genres were also proposing a genuine new pastoral, vision of home, the house, the household, the meeting place of mankind, the city glimpsed *from* the hill, the high vibrating place, the place sweet to the eye and sweet to the mind. If the house had been destroyed by the pursuing sins of the past, it must be rebuilt; if usurpers were living there it could be retaken, or better, the usurpers could be converted into family. If the upper rooms were inhabited by madmen or monsters, they could be driven out, or better, loved, joined, learned from. If the city were lost or poisoned or stolen, it could be seen still, with the right trick of vision, in the desert, on the plain, on the other side of the hinterland.

One thinks of Austen's frightening Bath or decaying Portsmouth or trivial Highbury first; but the artist herself thinks at last of *Persuasion*'s busy, energetic Union Street where Frederick Wentworth and Anne Elliot stride confidently up toward a future that had petered out in the fading energies of Kellynch Hall, and one can only guess how much of yearning would have accompanied the gentle mocking of the building of Sanditon. George Eliot's Florence is factionalized and corrupt up close, but the Frate, the spirit on the hill, and the historian herself, see a hidden true city in the mist of the usurped one. And when the veil "lifts," the psychic Latimer glimpses cities in the distance, mishapen, filled with the living dead, waiting for the enchantment to be lifted, the true citizens to come. Lawrence pays homage to the nonhuman powers folded in the heart of the mountains, sunk in the fertile lake, but in novel after novel, like Paul Morel, he keeps trying the "idea of the town," hoping at last to get it right.

Again, Lessing makes the clearest comments on this new pastoral. Two important novels of the early 1970s, *The Four-Gated City* and *Briefing for a Descent into Hell*, center on the achievement of a magic city; in both works a subtle use of science-fiction conventions allows her to claim both an imaginative and a real existence for these cities. Professor Charles Watkins of *Briefing* is "mad" to every perspective but his own, of course, when he reports on the journey that took him from ship to raft to shore to mountain to the city. He thought he had come only to blank rocks until his desire revealed to him that he was standing in "a very large and very fine city."[3] The city yielded to his mind successively what he sought there, when he sought it— first ruins, then dwelling places, finally, comment on current civilization, inhabitants half animal, then narrowly human. At last he sees the true inhabitants, residents of the sacred circle in the city's center, dwellers in the "crystal disc" where a man's perceiving five senses and the sixth, imagination, reveal a true universe vaster than he had thought. An unsympathetic doctor records only that a soiled, wandering, incoherent professor of classics raves that he was taken up in a flying saucer. A sympathetic doctor probes the other layers of meaning in the "patient's" narration and vaguely envies the energy and odd clarity of Watkins's imagination. An invisible narrator describes without comment or irony the descent of godlike beings to the mankind that is in need of "reminders" of its true nature and preternatural heritage. Watkins himself remembers, almost remembers, his home city, the interindividual community that is his real life. Trying to remember/discover it fully, he submits to shock treatment. And the "true" self who

[3] Doris Lessing, *Briefing for a Descent into Hell* (New York: Bantam Books, 1972), p. 49.

299

emerges in the letters that conclude the novel—routine, comfortable, solitary, and gently whimsical about his "breakdown"—is so clearly not the Watkins the reader knows that the effect, pure science-fiction Gothic, is not that a fine spirit has been "broken" or has "failed" but that it has been murdered and an alien mind, called normality, has taken over his body.

As for "the four-gated city," it was first created, or remembered, by the child Martha in Africa, "a city shining there in the scrub" (p. 216). Then it was laughingly recreated by Martha and her lover Mark Coldridge in the days of her modern unbelief, as an image, an archetype of the sought home, of communal wholeness, that went hidden as a "shadow city of poverty and beastliness" (p. 140) grew around and over it. Mark writes several versions of the archetype into short story, long story, novel, but he repudiates the book and the city during a "realist" phase of his artistic life. The book is later "taken up by the science fiction addicts" (p. 298) in the United States, through whose approving voices Mark begins to listen to his own book at last. But he doesn't listen closely enough; it is still for him, in the grip of the self-hater, the reducer, just an archetype, an imaginative construction. Readers who listen more closely write to him for the address of the city; they want to live there. He can tell them nothing. But Martha, whose search for the country of mutual mind, for the city of full humanity, is not merely literary, does have a kind of address. The city is accessible.

She reaches it first through the mind of her friend, Mark's "mad" psychic wife Lynda. Before she was told by the psychiatrists and forced by their shock treatments to listen to the voice of the self-hater driving her away from the country of mass consciousness, the child Lynda had assumed that everybody could hear what people were thinking, as she did. Frustrated equally by the artificiality of art and the elusiveness of life, the writer Mark imagines the city but is not prepared either to find it or to build it, although the tiny, nearly futile steps he makes toward the building of an alternate community to the dying England of the early 1970s bear fruit after the apocalypse that is Lessing's appendix to her novel. But using Lynda as her contact and model, Martha goes further. Older and stronger than Lynda was when she was frightened away from the city, Martha returns to the haunted house and journeys like Watkins, all the way there—"here, where else, you poor fool." This familiarity with the city and with the proper powers of human beings allows Martha, ten years into the apocalypse brought on by atomic and environmental carelessness, to recognize in the children being born in that time a new race, "guardians" to the human ideal, as the people of the real, hidden city have always been to us of the visible shadow city.

Lessing's breakthrough persons make their way *to* the city by way of music or images; Martha becomes like a radio or television receiver, "tuned in" or "plugged in" to the wavelength, and Charles Watkins at the start of his journey felt "like a barometer" set for "fair," like an instrument waiting painfully for "a higher, keener note" than usual to be struck from it, "for we were not strung to the same pitch as that for which we had been waiting" (p. 16). But both make their difficult, ambiguous way back *from* the city to ordinary life by way of words. "I gotta use words when I talk to you, Eliot," Charles laments to "Doctor Y," "I gotta use words" (p. 147). As he balances uneasily between the shadow (real?) city and the hidden (imagined?) city, he is asked to "try writing down" his thoughts. Obligingly he produces several narratives of journeys to the city, the heart of light—narratives full of time references and detail that, whatever their bizarre images or apparently discredited facts, offer their coherence and first-person control as their authority, as the crafty/innocent dialogues, the explosive lyrics, the passionate broken monologues of

301

Watkins offer their intense spontaneity as their authority. The authority (or is it just the relief?) of narrative in narrative is powerful and finally establishes its hegemony.

Yet as Coleridge observed, the imagination that uses words to "remember" is a secondary form, verging on that tertiary form, the "fancy"; the more coherent the narrative, the more it seems only a form of memory rather than of true discovery or creation. And it is not only to "Eliot" (which Eliot, one wonders?) or "Doctor Y" (why?) that "we gotta use words," obviously, but also to the "why" of our inquiring selves. So the resort to writing, the return to narrative, is an ambiguous business for Charles Watkins, who in the attempt to remember the hidden city risks falling prey instead to his old normal memories once he enters the mode of memory at all. We learn of his failure, his return to his normal self, in the letter in which he triumphantly announces to his university chairman, "I do remember all about the lecture series" (p. 275).

During her journey through the country of sound, Martha Quest writes notes, scribbles madly her discoveries, despairingly underlining, capitalizing, overpunctuating the words she finds to describe—how inadequately—what she "remembers." Her lover Mark, less adventurous but still plagued by the same intuitions as Martha, has written the narration of *The City in the Desert*, published it, and thereby lost the experience. As Martha returns with her scarcely legible bundle of notes to herself, Mark has just tried—pitiful, gallant, male effort—to write a narrative "Memorandum to Myself," desperately confined to the logic of points 1, 2, 3, 4, 5, about the state of the human race and what should be done to save it. But Mark has broken it off, as Martha did her notes, as the ghosts and the villains and the storytellers in the Gothic do. The novelists, Scott and Austen, Dickens and Eliot, Brontë and Lawrence and Lessing herself do what they can to guard the mystery of life from the sanities of narrative, even as they show forth the city by means of narrative. All, as heretics, are

committed to return with words to the community from the
convent cell where the name of god, the vision of the city,
suffices; all, as novelists, are committed to the clumsy communication of vision in narrative—as the harrassed visionary Watkins lamented, "I gotta use words." All, as artists,
are trying to escape from their own works before the
memory of the normal, the "real," overtakes and blots out
the memory, the discovery, of the high, the holy, the "here."

INDEX

Austen, Jane, 8, 21n, 118, 181, 294-295; *Emma*, 126, 128, 132, 139, 142, 144, 153-172; *Mansfield Park*, 128, 142-144, 151-153, 168; *Northanger Abbey*, 124-151, 161-164; *Persuasion*, 128, 135, 139, 146; *Pride and Prejudice*, 128, 142, 144; *Sense and Sensibility*, 128, 142, 144
automatism (repetition), 8, 59, 60, 81, 85, 89, 91, 185-186, 230, 235, 249, 274, 283

Becker, Ernest, 117-118, 120
Berryman, John, 15, 16
"between," 241-242, 245, 265, 291-292
Bloom, Harold, 11
Brontë, Charlotte, 5, 7, 21n, 60, 101-102, 113-117, 165, 179, 227
Brontë, Emily, 73n, 114
Burney, Fanny, 101, 130

Carlyle, Thomas, 249-250
Castle of Otranto, The (Horace Walpole), 6, 8, 11, 25-31, 42, 63, 66, 78-79, 104, 123, 219
Coleridge, Samuel Taylor, 4, 13n, 17, 45, 302
community, 5, 15, 18-20, 24, 45, 47-51, 57, 62, 71-72, 79, 87-88, 95, 108, 196, 303
Conrad, Joseph, 19, 101, 118, 231-233, 247

Dickens, Charles, 5, 101, 102, 108-113, 179, 197
dilation/decreation, 34, 41, 47, 50, 58, 65, 68-70, 75, 83, 204

Doctor Jekyll and Mr. Hyde (Robert Louis Stevenson), 8, 12, 67, 73, 78, 79-85, 90, 91, 228
Dracula (Bram Stoker), 9, 11, 30n, 34, 73, 84n, 85-95, 119, 232-233
dread (anxiety), 5-6, 8, 11, 15, 29, 116-118, 126, 138, 174-177, 182, 193, 215, 262, 296

eighteenth-century Gothic (fathers), 9, 31, 56-58, 66, 74, 82-83, 85, 110, 144, 188, 243, 298
Eliot, George (Marian Evans), 8, 21n, 34, 35, 118, 137, 139, 294-295; *Adam Bede*, 176-177, 182, 187; *Daniel Deronda*, 140, 161, 175-176, 186, 188, 194, 206, 209-230, 243; *Felix Holt*, 182; "Janet's Repentance," 176, 178, 191-192; "The Lifted Veil," 173, 183-187, 227; *Middlemarch*, 6, 173-175, 177-179, 203-206, 213, 216, 218-219; *Mill on the Floss*, 179, 187, 195, 200, 214, 225n; *Romola*, 175-176, 178, 187-205; *Silas Marner*, 179, 192
Eliot, T. S., 231, 235, 242, 293-294. *See also* haunting (the Dead Hand), prophecy (the Terrible Vision)

Fiedler, Leslie, 22
Fielding, Henry, 7, 35, 100-101, 121n, 130
Forster, E. M., 5, 6, 235, 289-290
Frankenstein (Mary Shelley), 9, 12, 19, 23-24, 33, 59, 62-73, 78-79, 137, 146, 160, 183-185, 256n
Frye, Northrup, 21

Library of Congress Cataloging in Publication Data

Wilt, Judith, 1941-
Ghosts of the gothic.

1. English fiction—History and criticism.
2. Gothic revival (Literature)—Great Britain.
3. Austen, Jane, 1775-1817—Criticism and interpretation.
4. Eliot, George, pseud., i.e. Marian Evans, afterwards Cross,
1819-1880—Criticism and interpretation.
5. Lawrence, David Herbert, 1885-1930—Criticism and interpretation.
I. Title.
PR830.T3W5   823'.0872'09   80-7559
ISBN 0-691-06439-3